Women, Work and Protest

Women, Work and Protest

A century of US women's labor history

edited by
Ruth Milkman

London and New York

First published in 1985
Reprinted 1987
by Routledge & Kegan Paul Ltd.

Reprinted 1991
by Routledge
11 New Fetter Lane, London EC4P 4EE

Simultaneously published in the USA and Canada by
Routledge
a division of Routledge, Chapman and Hall, Inc.
29 West 35th Street, New York, NY 10001

Set in Sabon 10 on 12 pt
by Kelly Typesetting Ltd., Wiltshire, England
and printed in Great Britain by
St. Edmundsbury Press Ltd., Bury St Edmunds, Suffolk

Library of Congress Cataloging in Publication Data

Women, work, and protest.
Includes index.
I. Women in trade-unions — United States — History —
20th century — Addresses, essays, lectures. 2. Sex
discrimination against women — United States — History —
20th century — Addresses, essays, lectures. I. Milkman, Ruth,
1954–
HD6079.2.U5W66 1985   331.4′0973   84-27732
ISBN 0-415-06592-5

For Nate

Contents

Tables

Notes on contributors

Deborah E. Bell is Assistant Director of Research and Negotiations at District Council 37, American Federation of State, County and Municipal Workers (AFSCME), which represents more than 100,000 municipal employees in New York City, approximately half of whom are women, She is a contract negotiator and labor economist, and develops union policy on working women's issues like play equity, child care, and the impact of new office technologies.

Ardis Cameron is a graduate student in American social and economic history at Boston College, and teaches history at the University of Massachusettes, Boston. She is presently completing a dissertation entitled 'Neighborhoods in Revolt: Wage Earning Women and Collective Action, Lawrence, Massachusetts, 1882–1912.'

Mary Frederickson is Assistant Professor of History at the University of Alabama, Birmingham. She is co-editor (with Joyce L. Kornbluh) of *Sisterhood and Solidarity: Workers' Education for Women, 1914—1984* (Temple, 1984) and is currently completing a book on the Southern Summer School for Women Workers.

Nancy Gabin is Assistant Professor of History at Purdue University. She has published articles in *Labor History* and *Feminist Studies*, and is at work on a book about women and the United Automobile Workers' union from 1935 to 1970.

Colette Hyman is a graduate student in history at the University of Minnesota in Minneapolis. She is currently at work on a dissertation on popular culture in the Popular Front, focusing on workers' theater.

Alice Kessler-Harris is Professor of History at Hofstra University in Hempstead, New York, where she also co-directs the Center for the Study of Work and Leisure. She is the author of *Women Have Always Worked* (Feminist Press, 1980) and *Out to Work: A History of Wage-earning Women in the United States* (Oxford, 1982). Her current research involves the impact of women's culture on the work process.

Marjorie Penn Lasky teaches history at Diablo Valley College in Pleasant

Hill, California. She is currently working on a doctoral dissertation in history at the University of California, Davis.

Priscilla Long has been a longtime activist in the movement for social change. She is a printer and was for ten years a member of the Red Sun Press collective in Boston. She is the author of the booklet *Mother Jones: Women Organizer, and her Relations with Miners' Wives, Working Women, and the Suffrage Movement* (1976). She now lives in San Diego and is completing a book on the Colorado Fuel and Iron Strike.

Martha May recieved her PhD from the State University of New York at Binghamton in 1984. Her publications include articles on the family wage in *Feminist Studies* and *Labor History*. She is currently completing a study of Progressive era social reform and family life.

Ruth Meyerowitz teaches Women's Studies and history at the State University of New York at Buffalo and is a former coordinator of its Women's Studies program. She is currently working on a book about the relationship between women auto workers and the UAW in the 1930s–1940s.

Ruth Milkman is Assistant Professor of Sociology at Queens College, City University of New York. Her publications include articles on women's labor history in the *Review of Radical Political Economics, Socialist Review, Feminist Studies*, and *Politics and Society*. She is currently writing a book on the sexual division of labor in the auto and electrical manufacturing industries in the first half of the twentieth century.

Sharon Hartman Strom teaches women's history at the University of Rhode Island. Her most recent publication is 'Challenging "Woman's Place": Feminism, the Left, and Industrial Unionism in the 1930s,' *Feminist Studies*, vol 9 (1983). She is currently at work on a book about women and clerical work between 1910 and 1950.

Rosalyn Terborg-Penn is Associate Professor of History and Director of African/Afro-American Studies at Morgan State University. She is the co-founder of the Association of Black Women Historians. She has co-edited two books: *The Afro-American Woman: Struggles and Images* and the forthcoming *Women in Africa and the African Diaspora*.

Roger Waldinger is Assistant Professor of Sociology, City College, City University of New York. His recent publications include two articles on the experience of recent immigrants in the garment industry, in *Social Problems* (1984) and in *Hispanics in the US Economy*, edited by M. Tienda and G. Borjas (Academic, 1984). He has also done work on the economic aspects of ethnicity, labor markets and the post-industrial city.

Editor's preface

Feminists have always been ambivalent about the relationship of women to trade unions. On the one hand, there is abundant evidence of women workers' ill-treatment on the part of organized labor. Many unions have a history of excluding women from membership altogether; virtually all have tended to exclude them from positions of power. And unions have often acted to reinforce rather than to challenge sexual inequality in the labor market. On the other hand, it is indisputable that unionized women are better off than their unorganized sisters. And unionism appears to have tremendous unrealized potential as an instrument for improving the situation of women workers.

The essays in this book seek to come to terms with this contradictory legacy as it has unfolded over the past century of women's labor history in the United States. They take up a wide range of specific subjects. Some are case studies of women's participation in individual unions, organizing efforts, or strikes; others examine broader themes in women's labor history, focusing on a specific period; and still others explore the situation of particular categories of women workers over a longer time-span. Although they are written from a variety of perspectives, all the essays share a preoccupation with the complex relationship between gender, consciousness, and working-class activism, in the context of the labor movement.

The history of women workers' relationship to trade unionism has only recently emerged as an object of serious scholarly inquiry, and the literature is still quite limited. In the past two decades, there has been an enormous outpouring of new research and interpretation in both labor history and women's history, yet the study of women and unions has remained marginal to both these fields. In labor history, despite the strong influence of social history and the movement away from narrow, institutional studies, the tacit presumption that the history of the working class is the history of male workers has been preserved intact. In this respect, the 'new' labor history has failed to remedy the defects of the old. An adequate historiography of women's relationship to formal working-class institutions like unions and parties is still lacking; nor have the recent efforts to reconstruct the history of working-class culture and consciousness been particularly concerned with women. Within the rapidly proliferating literature in women's history, there has been more attention to women workers and their role in the labor movement, but here the study of women's past experience in relation to family, sexuality and feminism has been pursued far more extensively.

Perhaps it is because the topic has been so neglected that so much of the recent work which has appeared in women's labor history has been essentially descriptive in nature. Interpretative efforts have been largely devoted to questioning the traditional assumptions about women's relationship to the labor movement, rather than to reaching an independent definition of the terrain of debate. Certainly, it was necessary to challenge the total invisibility of women in conventional accounts of labor history, and the initial efforts to unearth the record of women's militancy as workers and labor activists were bound to produce descriptive histories. But this led, implicitly or explicitly, toward an overly simplistic and highly romanticized conception of women's labor history. The old myths of women's lack of interest or involvement in labor struggle were effectively supplanted by new myths, which were equally one-sided and, indeed, the mirror-image of the old. In the new feminist orthodoxy, each discovery of female militancy was taken as evidence of a virtually limitless potential for women's activism in the labor movement – a potential thwarted primarily by the disinterest or active hostility of male-dominated unions. While yielding some valuable insights and motivating a substantial body of important research, this approach could not do justice to the complexity of its subject.

The essays collected in this volume offer more nuanced perspectives on women's labor history, and begin to examine issues which were neglected in the early, essentially compensatory literature. For example, rather than insisting in a general way on the existence of a huge untapped potential for female activism, these studies seek to specify the historical conditions which have encouraged women's militancy and those which have impeded it. And, in reconstructing the history of women workers' protest activities, several of these essays suggest that the mobilization of women has been especially effective when it has utilized organizational forms and techniques very different from those typically employed by men – forms that are rooted in women's own distinctive culture and life-experience. Also included here are efforts to begin to explain, rather than simply describe, the long history of male unionists' poor treatment of women workers. After all, insofar as men have an interest in promoting working-class unity, they might be expected to encourage women's full participation in unions, rather than to exclude them, and it is hardly self-evident why men's gender interest should prevail over their class interest in this regard. By examining the structural characteristics of unionism, on the one hand, and the impact of broader social ideology about gender on the labor movement, on the other, several of these essays shed new light on this critical problem.

The research collected in this volume also breaks new ground in regard to the period that it covers. The bulk of recent scholarship on women's relationship to unionism in the United States concerns the late nineteenth and early twentieth centuries. Even for this earlier period, the literature is sparse; but for the years after World War I, it almost disappears altogether (with the exception of a small group of studies of women and the United Auto Workers in the period immediately after World War II). This book begins to fill in some of the gaps. While the first few essays deal with the period before 1920, all the rest analyze more recent developments.

This emphasis opens up a range of new substantive issues as well, for there were a number of interrelated shifts in women's position, both in the paid workforce and in the labor movement, which began in the interwar years and then culminated in the post-World War II period. First, in the aftermath of the suffrage victory, with the growth of female participation in the labor force, the legitimacy of trade union claims to special protection for women began to wane, paving the way for the development of a labor movement commitment to the pursuit of gender equality in the workplace. At the same time, both in the labor movement and in the larger society, there was a shift away from the 'family wage' ideal – according to which male wages should be sufficient for family support, so that married women have no need to work outside the home – and women were increasingly regarded as individuals with the same rights to work as men. These changes, of course, coincided with the rise of industrial unionism, which greatly expanded the space available to women and women's concerns within the mainstream labor movement. The new constraints and possibilities shaping women's relationship to trade unions in the past half-century, then, were quite different from those operating in earlier years, and more directly relevant to the dilemmas facing women in the unions today.

The contributions in this volume extend the scope of the literature in women's labor history, both conceptually and in terms of historical periods covered. Nevertheless, there are many serious omissions as well. In particular, the one essay included here on African–American women and the labor movement does not compensate for the severe underrepresentation of women of color in this field. But if this book generates more research and rethinking about women's relationship to trade unionism, historically and in the present, its purpose will have been amply fulfilled.

New York City   R.M.
January 1984

1

Bread before roses: American workingmen, labor unions and the family wage

Martha May

For most of the twentieth century, American trade unions have both endorsed and actively pursued the ideal of a 'family wage' – a wage rate sufficient to support a male worker and his family. Contemporary feminists have often criticized the family-wage ideal and have pointed to the many difficulties it has presented historically for women workers in their struggle for equality. But whether the family-wage ideal historically constituted a class aspiration, which both women and men of the working class supported, or, alternatively, an effort to consolidate male supremacy within the working-class family, is a point of intense controversy among feminist commentators. In this chapter, Martha May offers an important new historical perspective on this debate. Tracing the early history of the family-wage ideal and its relationship to the American labor movement, May suggests that initially, in the nineteenth century, the family wage emerged as a working-class cause, supported by both sexes – and strenuously opposed by capital. Subsequently, however, as the pragmatic unionism of the American Federation of Labor became the dominant force within the labor movement, gender privilege superseded the claims of class, and the family wage became a cross-class ideal, supported by Progressive reformers as well as workingmen. In the long run, May contends, the impact of the family-wage ideal on the labor movement was extremely divisive; yet its origins were in a politics of class unity.

... should be paid a living wage rather than ... as determined by the laws of the universe,' ... writer in 1872, 'is pure and simple ... nineteenth century, employers and laissez- ... trenuously against the living wage capable of supporting a worker and his family. Forcing employers to provide for non-workers through the pay packet, they warned, would mean the demise of American industry. The very spirit of free enterprise was at stake.

In the Progressive era, however, the idea of a living wage won widespread acceptance. By 1918, the authors of a social survey of Philadelphia could state confidently:

> Nowadays very few persons object to the principle of a living wage. It is generally agreed that the humblest worker is entitled to a return for his services that will enable him to support himself and his family in decency and comfort.[2]

Once championed only by workingmen and labor unions, now the living-wage ideal was endorsed by Progressive social scientists, and even by some employers – notably Henry Ford, Elbert Gary and John D. Rockefeller – for whom it offered the promise of worker stability and productivity, and a bulwark against radical unionism.[3]

The living wage of labor, Progressives and paternalistic employers was in practice a family wage: the earnings of a male worker which were sufficient to support a dependent family.[4] As an ideal – and, indeed, it was more often a demand than an achievement – the family wage legitimated the division of labor by gender.[5] It encouraged the notion that female participation in the labor force merely supplemented family income, and served to justify unequal wage rates and sex segregation in the labor market.

Contemporary feminists agree on the consequences of the family-wage ideology for women; its historical *purpose*, however, remains ambiguous. Was the family wage a vehicle for male supremacy? Or was it, as Jane Humphries has argued, primarily an attempt by the working classes to retain autonomy?[6] Or, did the family-wage demand constitute an effort by workers to win better conditions by mobilizing values accepted throughout society in support of their complaints? Exploring these issues may help illuminate the processes through which sex segregation in the labor market is created and maintained, and how it might be overcome. Specifically, analyzing the historical origins of the labor movement's commitment to the family-wage ideal may help to explain the enduring tension between women workers and American labor unions.

This chapter examines the family-wage ideology of organized labor in two periods: the decades of its formation in the nineteenth century, and its operation in the early twentieth century. I will argue that, in the earlier period, the family-wage demand emerged as a working-class cause, which capital opposed but which both working-class men and women supported. Its meaning was transformed in the early twentieth century, however, as the class perspective of labor changed into a more pragmatic unionism. In the Progressive era, the family wage became a cross-class ideology, and now, within that ideology, issues of gender superseded the claims of class autonomy.

The family wage as a working-class demand

The family-wage ideology emerged in the first half of the nineteenth century as a response by workingmen to specific industrial and social conditions: the inadequacies of wage rates; the difficulties of securing subsistence; the relative fluidity of the labor market, with its high turnover rates, decreasing skill requirements, and technological innovations; and the presence of a powerful ideology defining gender roles. Fearful of the erosion of customary traditions of craftsmanship, a decline in status and decreasing wages, skilled workmen expressed serious concern about the effects of industrial development on family life. 'The name of freedom is but a shadow . . . if we are to be torn from our fireside for endeavoring to obtain a fair and just support for our families,' journeymen cordwainers in Philadelphia argued in 1806.[7] Similarly, at a Utica, NY convention in the 1830s, workers agreed that 'the mechanic with his family . . . has the honest right not only to a livelihood for himself and them, but to save from his earnings the means of education for his children, and comfort for himself in his old age.'[8]

The family wage represented a dual claim to subsistence and industrial justice to its early advocates: workingmen, organized in trades' societies and unions, demanded both sufficient wages and the rights due the industrious producer in a republic. Without fair wages, the workingman faced poverty and a diminution in status, as dependency upon industrial wages placed new constraints upon family resources. Under existing wage rates, frequently inadequate for the needs of one person, the working-class family would be unable to maintain a tolerable standard of living or retain its customs or traditions.[9]

Workingmen repeatedly condemned 'purse-proud aristocrats' and 'tyranny,' as labor's demands in the early industrial era centered around regaining status, recouping losses and reaffirming the laborer's basic rights, including the right to maintain a family. In demands for better educational standards, and in attempts to secure consumers' cooperatives, mechanics' lien laws and equitable methods of payment, workingmen recognized the connection between control over working conditions and over home life. The family wage became a first step toward ameliorating the precarious position of the workingman and his family under the new conditions of industrialization, a means to restore their dignity and equality. Male workers claimed that 'which the God of nature intended as their right, but which avarice denies them – a comfortable subsistence.' The family wage also promised a means to diminish capitalists' control over family life, by allowing workingmen to provide independently for their families. Cordwainers from Lynn, Massachusetts, complained in 1844 about an industrial system which robbed 'our families of support, our children of the benefits of the higher branches of education, and ourselves of the many comforts of life,' while enriching employers and creating 'anti-republican' distinctions.[10]

Through such rhetoric, workingmen expressed the belief that only 'producers' and their families faced the dislocations of family life resulting from industrialization. Only their wives and children experienced the pressures to join the labor force; only their children confronted the possibility of a lifetime of poverty and need. Divorced from other sources of income, workers claimed that only a fair wage rate stood between their families and the specter of poverty and starvation. As early as the 1830s, workers argued that if wives and children were forced to enter the labor market to supplement family income, the status of the workingman would be degraded. As labor organizer Seth Luther reasoned, 'we know ... that the *wives* and *daughters* of the rich manufacturers would no more associate with a *factory girl* than they would with a *negro slave*. So much for equality in a republican country.'[11] The National Trades' Union asked, 'is not avarice satisfied with a nation of Fathers and Sons, but our Wives and Daughters, the Loved Ones of our hearts and affections, shall be thrown into the spoilers' arms?'.[12] [One purpose of the family-wage demand was to spare the workingman's wife and children the degradation of factory labor. And, equally important, it was to insure that the workingman would retain his status within the family, and his right to a family structure resembling that of the more advantaged classes.]

Gender?

Workingmen left little doubt as to the form of family life they sought. William English, a leader in the National Trades' Union, wondered in 1835 if the time would arrive when 'our wives, no longer doomed to servile labor, will be the companions of our fireside and the instructors of our children.'[13] Without adequate wages, the workingman could not fulfill the normative prescriptions for a 'proper' family life. The family-wage demand asserted the social right of the working class to the ideal of family and gender roles embodied in the 'cult of true womanhood.'[Indeed, the family-wage ideology was heavily dependent on arguments about female domesticity and male responsibility.]The physical organization, the natural responsibilities, and the moral sensibilities of woman, prove conclusively that her labor should only be of a domestic nature,' declared the National Trades' Union.[14] In a speech delivered in 1867, William Sylvis of the National Labor Union inveighed in similar terms:

> It will be fatal to the cause of labor, when we place the sexes in competition, and jeopardize those social relations which render woman queen of the household. Keep her in the sphere which God designed her to fill, by manly assistance.[15]

The family-wage ideology operated by connecting class issues of subsistence and justice with gender, thus defining the relationship between men, women and work. The domestic ideal placed women in the home, while waged work received an increasingly masculine definition. Indeed, the 'cult of breadwinning' was featured promin- ently in the class ideology which developed among industrial workmen.[16] [But gender divisions remained subordinate to class claims; the working-class family ideology continued to be qualified by its emphasis on subsistence, justice and the demand for better hours and wages.] The similarity between the working-class family and its middle-class counterpart, workingmen argued, ended at the pay packet. Family relationships and idealized roles depended upon material conditions to sustain them: without family wages, the lady became a poor wife and 'breadgiver,' taking in boarders and laundry, or going out to work; while the industrious male laborer was transformed into an indigent, losing prestige and power not only in the shop, but also in society and in the home. In short, while the working-class ideology of family life idealized middle-class gender roles, it did so in the context of an analysis of social and material conditions.[17]

[The arguments for the family wage invoked the interests of the entire family, thus going beyond a simple assertion of gender privilege.] Workingmen consistently viewed their wage-earning responsibility as beneficial to their dependants. They argued against women's presence in the labor market at lower wage rates because it endangered this wage-earning responsibility and gave rise to a new and undesirable (in their view) type of family structure.

Protest by workingmen over a low-wage population of workers entering a trade was not confined to exclusionism directed at women. Journeymen also opposed the employment of unregulated apprentices, prison labor, unskilled workers and some immigrant groups.[18] But workingmen countered the perceived dangers of women's participation in the labor force with the rhetoric of gender division. Some claimed that women's innate moral virtue would be corrupted by factory employment, while others contended that women were better suited for manual work and should be prohibited as competitors with an unfair advantage.[19] Occasionally, male unions aided striking female workers. More often, though, male-dominated trades' societies and unions excluded women outright, or admitted them only in the hope of lessening the ill effects of female competition.[20] Prior to 1873, only two among the thirty-plus national unions then in existence admitted women to membership.[21]

The frequency of arguments for female exclusion and their conjunction with the family-wage demand have led a number of historians to theorize that these arguments motivated the family wage itself: job competition between genders led workingmen to use male privilege as a means to achieve access to better wages and conditions.[22] But the history of the family-wage ideology prior to 1890 suggests the need for reevaluation of this interpretation. Nineteenth-century sexual divisions must be understood in the dual context which they had for workingmen themselves: the shop as well as the home. The family wage, as a solution to the threats the workingman perceived to himself and to his family in the new industrial order, appeared *first* as a class demand for industrial justice, and a defense of traditional work and family arrangements. As the presence of women wage-earners in the labor market threatened to upset the balance between home and shop, and to diminish further the workingman's ability to have or maintain a family, the family-wage demand took on the additional aspect of female exclusion. The family wage promised to serve the male worker in the shop, by securing his right to better wages; it also maintained the family in the home, allowing women to fulfill their 'natural' role as wives and mothers, and allowing children to attain some education. The family wage promised to remedy class injustice by raising the standard of living of workers, and by assuring them family stability and security. 'Is it charitable, is it humane, is it honest, to take from the laborer, who is already fed, clothed, and lodged too poorly, a portion of his food and raiment, and deprive his family of the necessities of life?' iron-molders asked in 1859.[23] The family wage promised to resolve this inequity, to sustain family life and to protect family autonomy.

Yet, the family-wage demand ultimately exacted a higher price from its advocates. It worked against the interests of working-class men, women and families, by accepting and deepening a sexual double standard in the labor market. The family-wage ideal gave employers an easy means of undercutting wage rates and fostering competition among workers. It also confined both males and females to gender roles which impeded individual opportunity and expression. Equally important, the family-wage ideology discouraged any attempt to explore new, more egalitarian family arrangements within the context of industrialization. In defending the family through the family wage, working-class men and women placed family interests above individual need. This was especially significant for women, who shared in the advantages accruing to working-class families through the family-wage demand, but who at the same time faced the discrimination it legitimated, both in the shop and at home.

The problems inherent in the family-wage demand gradually became apparent, as the class character of the ideology's supporters underwent a dramatic shift in the Progressive era. Middle-class social reformers and activists came to embrace the family wage as a means of restoring social stability, while some employers recognized its possibilities as a means to control and divide labor. At the same time, within the ranks of organized labor, the family wage increas-
? ingly became a defense of gender privilege.[Labor's family wage, first predicated on the family, now served fully to rationalize male pre-rogatives, as women entered the labor market in growing numbers.]

The 'modern' family wage

As labor struggled for material improvements after 1890, the family wage played a crucial role in its demands. The dominance of the American Federation of Labor (AFL) indicated a new emphasis within labor's ranks on trade union issues of hours, wages and conditions; Samuel Gompers explained the philosophy of the modern trade union as 'economic betterment – today, tomorrow, in home and shop.'[24] Gompers called for

> a minimum wage – a living wage – which when expended in an economic manner, shall be sufficient to maintain an average-sized family in a manner consistent with whatever the con-temporary civilization recognized as indispensable to physical and mental health.[25]

Similarly, the family wage demanded by the AFL in 1907 was to be 'a constantly growing minimum wage ... sufficient to maintain [workers] and those dependent upon them in a manner consistent with their responsibilities as *husbands, fathers, men* and *citizens*.'[26] The AFL's position remained the same in 1919, when a spokesman summarized it this way:

> The workers are tired of having themselves, their wives and children, used as chips for our commercial, financial, and industrial gamblers ... What is the price we pay for children

free from factory life, for mothers burdened by no duties outside
the home, for fathers who have leisure for homes and families?
. . . The living wage is the right to be a man and to exercise freely
and fully the rights of a free man. That is the living wage, and to
realize it is the sure and true destiny of organized labor.[27]

This family-wage idea relied heavily on the male's right to an
improved standard of living as the family breadwinner, and implied
a fundamental difference between the rights of male and female
workers. Although the AFL pledged to organize women, and joined
in the call for female suffrage, affiliates continued to argue that
female workers reduced wage rates, and the federation took no
action against member-unions prohibiting female membership.[28]
Gompers himself contended in 1906, 'it is the so-called competition
of the unorganized defenseless women workers, the girl and the wife,
that often tends to reduce the wages of the father and the husband.'[29]
As Alice Kessler-Harris has suggested, the AFL tipped the scales
balancing female equality and exclusion toward the policy of
exclusion – never fully sanctioning gender restrictions, but maintaining barriers against female workers.[30]

Unlike the nineteenth-century labor movement's family-wage
argument, which reflected a broad-based response to industrialization, the AFL's family wage shifted the emphasis from the family
life to gender privilege. This paralleled the broader shift in the early
twentieth century to a pragmatic new unionism seeking material
improvements and union strength, rather than a class-based
movement for greater equality. [As the claim of class justice receded ?
as a motivation for the family-wage demand, the AFL argued for
improvements based on the male's primary role as worker and
breadwinner.] While rhetorically addressing the interests of a class of
producers, the federation pursued a family wage to legitimate higher
male wages. It implicitly promised the male unionist that only membership in an AFL affiliate would secure for him and his family an
'American standard of living.' In effect, the family now appeared as
one beneficiary of the male worker's claims, and not the reverse, as
had been the case in the nineteenth century.

The AFL differentiated between male and female workers in a
variety of ways – in its position on minimum wages, for example.
The federation opposed wage regulation for males, arguing that

legislation interfered with labor's ability to bargain and negotiate. At the same time, it recognized women, minors and government employees as exceptions requiring special protection. In 1913, the AFL resolved that women workers 'constitute a separate and more difficult problem. They are ... more easily exploited.'[31] The federation failed to object to the methods the states used to determine minimum wage levels, which in every case reflected the subsistence needs of single women, not of those supporting dependants. This sharply contrasted with labor's demand that the lowest male earnings should reflect the possibility that the male worker would be supporting a family, whether or not such a family was in fact present. The assumption was that all wage-earning women were single and left the workforce upon marriage; men, by contrast, should always be accorded higher wages because they might, one day, have families to support.

Gender-based wage differentials were also encouraged by the growing use of the family-wage idea in private and governmental budget studies and cost-of-living surveys, which figured minimum standards of 'health and decency' on the amount needed by a male breadwinner to support a dependent family. Labor's family-wage demands dovetailed with Progressive reformers' and social activists' insistence upon a male-supported family structure. As social worker Mary Conyngton advised, the 'friendly visitor' should 'properly use every means to make the wife see her duties as a homemaker, there should be no relaxation in the effort to make the man do his duty as breadwinner.'[32] A growing consensus appeared among such middle-class reformers that a family wage would allow working-class families to preserve 'proper' social values. Through the inculcation of thrift, sobriety and order, problems of poverty and social upheaval could be eliminated. A family composed of the male bread-winner, home-bound wife and obedient, Americanized children was central to this Progressive outlook. As early as 1904, economist John A. Ryan suggested that the economic vehicle for realizing this form of family life was the family wage.[33]

By World War I, the federal government had become a third advocate of the family wage, along with the Progressive and labor movements. The National War Labor Board used family-wage-based budget studies in its wage-adjustment determinations.[34] This practice produced debate over what constituted a family standard, and whether the government was encouraging an increase in standards of living. Many employers objected to the use of family wages in wage adjustments; one analyst noted that 'the attempt to set a budget-wage on the basis of the family's needs meant . . . the establishment of a family wage for all adult male employees, regardless of family responsibilities.'[35] While state support of the family wage did not result in the pernicious effects envisioned by its detractors, nor in the uniform achievement of a family-wage standard, it is significant that sectors of the state accepted its validity and urged its adoption. Once the family-wage ideology became part of a cross-class ideology, it had the status of a truism, an easily accepted statement on the best organization of life.

This cross-class acceptance of the family-wage standard in budget studies and wage determination initially appeared to benefit organized labor. But after World War I, it became a double-edged sword, as government determinations raised some wages while reducing others. The AFL returned to its former position against wage regulations after 1918.[36] Unions discovered that the family wage could be turned against the workingman by employers, as when family-wage rates connected to 'welfare' programs served to undercut union organization and divide the workforce.[37] Under these conditions, the AFL might have qualified or dropped its support of the family-wage notion, now employed to limit earnings and oppose organized labor. That the AFL affiliates continued to cite the male responsibility as family breadwinner to gain access to jobs and higher wages suggests this ideology remained useful in securing short-term goals. If the family wage no longer served to protect labor's family requirements at an optimal level, it still provided an advantage to the male worker in the shop.

Growing public concern over the impact of married women's participation in the labor force provided unionists with new ammunition to protect their jobs and prerogatives. After World War I, the family-wage idea reinforced the notion that most women worked temporarily, supplementing a male's earnings. Few people challenged the single woman's right to work; by the 1920s she was 'no longer expected to remain in the household of some related male protector.'[38] But the single woman eventually married and began her own family; then, as a Women's Bureau study stated, 'it is of manifest importance to know why so large a group of women with home responsibilities should be at work while the usual family providers are in evidence.'[39] Observers of the phenomenon of married women's waged work concluded wives' motivation for earning was family need.[40] This perception acknowledged the generally low rate of male earnings while rationalizing women's work, negating the idea of choice. Gwendolyn Hughes noted, 'as a rule, even mothers who worked from "choice" were simply making an effort to raise their families above a mere "subsistence" level.'[41] Although some commentators hailed married women's work as a sign of a positive, growing independence, most worried about the impact of mothers' absence from their children. Married women's work outside the home represented both a sign of new consumption needs and new household relationships; as Day Monroe viewed it, work for upper-class women was facilitated by the hired help who would assume their household duties. For working-class women, the 'problem' was more troublesome: who would ease the double burden they faced, of waged work and family responsibilities? The remedies suggested by analysts included mothers' pensions, family allowances, industry-supported child payments, and the family wage – all geared to ending the necessity for working-class married women to work.[42]

For organized labor, the continued popularity of the family-wage idea afforded male workers an opportunity to further their arguments for higher wage rates. Male unionists could demand first rights to jobs and pay increases because married women's employment only supplemented family income, and single women could expect to marry. Higher male earnings had an ideological legitimacy that women could not claim without asserting equal rights or denying the 'natural' organization of the family; the family wage provided a convenient means for male workers to retain their control of jobs and conditions.

The effectiveness of arguments for protection of male positions had a significant impact upon women workers. For example, in Highland Park, Michigan, the city council barred married women from city jobs in 1921, and followed that action by prohibiting all women workers, claiming that women displaced unemployed men.[43] In the 1920s, the Baltimore and Ohio Railroad agreed with the Brotherhood of Railway and Steamship Clerks to prohibit married women's work.[44] In the same decade, other unions simply excluded women entirely; the various unions representing elastic goring weavers, carpenters and joiners, and pattern-makers all denied women membership. In their twenty-fifth convention, the molders' union resolved that their leaders should 'give their best thoughts and effort in opposing the employment of female and child labor in jobs recognized as men's employment.'[45] While women workers as a category found themselves relegated to specific sectors of the labor market, married women's employment remained particularly suspect. The married women workers took work away from men who needed to labor. Some social analysts tried to counter such perceptions by arguing that women did not displace male workers; ironically, these advocates of women's expanded roles did not recognize that their defense admitted the importance – and the problems – of a sexually divided workforce.[46]

During the Depression, use of the family-wage argument to limit or prohibit women's employment accelerated. In 1930, the Economy Act's Section 213 mandated the discharge of one spouse in cases where both were federal government employees. This controversial legislation, directly based on the family-wage ideology, was proposed or adopted across the nation. In Kansas, the governor suggested barring women from employment if their husbands could support them. Syracuse, Racine and Seattle prohibited the employment of women whose husbands earned a 'living wage.' According to Lois Scharf, a 'virtual epidemic' of such legislation infected twenty-six states by 1939, some explicitly labeling the level at which a family income was sufficient to warrant discharge.[47] Despite the position of the national AFL that women workers should receive equal pay for equal work, some state and local federations, such as in Idaho, urged exclusion of married women.[48]

The family-wage ideology remained in full force, promoted by governmental agencies, AFL affiliates and social reformers. For the AFL, tacit support of the family wage was a pragmatic effort to defend falling wage rates, which declined 48 percent between 1929 and 1933.[49] Family-wage arguments continued to defend the male worker's right to a job at decent wages because of his gender and, by implication, his family responsibility. Overall, women's exclusion or lower pay seemed to be in the national interest, for the preservation of the nation's economy. But if the family wage rationalized discrimination against women in the name of the family, it returned

o most working-class households. Instead, it
ily earnings by reinforcing the exclusion of
r or lowering her wage rates, at a time when
the families of unskilled workers contained a
.[50] The family wage continued to serve only
s: the skilled unionists who could organize to
pursue jobs and oppose wage reductions.

Male privilege provided an extra claim to work and wages that unionists would not fully abandon until World War II, when the presence of women workers in jobs previously reserved for men forced them to support equal pay for women in order to protect their own postwar rates. [Under these conditions, the family-wage ideology no longer served the interests of unionized men. World War II also brought married women into the labor force in much larger numbers than ever before, a development which became permanent after the war.] This change in the composition of the female labor force gradually made the family-wage ideology anachronistic; [yet, within the organized labor movement, it dies hard.] To this day, one encounters expressions of the family-wage ideology among male unionists, and its resilience is one part of the explanation for the failure of organized labor to bring the ever-increasing number of women workers into its ranks.

Conclusion

The family wage illustrates a complex relationship between gender and class, one that rarely remained static. This wage form, and the ideology defining it, underwent a series of changes through the first 100 years of its operation. During the nineteenth century, it served as one argument for class justice and working-class autonomy. Workingmen perceived themselves denied access to a 'proper,' traditional family life, and they pressed their grievances about conditions in home and shop by citing family interests. There was little that was revolutionary or reactionary in their calls for family wages. They merely attempted to insure their families would not deviate from prescribed social norms: their demands were remarkably similar to the popular cultural descriptions of family articulated through an ideology of 'separate spheres.' What was crucial in the progress of the nineteenth-century family-wage ideology was the response to these demands outside the working class. No middle-class reformer incorporated the family wage into programs of relief for the poor, which continued to be premised on individual problems of intemperance and moral laxity. In the latter half of the nineteenth century, the family-wage demand also conflicted with employers' and governmental laissez-faire notions that wages should be strictly sufficient for an individual, with no guarantees of family minimums. [The class interests of capital and labor were opposed in the family-wage ideology, while the gender ?] interests of working-class men and women appeared to be united in efforts to achieve or maintain particular reproductive structures.[51]

By the turn of the century, organized labor addressed its full efforts to winning economic improvements through trade union strategies. [As the class perspective of labor changed into a more pragmatic ? unionism, Progressive activists and social reformers took up the issue of the working-class poor.] In seeking to reestablish social order, these predominantly middle-class men and women promoted the family wage as a solution to instability within the working-class family. The family wage became a cross-class ideology, with the issues of gender now superseding the claims of class autonomy. Progressive advocacy won widespread support for the family-wage ideology, but in a different form from the family wages pursued by organized labor. The Progressives' family wage, adopted by state and federal government agencies, and by some employers, was calculated at a minimum family level, while labor sought to maximize earnings. Middle-class use of the family wage, and some employers' acceptance of it, effectively limited the long-term economic advantages of the family wage to skilled labor.

Why did the family wage achieve an ideological hegemony? For reformers, this wage form promised to restore the 'traditional' family they believed would best provide stability and American values. Without adequate family wages, women and children were forced into the labor market, undermining the foundations of home life so essential to efficient social order. These goals corresponded with the needs of collective capital in several ways. The family-wage ideology reinforced the notion that women worked only to supplement family income, or temporarily as single women. This allowed employers to pay lower female wages without – in popular wisdom – endangering the social structure. But family wages served more subtle interests as well. They divided the workforce between genders, and between high- and low-waged sectors. An employer who awarded the family wage could blunt union activity and increase long-term profitability by reducing high labor turnover. The family wage also decreased overall working-class earnings by limiting female wages. When families sent several wage-earners into the labor force to earn a joint income sufficient for family needs, their wages together might easily exceed a minimum reasonable family-wage level.[52] In other words, family-wage payments tend to reduce wage costs of collective capital not by securing the unpaid domestic labor of the wife in the home, but by limiting her earnings and the amount paid to a family. Individual employers often failed to recognize this advantage, however, because of their short-term interest in hiring lower-paid females.

For organized labor, the impact of the family wage was, in the long run, detrimental. As unionists themselves occasionally argued, the existence of gender divisions allowed employers to undercut higher rates by using a low-waged workforce. In general, unionists chose to support female exclusion rather than pursue the gender equality which would have resolved the divisions in the interests of the entire working class. Motivated by the short-term goals of job protection and immediate material improvements, unionists maintained a commitment to the family wage to further their specific, limited needs.

The family wage also operated in the long-term interest of male workers, by perpetuating the legitimacy of gender privilege. While women workers struggled to convince employers – and society – of their need for fair wages and jobs, male workers found easier access to positions and power. In the twentieth century, this was facilitated by the abandonment of a class perspective in favor of pragmatism. Unionized workers defended their positions using whatever tools were readily available, including the ideology of sexual division. In the absence of a systematic, feminist class analysis, this probably appeared as the best choice for the trade union movement in the years before World War II. Ultimately, however, this path deepened the problems associated with a sexually divided labor force.

The family-wage ideology retained its power because it promised so much to so many: to reformers, order; to employers, profitability;

to unionized male workers, access and job control; to the unskilled, the hope of better conditions. The ideology reinforced class-specific goals while providing social stability. The one group which obviously did not benefit from the family wage was working women. Not only were their wages reduced – or terminated – by the family-wage ideal; there was also pressure from the definition of their work as unfeminine, selfish and detrimental to the social good. It is this legacy of the family wage, as much as its impact on the structure of the labor market and upon wages, which feminist organization still must confront.

Notes

1 Sidney Fine, *Laissez-Faire and the General Welfare State*, Ann Arbor, University of Michigan Press, 1956, p.60.
2 Bureau of Municipal Research of Philadelphia, *Workingmen's Standards of Living in Philadelphia*, New York, Macmillan, 1919, p.1.
3 I do not mean to imply that employers' use of the family wage was widespread; in general, it was the larger corporations with the capital to invest in strategies for long-term productivity which experimented with family-oriented 'welfare.' See Katherine Stone, 'Origins of Job Structures in the Steel Industry,' in Richard C. Edwards, Michael Reich and David M. Gordon, eds, *Labor Market Segmentation*, Lexington, D. C. Heath, 1975, p.54; Martha May, 'The Historical Problem of the Family Wage: The Ford Motor Company and the Five Dollar Day,' *Feminist Studies*, vol. 8, no. 2, Summer 1982, pp.399–424.
4 Progressive analysts also estimated the living wage for a single woman worker, and occasionally the single male. Family budget studies predominated, however, indicating both widespread concern about family life and the assumption that most Americans lived in a family unit. Faith M. Williams and Helen Connolly, *Bibliography on Studies and Costs and Standards of Living in the United States*, United States Department of Agriculture, Bureau of Home Economics, 1930; Shelby Harrison, *The Social Survey*, New York, Russell Sage Foundation, 1931; Charles Y. Glock, ed., *Survey Research in the Social Sciences*, New York, Russell Sage Foundation, 1967.
5 While the family-wage ideology promised to end poverty, average wages remained near or beneath estimated subsistence levels in the Progressive era. See, for example, Scott Nearing, *Financing the Wage Earner's Family*, New York, B. W. Huebsch, 1914; and Robert C. Chapin, *The Standard of Living among Workingmen's Families in New York City*, New York, Russell Sage Foundation, 1909.

6   See Heidi Hartmann, 'The Unhappy Marriage of Marxism and Feminism: Towards a More Progressive Union,' *Capital and Class*, vol. 8, summer 1979, pp.1–32, and Jane Humphries, 'The Working-Class Family, Women's Liberation and Class Struggle: The Case of Nineteenth-century British History,' *Review of Radical Political Economics*, vol. 9, fall 1977, pp.25–42.

7   David Saposs, 'Colonial and Federal Beginnings,' in John R. Commons, *et al., History of Labor in the United States*, vol. 1, New York, Macmillan, 1918, pp. 141–2.

8   Mary P. Ryan, *Cradle of the Middle Class: The Family in Oneida County, New York, 1790–1865*, New York, Cambridge University Press, 1981, p.131.

9   Historians continue to debate the 'typical' standard of living of skilled and unskilled working-class families in the nineteenth century. Most argue that unskilled laborers received wages sufficient for the support of a single person, while skilled workers' wages could range from levels beneath poverty to a comfortable family standard. For some members of the working classes, the family wage was obviously a potential means for gaining adequate subsistence. See Clyde Griffen, 'Workers Divided: The Effect of Craft and Ethnic Differences in Poughkeepsie, New York, 1850–1880,' and Leo F. Schnore and Peter R. Knights, 'Residence and Social Structure: Boston in the Antebellum Period,' both in Stephan Thernstrom and Richard Sennett, eds, *Nineteenth-century Cities: Essays in the New Urban History*, New Haven, Yale University Press, 1969; Norman Ware, *The Industrial Worker, 1840–1860*, Boston, Houghton Mifflin, 1924; Bruce Laurie, *Working People of Philadelphia, 1800–1850*, Philadelphia, Temple University Press, 1980; and Steven Dubnoff, 'A Method for Estimating the Economic Welfare of American Families of Any Composition, 1860–1909,' *Historical Methods*, vol. 13, no. 3, pp.171–80.

10 Philip Foner, *History of the Labor Movement in the United States*, vol. I: *From Colonial Times to the Founding of the American Federation of Labor*, New York, International Publishers, 1947, p.120; John R. Commons, *et al., A Documentary History of American Industrial Society*, New York, Russell & Russell, 1958, vol. 8, p.234.

11 Seth Luther, *Address to the Working Men of New England*, pamphlet reprinted in Philip Taft and Leo Stein, eds, *Religion, Reform, and Revolution: Labor Panaceas in the Nineteenth Century*, New York, Arno, 1970, p.1.

12 Commons, *Documentary*, vol. 5, p.284.

13 Helen Sumner, *Report on the Condition of Women and Child Wage Earners in the United States*, vol. 9: *History of Women in Industry in the United States*, Washington, 1910, p.29.

14 Commons, *Documentary*, vol. 6, p.281.

15 James C. Sylvis, *The Life, Speeches, Labors, and Essays of William H. Sylvis*, Philadelphia, Claxton, Remsen & Haffelefinger, 1872, p.220.

16 The 'cult of breadwinning' has received little attention from historians, and its origins and developments remain sketchy at best. The masculine ideal dates at least to the patriarchal family of colonial America, in which men held legal and economic responsibility for family affairs. See, for example, Philip Greven, *The Protestant Temperament: Patterns in Child Rearing, Religious Experience, and the Self in America*, New York, Alfred A. Knopf, 1977; Mary Beth Norton, *Liberty's Daughters: The Revolutionary Experience of American Women, 1750–1800*, Boston, Little Brown, 1980. See also Linda Schneider, 'The Citizen Striker: Workers' Ideology in the Homestead Strike of 1892,' *Labor History*, vol. 22, no. 4, winter 1981, pp.52–63.

17 An excellent example of this may be found in the speeches of National Labor Union leader William Sylvis. See Sylvis, *Life, Speeches, Labors*.

18 See John Higham, *Strangers in the Land: Patterns of American Nativism, 1860–1925*, New York, Atheneum, 1971; John B. Andrews, 'Nationalisation,' in Commons, *History of Labor*, vol. 2, especially pp.3–10; Ware, *The Industrial Worker*.

19 Ware, *The Industrial Worker*, pp.77–80; Commons, *Documentary*, vol. 8, pp.134–49.

20 See, for example, Carol Turbin, 'And We Are Nothing But Women: Irish Working Women in Troy,' in Carol R. Berkin and Mary Beth Norton, eds, *Women of America: A History*, Boston, Houghton Mifflin, 1979, pp.202–21.

21 Gerald Grob, *Workers and Utopia: A Study of Industrial Conflict in the American Labor Movement, 1865–1900*, Evanston, Northwestern University Press, 1961, p.55.

22 For example, see Hartmann, 'The Unhappy Marriage,' and Alice Kessler-Harris, *Out to Work: A History of Wage-earning Women in the United States*, New York, Oxford University Press, 1982, p.68.

23 Sylvis, *Life, Speeches, Labors*, p.32.

24 Samuel Gompers, *Seventy Years of Life and Labor*, New York, E. P. Dutton, 1925, p.286. See also Grob, *Workers and Utopia*, p.133.

25 James Boyle, *The Minimum Wage and Syndicalism*, Cincinatti, Stewart & Kidd, 1913, p.73.

26 American Federation of Labor, *History, Encyclopedia, Reference Book*, American Federation of Labor, Washington, DC, 1919, p.7.

27 David Saposs, *Readings in Trade Unionism*, New York, George H. Doran, 1926, p.270.

28 Ruth Milkman, 'Organizing the Sexual Division of Labor: Historical Perspectives on "Women's Work" and the American Labor Movement,' *Socialist Review*, January–February 1980, pp.95–144; Women's Bureau, Bulletin no. 12, 'The New Position of Women in American Industry,' Washington, DC, 1920, p.157.

29 Alice Kessler-Harris, ' "Where are the Organized Women Workers?",' *Feminist Studies*, vol. 3, no. 1/2, fall 1975, p.96.

30 *Ibid.* See also Ann Schofield, 'The Rise of the Pig-Headed Girl: An

Analysis of the American Labor Press for their Attitudes toward Women, 1877–1920,' PhD dissertation, State University of New York, Binghamton, 1980.

31 Taft and Stein, eds, *Religion, Reform and Revolution*, p.146.

32 See Mary Conyngton, *How to Help: A Manual of Practical Charity*, New York, Macmillan, 1909, p.131.

33 John A. Ryan, *The Living Wage*, New York, Macmillan, 1906.

34 Selig Perlman and Philip Taft, 'Labor Movements,' in Commons, *Documentary*, vol. 2, p.408.

35 Don Lescohier, 'Working Conditions,' in Commons, *Documentary*, vol. 3, p.72.

36 Perlman and Taft, 'Labor Movements,' p.452.

37 See May, 'Historical Problem of the Family Wage.'

38 Day Monroe, *Chicago Families: A Study of Unpublished Census Data*, Chicago, University of Chicago Press, 1932, p.31.

39 Women's Bureau, Bulletin no. 23, 'The Family Status of Breadwinning Women,' Washington, DC, 1922, p.42; Women's Bureau, Bulletin no. 30, 'The Share of Wage-earning Women in Family Support,' Washington, DC, 1923, p.1.

40 See Winifred Wandersee, 'Past Ideals and Present Pleasures: Women, Work, and the Family, 1920–1940,' PhD, University of Minnesota, 1976; Robert and Helen M. Lynd, *Middletown: A Study in American Culture*, New York, Harcourt Brace & World, 1929, pp.26–7; and Lois Scharf, *To Work and to Wed: Female Employment, Feminism, and the Great Depression*, Westport, Greenwood Press, 1980.

41 Gwendolyn S. Hughes, *Mothers in Industry*, New York, New Republic, 1925, p.25.

42 *Ibid.*, p.17; Monroe, *Chicago Families*, pp.1, 185.

43 *New York Times*, November 28, 1921.

44 Scharf, *To Work and to Wed*, p.44.

45 Women's Bureau, Bulletin no. 12, 'The New Position of Women in American Industry,' Washington, DC, 1920, p.57.

46 See Kessler-Harris, *Out to Work*, p.296.

47 Scharf, *To Work and to Wed*, pp.42–56; Lorine Pruette and Iva L. Peters, eds, *Women Workers Through the Depression*, New York, Macmillan, 1934, p.104.

48 Scharf, *To Work and to Wed*, p.131.

49 Broadus Mitchell, *Depression Decade: From the New Era Through the New Deal*, New York, Holt Rinehart & Winston, 1947, p.270.

50 In 1930, 78 percent of the employed population was male and 22 percent was female. Lescohier, 'Working Conditions,' p.35. Day Monroe discovered that in Chicago in 1920, 57 percent of families of unskilled workers were supported by a sole male breadwinner (Monroe, *Chicago Families*). A later study of Chicago families by Leila Houghteling reported that for over two-thirds of unskilled marriage wage-earners, a male's earnings were insufficient to provide a standard of living

comparable to that awarded by charities (Houghteling, The *Income and Standard of Living of Unskilled Laborers in Chicago*, University of Chicago Press, 1927).

51 Fine, *Laissez-Faire*; Robert Bremner, *From the Depths: The Discovery of Poverty in the United States*, New York University Press, 1967, p.4.

52 A comparison of English and American standards of living at the turn of the century by Peter Shergold illustrates the point: when examined on the basis of male earnings, American working-class incomes appeared higher than those of English laborers. When female earnings were added to family receipts, English families enjoyed a higher family standard. See Peter Shergold, *Working-class Life: The 'American Standard' in Comparative Perspective, 1899–1913*, University of Pittsburgh Press, 1982.

2

Labor organizing and female institution-building: The Chicago Women's Trade Union League, 1904–24

Colette A. Hyman

Are women workers essentially like their male counterparts, or do they have distinctive characteristics and needs which demand special attention from labor organizers? Contemporary American feminists tend to be suspicious of any assertions that women workers are 'different' from men, and blame women's underrepresentation in the labor movement on sexism and on the unions' relative lack of interest in organizing women. An earlier generation of feminists, however, had a very different point of view, as Colette A. Hyman demonstrates in her analysis of the Chicago Women's Trade Union League in the early twentieth century. The league developed strategies for organizing women which built directly upon the cultural norms that separated women workers from men – in effect, embracing rather than challenging those norms. While the trade unions focused almost exclusively on workplace issues in their organizing efforts, the league sought to draw women into the labor movement through much broader appeals, addressing women's concerns within the community as well as the workplace. Hyman shows how the league's middle-class leaders, drawing on their experience in the settlement house movement, successfully utilized 'woman-centered' organizing techniques in the female working-class and immigrant communities of early-twentieth-century Chicago.

In her long years as an organizer for the Boot and Shoe Workers' Union and for the Chicago Women's Trade Union League (WTUL), one of the most valuable lessons that Mary Anderson learned was that 'to get women into the trade union movement required a technique that was different from organizing men.' One aspect of this technique was securing 'nice places for the girls to meet in order to lure them to come.' The Chicago WTUL placed great emphasis on this tactic. In 1913, it successfully petitioned the School Board to allow trade unions to hold meetings in the schools rather than above the saloons. 'Women who are members of unions,' the resolution read, 'do not attend the meetings because of the proximity to the saloon.'[1]

In seeking acceptable meeting places for women, the WTUL was attempting to overcome some of the obstacles to women's labor activism without challenging the rigid cultural norms of the day. The league's entire approach to organizing women workers was shaped by Anderson's precept that getting women into the labor movement required strategies distinct from those used to organize men. In contrast to the established unions, the WTUL took into account the whole of women's lives, not just their lives as wage-workers. The strategies that the league developed encompassed women's domestic responsibilities as well as cultural standards that severely limited women's participation in activities outside the home.

By its very structure, the organized labor movement at the turn of the century all but excluded working women. The American Federation of Labor (AFL), which set the norms for labor organizing in this period, sought to mobilize skilled workers, the vast majority of whom were white, native-born men; the majority of working women were unskilled immigrants. In many cases, women were automatically unionized where men had succeeded in effecting a closed-shop agreement, or unions organized women in order effectively to protect the earning power of men. Generally, however, as one contemporary female observer put it, 'the real effort expended in actual organizing among women is indeed a negligible factor.'[2]

Historians who have tried to account for the limited representation of women in the labor movement have largely focused on the lack of attention to organizing women on the part of the established unions. For example, in *The Rising of the Women*, Meredith Tax argues that women

> were unorganized because they have just become workers;
> because they had so much work to do at home that they could

hardly move; because their husbands, boyfriends, and fathers did not let them go to meetings; because they earned so little that they could not afford to take extra risks; and because no one would organize them. And when anyone tried, women often showed that, despite all these barriers, they were raring to go.[3]

Tax presents an account of what happened 'when anyone tried' to organize women. She recognizes the existence of special obstacles that limited women's participation in the labor movement, but her analysis does not extend to women activists' systematic efforts to overcome those obstacles.

The WTUL occupies a central place in the history of women in the labor movement precisely because it was one of the first labor organizations directly to confront the culturally imposed limitations on women's activities and their domestic responsibilities in attempting to draw them into the union movement. In the varied activities and programs that it developed for women workers, the WTUL consistently took women's special needs into account. In designing women-centered organizing strategies, the WTUL took advantage of already existing networks among women, and helped to create new ones in order to facilitate women's collective action. The league focused its activities on the existing women's community, while simultaneously working to reshape that community.

These strategies were born out of women's experience in the various groups and organizations that constituted 'social feminism' in the late nineteenth and early twentieth centuries, and particularly the settlement houses. It was through this work that the middle-class women who came together to form the WTUL learned about women's networks and about the importance women attached to traditional institutions. Most of the early and more successful work of Hull House and other settlement houses was with women, although they were also strongly dedicated to the labor movement, providing meeting places for unions and support during strikes.[4]

While settlement house leaders were among the founders of the WTUL and were active in each of the first three chapters that were formed (in New York, Boston and Chicago), the connection between the settlement house movement and the WTUL was particularly strong in Chicago. The first officers of the Chicago league were all settlement house residents, and the WTUL held its meetings at Hull House, until it moved to a building downtown occupied by other union offices.[5]

It was through their settlement house work that the middle-class women who helped shape the Chicago WTUL learned about the issues facing working-class women, and about the familial and communal networks that existed among them. This education molded their whole analysis of the needs of working women. The settlement house was also the avenue through which working-class women, at least initially, came into the WTUL. The women who brought their children to Hull House for kindergarten, or who came themselves for sewing classes, got to know the middle-class women who later would organize WTUL outings, socials and meetings. Subsequently, these same working women, with their friends and female kin, attended league meetings and became involved in the organization.

The Chicago chapter of the WTUL is certainly not unique for its involvement with settlement houses. However, it does stand out for its continued involvement in labor struggles long after other chapters – most notably the New York chapter – began shifting their focus to protective legislation campaigns. The Chicago chapter also benefited from that city's strong tradition of labor activism and previous attempts at cross-class cooperation among women. These traditions greatly enhanced the league's ability to work with male-dominated labor organizations, in particular the Chicago Federation of Labor.[6] These factors all combine to make the Chicago WTUL a fruitful case study for examining the league's organizing strategies, and for examining the more general use of women-centered strategies for organizing women into labor unions.

The WTUL's strategies and the activities that constituted them can be separated into two broad categories: direct participation in strikes, labor negotiations and the establishment of unions, on the one hand; and the whole range of activities designed to promote unionization among women, on the other. The latter included social events, educational programs, publication of the 'Women's Department' in the Chicago *Union Labor Advocate* and, later, of the monthly *Life and Labor*.

The wave of garment-workers' strikes of 1909–10 in New York and Philadelphia washed over Chicago the following winter, placing the Chicago WTUL in an important role as organizer and negotiator as had been the case in New York and Philadelphia.[7] When the workers walked out of the Hart, Schaffner and Marx factories, they first approached the United Garment Workers of America (UGWA) for assistance. As support from the union was not forthcoming, strikers sought assistance from other sources. Within a few weeks of the walkout, they appealed to the WTUL, at first asking for speakers for their meetings. The league soon became a major actor in the struggle, and contributed to its resolution at two levels. The organization was represented by Margaret Dreier Robins and Agnes Nestor on the Joint Strike Conference Board (composed of representatives from the UGWA, the Chicago Federation of Labor and the Strikers' Executive Committee). The WTUL also set up its own strike committees.

Robins's and Nestor's participation in these successful negotiations between manufacturers and workers won them and the WTUL the respect of the Chicago labor movement. In fact, Robins was elected to the Chicago Federation of Labor Executive Committee shortly afterward. The high esteem in which the labor community held Robins and the WTUL, as a result of their participation in this major strike and in other smaller ones, served the league well. Because the league had established its credentials in the labor movement, male labor leaders looked favorably upon its other programs that addressed women's special needs as women.

While the WTUL participated in countless other strikes in Chicago in the next ten years, none was as large as the garment-workers' strike and none required an effort on the same scale. However, the league's involvement in that strike was characteristic of its later work in unionizing women, as well as its activities with working women in general, and reflects its dedication to building community among women workers. The work of two of its strike committees most directly represents the WTUL's concern with community issues: the Rent Committee and the Relief Committee. The Rent Committee worked to persuade landlords and lodging-house keepers to wait for their payments until the strike was over. The committee also found lodging with families for many hundreds of single women and men strikers, and provided relief to those whom they could not accommodate in this way.[8]

The essential work of feeding the strikers fell to the league's Relief Committee. The WTUL maintained a lunch-room where strikers on picket duty could buy sandwiches at cost; the owner of the bakery where the league served lunch donated the space. The league's Relief Committee also ran the food commissaries set up by the Joint Conference Board. Six stores were opened, serving 50,000 people daily. Each store had one superintendent and employed five or six strikers as clerks. The Relief Committee visited the stores every day and maintained contact with the suppliers.[9] This commissary system was acknowledged by many – including John Fitzpatrick, president of the Chicago Federation of Labor – as the WTUL's most important contribution to the strike effort and to the labor movement.

At the same time as playing a key role in providing food and lodging for striking workers, the league also mobilized the whole community. Finding lodging for single workers with families solidified the working-class community by involving these families directly in the struggles of strikers. In the commissaries, strikers worked together to provide one another with food. This was especially crucial for the continued participation of women strikers, since the responsibility for feeding the family was otherwise the woman's. The league's work defused the divisiveness that often results from long strikes by drawing everyone into the struggle, and by making the resolution of the strike a community-wide project.

The league also worked to maintain solidarity among strikers by working with different immigrant groups in their own languages. A Jewish woman and an Italian woman worked with Agnes Nestor to organize the striking workers and their communities. Each of these two women worked in her own ethnic community, organizing meetings and explaining the negotiation and unionizing process. The league also printed leaflets in the native languages of the strikers.[10] Employers often used ethnic diversity to keep workers divided, and native-born unionists often saw this as too big an obstacle to overcome in creating worker solidarity. In contrast, the WTUL took on the challenge of working with a multilingual constituency and used workers' native languages to draw them into, and maintain, participation in the labor struggle. This was a particularly powerful strategy in working with women, because in many immigrant communities women tended to learn less English than men.

The WTUL's later involvement in strikes and in organizing women outside of strikes owes much to its experience in the garment-workers' strike of 1910–11. During that long winter, league members put their analysis of the needs of working women into action and learned more about both those needs and the obstacles to women's participation in the labor movement. The tactics and strategies they used – most importantly, the effort to address women in their own communities – grew out of earlier experiences in strikes, and would be further refined in later strikes and adapted to non-strike situations, as well.

League women well understood the intimidation that occurred on picket lines, and used to advantage the knowledge that a woman is much more likely to respond favorably when approached in a situation in which she feels safe. Establishing this personal contact is a theme that runs throughout discussions within the WTUL about how to draw in the more hesitant, timid women. For example, several years before the garment-workers' strike, Ellen Lindstrom, then vice-president of the Chicago WTUL, and long-time organizer for the Special Order Clothing Makers, enthusiastically promoted the tactic of home visits following contact with workers on the picket lines. She had learned to watch the shops for strike-breakers and had then gone to talk to the women in their homes. 'Many girls who will not listen to persuasion on the street will listen when talked to in a friendly way,' she concluded.[11] During the 1910–11 strike, this approach was expanded to involve the Jewish and Italian organizers, whose special task was to address strikers in their own, familiar surroundings.

After the garment-workers' strike, the WTUL used home visits to educate women about unions. In their special efforts to overcome linguistic and cultural barriers to the unionization of Italian women, the league collected their names from a list of women receiving milk during the strike, and visited them in their homes. According to Agnes Aitken, who designed the program to reach Italian women, 'the visits were made as from old friends, to learn how the families were getting along, to encourage their joining the unions and the Women's Trade Union League.'[12] From their activities in settlement houses, middle-class league members had learned about the importance of home life for Italian women, and they drew on this experience in their efforts to attract these women to the labor movement.

The WTUL considered work with women already in trade unions to be equally important. The league held official consultations to assist women's union locals in stabilizing their structure and membership. League organizers often performed the duties of a business agent until the union was able to do so itself; in some cases, the WTUL organizer held almost daily conferences with officers and members of AFL-affiliated unions. In the summer of 1923, when the International Ladies' Garment Workers' Union (ILGWU) began an organizing drive in Chicago, it called on the WTUL for assistance in leafleting in its educational campaign. The ILGWU also asked the league to form 'committees to interest public-spirited women' in the campaign.[13] The league had become a recognized source of valuable assistance in women workers' unionizing efforts.

While the WTUL's work with the ILGWU and other unions gave it standing in the male-dominated labor movement, what was unique in its approach was the broad spectrum of activities it sponsored to promote unionization among women. These activities reflected the league's understanding that organizing women required strategies that were different from those used to organize men. Because all WTUL activities were developed for the purpose of drawing women into the union movement, they can be seen as part of an expanded concept of union organizing. The tools that the Chicago WTUL used in mobilizing its constituency included social gatherings, neighborhood organization through district committees, personal testimonies and its own information media. The league's most influential activities were its educational programs, which sought to promote self-organization and to train women workers as leaders, and which also taught the league's constituency English.

Among the activities that the WTUL sponsored, social gatherings of various sorts took a prominent place. Afternoon teas and storytelling were features adopted early on by the league to make its offices more attractive to women workers, and through its middle-class members and other supporters, it was able to secure funds from the very start for receptions, 'social Sunday afternoons,' Halloween balls and summer picnics. The league has been criticized, perhaps justifiably, for the 'uncomfortably aristocratic air' of some of its activities. But the WTUL organizers designed their programs to be compatible with their constituency's shared values and experiences as women and as members of specific ethnic groups.[14] Indeed, the WTUL's success in sustaining its ethnic and class diversity is attributable in part to the conscious use of 'social features' as a 'bonding mechanism among members from varied backgrounds.'[15] The WTUL recognized young women's needs for acceptable social activities and, to a certain extent, sought to shape their social life in ways that would promote union organizing.

Margaret Dreier Robins and other league members strongly emphasized these 'gay times' and sought to identify union activism with sociability and camaraderie. This was crucial in retaining the league's wage-earning constituency, because women engaging in union activities ran the risk not only of losing their jobs, but of attracting the wrath of their families and the ostracism and ridicule of their peers, as well. The WTUL tried to counter these powerful strictures by creating a community of women with similar experiences where their activism was a central value.

In creating this community, WTUL members understood the importance of incorporating, as much as possible, existing networks among working-class women. In 1908, the WTUL set up district committees 'for the purpose of holding meetings in the different sections of Chicago and also for the purpose of bringing together into personal relationship . . . members who live in the same vicinity, thus helping them to form district centers of the League.'[16] Through the district committees, social gatherings were held in the various working-class neighborhoods of the city, and the league attracted many members who would not have joined otherwise. Three years later, a report on the district committees indicated that district parties continued to enjoy great popularity and success.[17]

The WTUL's neighborhood organizing was particularly effective because it was rooted in the women's most familiar surroundings. The downtown area where the WTUL had its offices was foreign territory for many women whose domestic chores, employment and social activities kept them within the confines of their own neighborhoods. The district committee was an appropriate complement to other WTUL activities that took place downtown, and was based on the same principle of developing personal relationships among women. Women who could not or would not go downtown could have similar experiences in a much more familiar, comfortable location. A testimony to the success of the Chicago neighborhood committees is the establishment of a similar program in New York three years later.[18]

The personal contact which the WTUL, like the settlement houses, relied upon to attract its constituency was developed through another very direct, individual tool that the league used: the personal testimony. At monthly meetings, members often talked about their experiences at work, during strikes and in the home. At the First Interstate Conference of the National WTUL, held in Chicago in 1907, after speeches by Margaret Dreier Robins and other WTUL and union officials, Robins opened the floor for discussion and asked delegates to talk about what they had accomplished. Several women spoke up and offered personal testimony about their unions.[19]

The forum that the WTUL provided for women workers served two purposes. First, women were able to speak publicly about their experiences and develop a sense of self-confidence. At the same time, other women learned of successful activities of women very much like themselves in a way which created a sense of the real possibility of organizing in their own shop. Testimony by other working women served to bring unions away from the realm of male bureaucrats and into the realm of the everyday life of working women.

Personal accounts about working conditions and organizing were also conveyed in written form. Shortly after its founding, the Chicago league, and later the national league, estalished its own network of communication first in the *Union Labor Advocate* 'Women's Department,' and then in the monthly WTUL magazine *Life and Labor*.

The Chicago *Union Labor Advocate* was a privately published monthly magazine closely tied to the Chicago labor movement. During the first decade of the twentieth century, the *Advocate* was the official organ of numerous labor bodies, including the Chicago Federation of Labor. Beginning in December 1904, the Chicago WTUL assumed responsibility for the magazine's 'Women's Department,' edited by Anna Nicholes, WTUL secretary. In 1908, the national league, which had its headquarters in Chicago, made the *Advocate* its official organ as well, and Alice Henry, a journalist recently arrived from Australia, took over the expanded section.[20] These pages contained reports on the Chicago WTUL's monthly meetings, and on NWTUL conventions, articles on the activities of other WTUL branches, accounts of strikes and organizing activities among women workers, and brief personal reports from both working women and middle-class 'allies.'

WTUL members placed great value on information about the

labor movement, an important factor in effective organizing and in the development of a vital network among women labor activists. The league's goal in publishing the 'Women's Department' was to provide

> a medium for the exchange of ideas on all industrial questions, especially those relating to the work and conditions of women and children, to give news items concerning all unions in which women are members, so that each may be informed of the movement, generally and to stimulate and encourage organization.[21]

Shortly after making the *Advocate* its official organ, the NWTUL increased the circulation of the 'Women's Department' by reprinting these pages and distributing them to other chapters. By 1910, however, local chapters of the WTUL, which were growing in number and membership, wanted a magazine of their own, and the NWTUL's Executive Board decided to begin publishing *Life and Labor*. In so doing, it was following the example of other women's organizations, like the Women's Christian Temperance Union, which had found the publication of its own monthly magazine of great use in keeping its constituency unified and active.[22]

Life and Labor, first published in January 1911, offered a broad spectrum of reading. It included the same range of contents as the *Advocate*'s 'Women's Department,' but in vastly expanded form. In addition, it provided information on the women's suffrage campaign, at both the national and state levels, and on the movement for protective legislation. *Life and Labor* also published reviews of books about women and work, historical notes about women, and even serialized classic novels like *Les Misérables*, *A Tale of Two Cities* and *The Last of the Mohicans*. Following the practice of other magazines, *Life and Labor* printed letters from its readers – such as the one by Anna Rudnitzky, an active organizer in the garment-workers' strike, which is practically an advertisement for unionism and for the WTUL: '[The union] makes us stronger and it makes us happier and it makes us take more interest in life,' wrote Rudnitzky. 'Now the [WTUL] has helped me so much and the union has helped me so much and I want to help others.'[23]

The use of personal accounts like this one was a central aspect of *Life and Labor*'s effort to create and sustain a community of like-minded women. In 1920, the magazine published three prize-winning essays submitted to the WTUL's competition on 'Why I Joined My Union and What It Has Done for Me.' Each essay refers to the personal, emotional benefits of unionization, as well as the material improvements in wages and working conditions.[24] Together, they present strong models for union activism among women and create the sense that it is indeed possible for women to work together to improve their working conditions without sacrificing what is important to them as women.

The expanded format of the WTUL's publication allowed the league to provide readers with educational material as well, and this soon became integral to the purpose of *Life and Labor*. In addition to being a lifeline between women in the unions and an organizing tool, *Life and Labor* also became a serialized textbook for the woman organizer. WTUL leaders provided two kinds of resource material in *Life and Labor*: women workers needed to learn both about the substance of collective bargaining and about the practical processes of conducting union business. For the first, *Life and Labor* published reading lists and syllabi from courses on labor history and labor relations. The second task was more challenging; for information about unions and labor law by itself was not effective in helping women overcome the socialization into passivity that left them ill-equipped to bargain with employers or to speak up at male-dominated meetings. Providing personal accounts by women who had become active in their unions was but one approach in this education of women workers as activists. *Life and Labor* also sought to provide its readers with 'how to' guides on the process of union business. For example, in 1911 Margaret Dreier Robins published a series of articles on parliamentary law, directed specifically at women workers inexperienced in meetings and intimidated by parliamentary procedures. In 'How to Take Part in Meetings,' Robins presented examples of women's participation in meetings, why they were not effective, and how they could be made more effective. By her fifth lesson, she was encouraging women to overcome their fear and learn to preside at meetings.[25] The series was later published as a separate pamphlet, *Self-government in the Workshop*. Articles like these went hand-in-hand with personal testimonies by women activists in encouraging women to take control of their working lives.

League members were fully conscious of the potential that their publication had for teaching women what they needed to know in order to become effective unionists. However, they also realized that much more was needed, especially since a large proportion of their constituency knew little or no English. Educating working women was central to the WTUL's goal of organizing women workers, and WTUL organizers saw this as crucial to forming stable unions. Robins stated this explicitly in *Self-government in the Workshop*:

> Believing then as we do now in the right to self-government in the workshop, and recognizing that we can only win this battle for industrial permanency by united action, the Women's Trade Union League stands pledged for trade union organization. *This is a great educational task* [emphasis added].[26]

The WTUL sought to educate women workers in two ways: to teach them about unions and to teach them English. The combination of the two approaches involved an understanding of the difficulties inherent in organizing women workers, and of the particular difficulties in reaching immigrant women. The league's approach to educational work also blurred the distinction between educational and organizational work, and thus implicitly suggested a redefinition of the process of union organizing.

In the aftermath of the massive garment strikes of 1910–11, officers of the Chicago WTUL felt the need for trained women organizers very acutely. In 1914, the national WTUL, whose headquarters were in Chicago, worked closely with the Chicago league in organizing and directing a new Training School for Women Organizers. The program was divided between class time and field work. The two students who enrolled in the school's first year attended courses on trade union organization, industrial organization, trade agreements, labor history, public speaking, bookkeeping and writing. Their field work, under the direction of Agnes Nestor and Mary Anderson, consisted of visiting unions, attending shop meetings and street meetings, and learning the responsibilities of union executive officers – such as initiating new members, taking reports of grievances, adjusting grievances and conferring with employers. By 1916, the school's enrollment had increased to nine students. For women who could not come to Chicago, the school offered correspondence courses in business English, trade agreements, injunctions and industrial history. The school was the first full-time labor school in the United States, and for many years, it remained the only one that provided field training as well as academic training. Students found the program very useful and Anderson, herself a long-time organizer, considered the program to be 'one of the most important things that was done for women in the trade union movement.'[27]

The Chicago WTUL's efforts to teach English to immigrant women workers began in 1908 with classes taught by volunteers from the Chicago Federation of Teachers. In 1911, the league initiated a more aggressive campaign to teach immigrant women English. Just as the garment-workers' strikes had pointed to the need for trained, experienced leadership, they also showed the importance of knowing English for working women, and the 'need of much close personal contact secured by this communication.'[28] The WTUL sought to integrate its English lessons with the daily lives and cultural forms of immigrant women. The lessons were mostly taught in women's homes, so that women could acquire the language skills that would help them organize more effectively, while remaining within the cultural boundaries limiting women's activities outside the home.

The Chicago league placed special emphasis on teaching English to Italian women because of 'difficulty met in adjusting some of their time-honored customs to the new conditions in this country, as, for instance, the home life of the women.' Italian women in all cities were among the most difficult to organize, and in Chicago, the WTUL was determined to change this pattern. In recognition of the fact that most Italian women abided by the custom of staying at home evenings, and therefore rarely attended night courses, the WTUL's Education Committee resolved to teach classes in Italian women's homes. In the course of the classes, women would discuss such topics as accidents, health care, and the Immigration and Naturalization Service. 'By degrees confidence was established and it was not long before family interests were discussed.'[29] Women learned English in a way that developed personal relationships, forming networks that could later be drawn upon for support during organizing campaigns or during a strike.

These networks were solidified through a wide range of WTUL-sponsored social and cultural activities. The league's educational programs combined English classes with parties, music, and trips to parks on weekends. To give extra incentive to women to join the union in their trade, all these activities were offered free of charge to women who showed a union card.[30] In setting this standard, the WTUL, presented women reticent about joining a union with immediate benefits. For the WTUL, teaching English was a point of entry into these women's lives through which lessons of unionism could be taught. It was the first step in female institution-building among immigrant women.

The most concrete way in which the league combined English lessons with union lessons was through the use of a textbook prepared by the New York WTUL. Realizing that once students had acquired a certain amount of English vocabulary, it was difficult to find lessons that were interesting and stimulating, New York league member Violet Pike wrote a new text, *New World Lessons for Old World Peoples*, which taught the advantages of unionism at the same time as it taught vocabulary. The primer was published in Lithuanian, Italian, Yiddish, Bohemian and English, and contained illustrated stories contrasting union and non-union conditions. The lessons were designed to provoke lively discussion and to stimulate students to think out their own answers to the various questions surrounding unionization. The characters in the stories were women, mostly single immigrant women, like the majority of those using the text. The book presented as role models women living in the same kinds of communities as the students themselves, explicitly suggesting that they could be active in unions and work toward improving their working conditions without forsaking their community.

Lesson five, for instance, 'A Trade with a Union,' puts forth in simple English a young woman's understanding of how a union has helped her friend and how it could help her. The friend tells of her shorter working hours, extra pay for overtime, and higher wages, but she does not gloss over the work involved in unionizing her shop:

> It took a long time.
> It took a great deal of hard work.
> But now our union is strong.
> We girls are proud of it because we made it.
> It was worth the hard work.[31]

In a few short lines, women with a beginner's knowledge of English, and, presumably, of unionism learned both an English lesson and a lesson in unionism. The emphasis throughout the textbook is on the activism of the working women themselves, and on their own accomplishments.

In Chicago, the primer was used by tutors from the Chicago Federation of Teachers and specifically trained teachers speaking English and the native language of the students. Supplies were supplemented by a circulating library loaned to the league by private individuals and by the Chicago Public Library. The Chicago *Journal* hailed the publication of the book as 'the basis of a crusade of education never before undertaken in Chicago.'[32]

WTUL members had a complex understanding of how language works in community cohesiveness and in movement-building. Accepting workers' native language as a communal institution that could be used to advantage in drives to involve women in the labor movement, the league hired organizers to address women in their native language and printed leaflets in different languages to reach women who understood little or no English. At the same time, the WTUL could not ignore the need for a common language among its constituency, and the need for these women to communicate effectively with employers, union officials and one another. Out of this grew a diversified program to teach women English, one that respected and used community norms while also teaching valuable lessons in unionism.

From the beginning, the WTUL realized that in order to achieve even a small part of its program of organizing women into unions and improving working conditions, it needed to take a deep interest in all phases of community life. Therefore, the league attempted to come to terms with the totality of working women's lives, at home as well as at work. Their lectures, classes, leaflets and social activities indicate a recognition among members that a young woman's role at work was closely related to her role at home, and that her involvement as a unionist was related to her social and cultural life as a single young woman.

In providing spaces and organizing events where women with shared experiences could learn from one another to take greater control over their lives, in providing publications where women could learn about a large variety of topics relevant to the labor movement, and in using women's homes to teach about unionism while teaching English, the WTUL taught women practical lessons about organizing. The league also provided women with opportunities to develop relationships with other women, and thus was instrumental in establishing the networks necessary to building a working women's movement.

There are no precise figures on the number of active union members that WTUL strategies drew into the labor movement. However, the Chicago league continued to expand through the early 1920s, suggesting that its programs were indeed quite successful. The continued growth of WTUL activities in the years after World War I is especially remarkable in light of the rightward swing of public opinion and the upsurge of anti-radical and anti-union activities at the time. The WTUL's already difficult task became even more difficult in this increasingly hostile climate. By 1925, after unionists in industries that employed large numbers of women had been defeated in several important strikes, the Chicago WTUL followed the example of most other league chapters and shifted its focus to protective legislation.

None the less, the WTUL left an important mark on the labor movement. The 'new unionism' that emerged in the garment industry after the strikes of 1909–10 owed a large part of its innovation to programs inspired by the WTUL. Beginning in 1914, female members of the International Ladies' Garment Workers' Union in New York formed separate female institutions within that union – the Unity Center, for example, which promoted women's continued activism through classes, social activities and, later, a vacation resort.[33] A strong emphasis on workers' education, which distinguished unions like the ILGWU and the Amalgamated Clothing Workers of America from older entrenched craft unions, is a testimony to the impact of the WTUL's educational programs on unions. Later on, other WTUL tactics, like home visiting, were incorporated into the organizing drives of the Congress of Industrial Organizations. Moreover, contemporary women's labor organizations see themselves as following in the footsteps of the WTUL, which was the first organization systematically to approach the organization of women into unions with women-centered strategies. Today, unions like the Coalition of Labor Union Women adopt

WTUL tactics to bring together female unionists to work toward increasing their power and effectiveness in their unions. The Chicago league, and the WTUL as a whole, began a tradition which lived on in the labor movement for decades after they ceased their direct participation in labor struggles.

Notes

1 Mary Anderson, *Woman at Work*, Minneapolis, University of Minnesota Press, 1951, p.52; 'Want Schools for Meetings,' Chicago *Record Herald*, October 13, 1913, University of Illinois–Chicago Circle, Manuscript Collection, WTUL Clippings Collection (hereafter: WTUL Clippings).

2 Theresa Wolfson, *The Woman Worker and Trade Unions*, New York, International Publishers, 1926, p.105.

3 See Meredith Tax, *The Rising of the Women: Feminist Solidarity and Class Conflict, 1880–1917*, New York, Monthly Review Press, 1980, p.32.

4 Allen F. Davis, *Spearheads for Reform: The Social Settlements and the Progressive Movement*, New York, Oxford University Press, 1967, pp.105–6.

5 Jane Addams, *Twenty Years at Hull House*, New York, Macmillan, 1910, p.22.

6 For a more detailed presentation of the factors that allowed the WTUL in Chicago to become and remain active in union organizing, see Colette A. Hyman, 'The Chicago Women's Trade Union League: Labor Organizing and Female Institution-Building, 1904–1924,' MA thesis, University of Minnesota, 1982, pp.5–11.

7 N. Sue Weiler's article 'Walkout: The Men's Garment Workers' Strike, 1910–1911,' *Chicago History*, vol. 8, no. 4, winter 1979, pp.238–49, provides a complete account of the strike in Chicago.

8 Chicago WTUL, 'Official Report of the Strike Committee – Chicago Garment Workers' Strike, Oct. 29, 1910–Feb. 18, 1911,' Chicago Historical Society (hereafter: CHS), p.20.

9 *Ibid.*, pp.13–18.

10 'Garment Workers' Strike,' *Union Labor Advocate*, vol. 11, no. 11, November 1910, p.79. (Microfilm edn: *The Papers of the WTUL and its Principal Leaders*, Publications Series. All citations from the *Union Labor Advocate* refer to this microfilm edn.)

11 'Report on WTUL Monthly Meeting,' *Union Labor Advocate*, vol. 5, no. 5, May 1904, p.12.

12 Agnes Aitken, 'Teaching English to Our Foreign Friends' and 'Among Italians,' *Life and Labor*, vol. 1, no. 10, October 1911, pp.309–11. (Microfilm edn: *The Papers of the WTUL and its Principal Leaders*,

3

Bread and Roses revisited: Women's culture and working-class activism in the Lawrence strike of 1912[1]

Ardis Cameron

The 1912 strike of immigrant textile-workers in Lawrence, Massachusetts, has generally been viewed by feminist labor historians as illustrative of the vast potential for female workers' militancy — a potential seldom realized in the early twentieth century due to the predominance of exclusionary craft unionism in that era. At Lawrence, the highly inclusive industrial syndicalism of the Industrial Workers of the World (IWW), in sharp contrast, allowed for full-scale female participation in labor militancy and, also, put forward demands which reached far beyond the narrow, economic orientation of the craft unions. It was a strike, as James Oppenheim's famous song put it, for 'bread and roses.' In this chapter, Ardis Cameron presents a new perspective on this much studied strike. Using new data from oral history interviews as well as extensive primary research, Cameron suggests a far more complex view of the Lawrence events than previous historians have offered. She points to the critical contributions of pre-existing female community networks, and a longstanding 'women's culture,' to the innovative tactics used by the Lawrence workers. Rather than attributing the militancy of the women strikers to the IWW's structure and organizing approach, as others have done, Cameron suggests that the line of causality flowed in the opposite direction: the women's militancy, rooted in 'the convoluted yet ordinary web of female daily life,' was the basis for the success of the IWW-led strike.

On January 11, 1912, a group of about 100 women waited in the weave room of the Everett Mill to see if their pay envelopes had been cut. A recent Massachusetts law had reduced the maximum hours of work for women and children from 56 to 54 hours per week and the mills had hinted that the subsequent loss in production would be made up in lower wages. Loomfixers, highly skilled male workers, had responded by setting up committees in all mills that employed fixers and planned to strike as a group, but to stagger their protest from mill to mill so that 'all members could cooperate but remain working until their turn came.' Local 20 of the IWW had made similar plans. On January 5, the IWW had written to William Wood, president of the American Woolen Company, requesting a meeting to discuss the entire question. On January 9, 200 black boys had walked out, but they quickly returned when the traditionally rebellious mule spinners, who depended on the quick hands and feet of the boys to operate their machines, rounded them up and angrily pointed out that it wasn't the right time of year for a strike. 'Besides,' shouted one spinner, 'we are married men and do not take kindly to the action of boys.'[2]

These independent strategies, however, were quickly forgotten when the female operatives at the Everett discovered their pay was short. Throwing down their aprons and grabbing picker sticks, the women marched out of the mill and called for others to follow them. They stood on one another's shoulders to shout orders, and sent 'flying squadrons' of men and women through all the other mills to recruit supporters and shut down machines. Carrying American and Italian flags, 3,500 marchers linked arms and stormed the city's major mills, slashing power belts, smashing windows, and breaking down mill gates to release other workers. By January 13, 25,000 operatives had gone out. The 'Bread and Roses' strike of 1912 was under way.[3]

Coming on the heels of the 1909 strike at McKees Rocks and the 'Uprising of the 20,000' shirtwaist-makers in the Lower East Side, the strike at Lawrence climaxed a series of proletarian revolts. Its success gave renewed legitimacy to the class-conscious factions in the labor movement, and demonstrated an alternative to the craft-union strategy of the American Federation of Labor. As David Montgomery has suggested, these mass industrial strikes made skilled workers, increasingly under attack from scientific management and technological change, more willing to align themselves with the unskilled, providing a strong fillip for the 'new unionism' which characterized the years between 1909 and 1922.[4]

The Lawrence strike was extraordinary both in its tactics and in the quantity and diversity of the participants. Almost 30,000 men, women and children struck, and forty nationalities were represented in their ranks. Contemporaries wrote extensively about the 'Revolutionary Strike,' the 'Industrial War,' the 'Revolt of the Masses' and the 'Boiling Over of the Melting Pot.'[5] Almost without exception, they describe a city in revolt, and they repeatedly express horror, delight or confusion over the vast numbers of striking women who, as one judge noted, 'have lots of cunning and also lots of bad temper.' 'They're everywhere,' complained another town official, 'and it seems to be getting worse and worse all the time.' Some observers blamed the extreme militancy not on the IWW, but on 'unruly and undisciplined female elements.' 'Just as soon as women disregard constituted authority by catching and tearing officers' coats,' bemoaned a Massachusetts judge, 'why, then you have the foundation for all that follows.' For many, the women's leader, Elizabeth Gurley Flynn, was the symbol of the ubiquitous female militant. 'Partly a Joan of Arc, partly an Emma Goldman,' explained one newspaper editor, 'but Flynn is more than either, a reincarnation of the militant and maddened women who led the march of the Commune from Paris to Versailles.'[6]

Until recently, these women represented what historians defined as pre-political, even marginal actors in working-class political life, and their efforts have often been neglected in the historiography of worker militancy. Most did not belong to unions or political parties, and joined the IWW only during the strike, deserting it soon after. Although evidence is sketchy, most activists seem to have come to Lawrence from traditionally rural or recently industrializing areas, although there were important exceptions to this pattern.[7]

It would be a mistake, however, to view these women as outside or peripheral to working-class militancy and consciousness. The bonds which nourished female friendships and alliances (often identified as characteristic of pre-industrial cultures) also helped sustain neighborhood networks in an industrial setting. Ties between women provided a necessary organizational base for collective efforts and helped to maintain strike discipline and promote class consciousness. In Lawrence, women's efforts in the neighborhoods broadened the critique of capitalist development to include not only wage disputes, but issues of daily community struggle. It was, after all, a strike for bread, and for roses too. The extensive scope of the strike, whereby nearly every mill in the city was shut down, demonstrated almost universal participation in strike activities, concretizing widely shared notions of commonality and justice – or what strikers labeled 'a square deal.' 'We stick together now,' explained one female mender, 'all of us, to bring about a settlement according to our ideals, our ideas of what is right.'[8]

Understanding the role of working-class women in workers' struggles means exploring topics once eschewed by the labor historian: the family, the household and what historians of women have called the 'bonds of womanhood.' By placing women at the center of community struggle and collective actions, historians like Sheila Rowbotham and Temma Kaplan have begun to challenge the prevailing assumption that male-defined trade unionism is the essential form of working-class organization. Unlike the work of the new labor historians, which tends to neglect the role of the non-wage earner in class formation, these studies call attention to the importance of neighborhood activity and daily life in honing class consciousness and assessing power relations. By extending the definition of class beyond (but not necessarily excluding) relations of production, Kaplan and Rowbotham have located working-class political organization in the daily lives not only of the wage-earner, but also of those groups who, though 'formally outside of capitalist production, are still part of the working-class social network.'[9]

Since the Lawrence strike is a primary historical example of a workers' struggle which drew extensively on community networks, and since it involved such a large and disparate group of women, it offers a particularly good opportunity to explore the relationship between the traditional sphere of working women – the home, the marketplace and the streets – and working-class activism. What sorts of conditions allowed ordinary women, both housewives and wage-earners, collectively and militantly to protest their situation? How did women's collective efforts promote community cohesiveness and neighborhood discipline? How was women's traditional sphere used to mobilize community action and solidify class consciousness? And finally, did participation in the strike change women's consciousness of themselves? How did their activism alter their personal relationships and traditional subservience to men?

We can begin to answer some of these questions by reconstructing the experiences of women who participated in the Lawrence strike. This chapter draws on research into the lives of more than 114 working-class women who were active in the strike, culled from newspaper accounts, arrest records, hospital reports and government investigations. These women were the most militant of the rebels – those, as one striker put it, 'who had drunk of the cup to the very dregs.'[10] This essay looks at collective action from the inside, examining the ways in which women's daily experiences and resources helped transform working-class neighborhoods into networks of militant, collective struggle.

The founders of the city of Lawrence had, from the start, envisioned an industrial boomtown and worked hard to insure high profits and maximum productivity. The machine-tending nature of the textile industry, which required increasingly less skill, encouraged management to establish patterns of labor recruitment and a system of social control that it hoped would provide the mills with a docile and vulnerable workforce. Semi-skilled and unskilled immigrants were actively recruited throughout Lawrence's history so that, in the decades before World War I, the city's neighborhoods contained large proportions of immigrant workers, the majority of whom were women. By 1910, Lawrence was one of the world's largest woolen textile centers and fully three-quarters of the city's 85,000 people directly depended on the mills for their livelihood. Of the 60 percent who actually toiled inside the factory gates, well over half were women and children.[11]

Typically, these women lived in densely crowded neighborhoods which surrounded Lawrence's vast mill district. In the center of the working-class community, an area known as The Plains, a 1911 survey of five half-blocks revealed an average of between 300 and 600 people per acre. As one historian has pointed out, 'Only 3 blocks in Harlem contained more densely crowded streets.' Among the women who made these streets their home, most either worked in one of the city's mills, or lived in a household of textile operatives. Either way, women were essential breadgivers in Lawrence as few families could secure the 'necessaries of life' without female labor.

This was especially evident in immigrant families. Of 292 foreign-born homes surveyed in 1909, only 18 percent consisted of households in which the husband alone provided the family's entire income. While Lithuanian and Polish families tended to supplement income with boarders and lodgers, thereby utilizing female labor in laundering, sewing, cleaning and cooking for tenants, the French (77 percent), Syrians (42 percent) and Southern Italians (37.5 percent) relied heavily upon the mill earnings of wives and children. 'In Lawrence,' observed the *New York Call*, 'all the family must work, if the family is to survive.'[12]

The selective nature of the immigration process also insured that households included a broad range of familial and non-familial social relationships. Government investigators found that defining these numerous entanglements was often tortuous, and eventually settled on describing a household in these neighborhoods as any arrangement 'consisting of one or more families, with or without boarders or lodgers as well as all groups of persons living together, no family included, or various combinations of family, groups and boarders and lodgers.'[13] As one former striker explained:

> One of my life-long friends and I first met as bedsisters in a friend's place – you know, what they called a tenement. There was a saying, 'The beds were never cold.' Well, sure, back then you see this is how you lived – you slept in shifts. We all lived like one then. One kitchen we all used and we all knew each other.[14]

Such collective living arrangements facilitated daily exchange and the sharing of goods, services, and mutual concerns. For women, traditional domestic responsibilities such as child care, laundry, food preparation, sewing and nursing, also encouraged mutual support among female neighbors and kin, and secured the household as well as other communal spaces as women's prerogatives. Both before and during the strike, those local centers of female activity – grocery stores, streets, stoops, bath houses, kitchens – also enhanced women's concepts of material rights and sustained efforts to negotiate and agitate for economic justice. As a former weaver who shared rooms with a girlfriend and her uncle commented:

We met a few months before the strike, but both worked at

different mills. We'd (all of us girls) be together sure, in the kitchen, wherever – and we talked. Of course, we all knew our pay, we compared all the time. Better pay, we'd go get it.[15]

Comparing wages and prices was also a common ritual for women and girls who shared their daily commute to and from the factory gates:

We'd all meet at a certain corner on our block in the morning, it was very dark, you know. We worked very early, came home in the dark too. Well, we'd get our girlfriends together and we'd walk each other to the mills. We'd talk about everything, but always, too, about our pay, oh sure.[16]

Several women recalled shopping with their mothers or friends where grocery stores served as social centers as well as forums for price discussions. As one activist recalled:

The shops had chairs and we'd take the chance to catch up. We compared prices with our neighborhood and the other Italian markets, then we'd go to the other grocery stores and do the same. Everyone was there, and the stores stayed opened till late at night.[17]

Such spaces had important implications for popular organization during the strike. Street corners and stores were transformed into daily information and decision-making centers; for despite the disruption in wage patterns, women and girls continued domestic routines. As one striker put it, 'We'd all want to know, "what to do, what to do?" Everyone was out, so we'd meet, at our corner, and, oh, everywhere.'[18]

The sources of women's culture in the multi-ethnic neighborhoods of Lawrence began here, in the web of informal relationships that were nourished and sustained by women as they performed their customary tasks of mutual help, daily exchange, breadwinning and food preparation. The grocery, where mothers and daughters shared timely gossip as well as daily price indexes with other women, was a critical contact-point where a woman's aptitude for obtaining a 'just price' underscored both her individual and public importance in regulating and adjudicating the community's moral economy. Prices and wages were discussed with keen and almost daily interest, and women held sharp and exacting notions of what one was entitled to.

Finances were calculated to the penny and converted into hard-headed notions of worth. Several women recalled the Lawrence strike as 'the strike for three loaves,' and most remembered not only that the pay was short, but that it was precisely thirty-two cents short. The streets, which allowed for public scrutiny as well as space for personal exchange; the tenement stoops, where mothers patrolled their blocks and supervised community activity; and kitchens, where nurturance and communal cooperation occurred daily – all sustained close-knit, female-centered networks.[19]

Often unencumbered by traditional sources of restraint, such as older siblings, grandparents, village life, or, in the case of the Lithuanians and Poles, the established church, their networks allowed women collectively to confront their situation from the focal-point of their lives as they straddled the challenges of womanhood and the demands of wage labor.[20] Both the exigencies of migration and the harsh reality of Lawrence mill life intensified the need for mutual assistance and daily reciprocity. Bonds that were formed along informal networks were strengthened and reinforced in the constant struggle for survival so that sharing responsibilities, both in the home and in the workplace, helped provide a communal and holistic context for individual action. 'We are not egged on by anyone or forced to go upon a picket line,' explained one female striker. 'We go there because we feel that it is but duty.'[21]

In no way was women's collective duty more vigorously expressed than in the daily attempts to discipline their neighborhoods and prevent community dissension. Both soldiers and scabs knew from personal experience that these networks could be transformed into effective sources of resistance and militancy. Of the 130 women formally arrested during the strike, almost 90 percent were charged with assault on an officer or intimidation.[22] Guarding the streets from third- and fourth-floor windows, women at times poured scalding water on work-bound neighbors. Hanging out of these makeshift watchtowers, others joined in, throwing stones along with heated insults. The IWW shrewdly took advantage of these opportunities to prevent scabbing and provided several female leaders with cameras so that they could follow those neighborhood 'traitors' and photograph them. Women shadowed their victims and then, amidst great hissing and hooting, ceremoniously hung his picture or her image in the local grocery store.[23]

In most cases, however, sisterhood and communal unity were maintained in the household, where traditions of reciprocity and sharing were now systematized for political struggles. Among activist households, 23 percent were headed by women dependent on strikers' wages. Solidarity, it seems, overrode immediate financial losses. Mothers often converted their homes into soup kitchens for hungry strikers or provided child-care while younger women picketed or paraded. One former striker recalled how her mother would open up the kitchen 'to all the kids on the block. She'd make bread or pizza and everybody would be there – all during the strike. My brother was very active, so we didn't see too much of him, you know he was in jail or at the IWW. So my mother makes sure no one goes hungry or cold, not on our block.'[24] Others, less well off, served at soup kitchens or organized fund-raising drives at stores, restaurants, and other businesses, asking for money or food. 'If they don't help you now in your hour of need,' proclaimed a popular IWW leader, 'you know how to treat them.'[25] And most women did. Unsympathetic stores were boycotted and any that refused credit or food found red scab signs on their front doors. On the whole, however, local shops contributed to the effort and ran soup kitchens as well as supplying food to strikers and their families.

During the strike, plans to care for children and thus prevent the 'lash of youthful hunger' from driving women back to work utilized communal child-care patterns and established boarding practices already woven into workers' lives. Typically (before the strike) working mothers had turned to neighbors who took in children at modest fees, or, in some cases, had sent their young into the country-side during the work week and collected them again on Sundays. The famous strike tactic of sending Lawrence's children to socialist and anarchist sympathizers in New York and Philadelphia, the so-called 'children's exodus,' was in many ways an extension of this method of child-care, successfully merging radical political strategy with customary practice.[26]

The composition and structure of the women's networks had an important bearing on the character and effectiveness of the strike, as well. Ages of female activists ranged widely, from 13 to 48 years. The mean age was 26, with the 20–4 and 25–9 categories containing the highest concentrations. Alliances between generations of women fortified class solidarity and often inspired new forms of collective

Convention, Trinidad, Colo., September 16, 1913, in E. L. Doyle Papers, WHD/DPL.

10 *Read the Grievances of the Colorado Coal Miners*, UMWA Papers, File: District No. 15, 1913, Washington, DC.

11 Mary Thomas O'Neal, *Those Damn Foreigners*, Hollywood, California, Minerva Printing & Publishing, 1971, p.67.

12 Mother Jones's speech at Starkville, Colorado, September 24, 1913, *CIR Report*, vol. 8, p.7,253.

13 *Ibid.*

14 Colorado Bureau of Labor Statistics, *12th Biennial Report, 1909–1910*, Denver, Smith Brooks Printing, p.127.

15 John McLennan testimony, *CIR Report*, vol. 7, p.6,529.

16 Mary Thomas testimony, *CIR Report*, vol. 7, p.6,354.

17 Colorado Bureau of Labor Statistics, *12th Biennial Report*, p.27.

18 Waleryon Korda to President Woodrow Wilson, April 29, 1914, National Archives, RG60 (Department of Justice), File 168733-a.

19 John McQuarrie testimony, *CIR Report*, vol. 7, p.6,782. McQuarrie quoted in Inis Weed, 'The Miner as Citizen,' Committee on Industrial Relations Papers, Box 10, 'Coal Mine Strike,' National Archives, RG174 (Department of Labor).

20 Lindsey exhibit no. 5, *CIR Report*, vol. 8, p.7,388.

21 Joseph M. Patterson testimony, *CIR Report*, vol. 7, p.6,784.

22 Patterson exhibit no. 1, *CIR Report*, vol. 8, p.7,269.

23 Lillian Green, 'Resent Insult – Mother Jones,' Denver *Times*, December 17, 1913.

24 O'Neal, *Those Damn Foreigners*, pp.33–4.

25 *Ibid.*, p.100.

26 Pearl Jolly testimony, *CIR Report*, vol. 7, p.6,354; Operators exhibit no. 101, *Cong. Hearings*, vol. 2, p.6,615; *Nationalities Employed in the Mines of Colorado during the Year 1912, and the Percentage*, UMWA Papers, File: District No. 15, 1912, Washington, DC.

27 Charlotte Erickson, *American Industry and the European Immigrant, 1860–1885*, Cambridge, Mass., Harvard University Press, 1957, p.86.

28 Mary Petrucci testimony, *CIR Report*, vol. 8, p.8,190.

29 John McLennan testimony, *CIR Report*, vol. 7, p.6,531.

30 Helen Ring Robinson quoted in 'Army of Women,' *Denver Post*, April 26, 1914, p.6.

31 'The West Report on Ludlow,' Committee on Industrial Relations Papers, Box: 'Colorado Strike,' National Archives, RG174 (Department of Labor).

32 Report of the Military Commission, May 2, 1914, *CIR Report*, vol. 8, p.7,311.

33 O'Neal, *Those Damn Foreigners*, p.73.

34 *United Mineworkers' Journal* (hereafter: *UMWJ*), September 25, 1913, pp.2 and 12; O'Neal, *Those Damn Foreigners*, pp.87–8; *RMN*, September 9, 1913, p.4; *RMN*, September 15, 1913, p.3.

35 E. L. Doyle testimony, *CIR Report*, vol. 7, p.7,067; and E. L. Doyle, Minutes of the Policy Committee, E. L. Doyle Papers, WHD/DPL.
36 E. L. Doyle testimony, *CIR Report*, vol. 7, p.7,017.
37 *RMN*, September 16, 1913, pp.1 and 5.
38 O'Neal, *Those Damn Foreigners*, p.101.
39 E. L. Papers, envelopes nos 11 and 18, WHD/DPL; John McLennan testimony, *CIR Report*, vol. 7, p.6,526; O'Neal, *Those Damn Foreigners*, p.108.
40 *The Miners' Magazine*, October 23, 1913, p.6; O'Neal, *Those Damn Foreigners*, p.112.
41 Priscilla Long, interview with Mike and Katherine Livoda, Denver, Colorado, January 1977.
42 *Ibid.*
43 O'Neal, *Those Damn Foreigners*, p.114.
44 *RMN*, October 22, 1913, p.3; *UMWJ*, October 30, 1913, p.1; clipping stamped October 20, 1913, John Chase scrapbook, WHD/DPL; E. L. Doyle, Minutes of the Policy Committee, E. L. Doyle Papers, envelope no. 11, WHD/DPL; O'Neal, *Those Damn Foreigners*, p.113.
45 Van Cise exhibit no. 2, *CIR Report*, vol. 8, pp.7,325–6.
46 Statement of Robert Burroughs, Hildreth Frost Papers, Box 1, Colorado State Historical Society, Denver, Colorado.
47 Karl Linderfelt testimony, *CIR Report*, vol. 7, p.6,883.
48 Mary Hannah Thomas testimony, *CIR Report*, vol. 7, p.6,359.
49 Clipping, 'Mother Jones Put Out of Mine Town,' Mother Jones Papers, Box 2, File: Colorado 4, Catholic University of America, Washington, DC; 'Troops Deport Mother Jones,' *RMN*, January 5, 1914, p.2; clipping, 'Mother Jones Deported by Militia,' John Chase scrapbook, WHD/DPL.
50 'Denver Suffragists Raise Cry at Expulsion of Mother Jones,' *RMN*, January 7, 1914, p.1; 'Mother Jones Divides Women,' *RMN*, January 12, 1914, p.4.
51 *UMWJ*, January 22, 1914, p.17; *RMN*, January 7, 1914, p.1; *RMN*, January 12, 1914, p.4; *RMN*, January 13, 1914, p.8.
52 *RMN*, January 16, 1914, p.4.
53 Report of the Commanding General to the Governor, 'The Military Occupation of the Coal Strike Zone by the Colorado National Guard, 1913–1914,' WHD/DPL.
54 'Great Czar Fell,' *UMWJ*, January 29, 1914, p.4; clipping in *Trinidad Free Press*, George Minot Papers, WHD/DPL; *RMN*, January 23, 1914, p.1; *Denver Post*, January 23, 1914, p.9; J. W. Brown, 'Military Despotism in Colorado,' *UMWJ*, March 26, 1914. p.2.
55 Report of the Commanding General.
56 *RMN*, January 23, 1914, p.1.
57 Lieutenant C. A. Conner to Captain Frost, April 14, 1914, Hildreth Frost Papers, WHD/DPL.
58 Helen Ring Robinson testimony, *CIR Report*, vol. 8, p.7,211.

59 M. G. Low testimony, *CIR Report*, vol. 7, p.6,853.
60 Helen Ring Robinson testimony.
61 Mary Thomas O'Neal to Arthur Biggs, president District No. 15, UMWA, June 5, 1970 (in author's possession).
62 Mrs Dominski testimony, *CIR Report*, vol. 9, p.8,186; Mrs Ed Tonner affidavit, *CIR Report*, vol. 8, p.7,384; Mrs Petrucci testimony, *CIR Report*, vol. 9, p.8,194; William Snyder testimony, *CIR Report*, vol. 7, p.6,853; Ometomica Covadle affidavit, Leyor Fylor affidavit, Mrs James Fylor affidavit, William Snyder affidavit, Virginia Bertoloti affidavit, Juanita Hernandez affidavit, Mrs Ed Tonner affidavit – all in Committee on Industrial Relations Papers, National Archives, RG174 (Department of Labor); Mrs Lee Champion speech, May 21, 1914, Washington, DC, in Ellis Meredith Papers, Colorado State Historical Society, Denver; McGovern, 'The Colorado Coal Strike,' p.286.
63 O'Neal, *Those Damn Foreigners*, pp.133–4.
64 Pearl Jolly speech, Mayt 21, 1914, Ellis Meredith Papers, Colorado State Historical Society; Pearl Jolly testimony, *CIR Report*, vol. 7, p.6,357.
65 Juanita Hernandez affidavit; William Snyder affidavit; William Snyder testimony.
66 Mary Petrucci testimony, *CIR Report*, vol. 9, p.8,094; clipping, Lucy Huffaker interview with Mary Petrucci, Mother Jones Papers, Box 2, File: Colorado 4, Catholic University of America, Washington, DC.
67 Pearl Jolly testimony, p.6,351.
68 Lucy Huffaker interview with Mary Petrucci.

5

Another look at the International Ladies' Garment Workers' Union: Women, industry structure and collective action

Roger Waldinger

*The 1909–10 New York City shirtwaist-workers' strike, the famous
'Uprising of the 20,000,' is a classic example of female industrial
militancy, and has figured prominently in the debates about women
workers' relationship to unionism in the early twentieth century.
This dramatic strike led to the transformation of the International
Ladies' Garment Workers' Union (ILGWU) from a craft union into
a massive industrial union which, from 1910 through the 1930s,
included more women workers than any other single union in the
country – this despite large fluctuations in membership levels in the
ILGWU over the years. In this essay, Roger Waldinger situates the
unionization of female garment-workers in its broader context,
analyzing the social and demographic characteristics of the
workforce, changes in production technology and shifts in the
structure of the industry over the first three decades of the twentieth
century. He argues that while strike activity was always endemic
among women garment-workers, a precondition for the creation of
the durable industrial unionism which emerged in 1910 was the
relative stability of industrial conditions – a stability which was
subsequently undermined, with severe consequences for the
ILGWU. Waldinger also explores the reasons for women's
underrepresentation within the union's leadership structure, despite
their vast numbers among the membership, pointing to exclusionism
in the power centers of the union, on the one hand, and the cultural
and structural constraints on women's activism, on the other.*

What is the hidden history of women workers? Historians have tended to concentrate on one question: did employment prove emancipatory, leading women to protest and, through protest, to question fundamental values – or did it simply reinforce the prevailing definition of women's place and role in the sexual division of labor? Those working in the field of women's labor history often write as if either perspective – conflict or subordination – provides a satisfactory explanation for the ambiguous experience of early-twentieth-century women workers. On the one hand, some historians seek to recover women's roles in the prominent labor conflicts of the period, arguing, as does Barbara Wertheimer in her popular account of women's labor struggles, that 'We Were There'[1] A more sophisticated treatment is offered by Alice Kessler-Harris. She notes that cultural patterns, the hostility of male workers, and the indifference (if not antagonism) of established unions impeded organizing among women workers, but contends that 'despite reluctance, women still could be devoted and successful union members' who 'often outdid men in militancy.'[2] Similarly, David Montgomery acknowledges that activist women often departed from the life-styles typical of the turn-of-the-century rank and file. Yet he maintains that it is 'misleading to distinguish categorically between representative passive women and exceptional activists,' given the high level of conflict that characterized the labor scene during the first two decades of the twentieth century.[3] Altogether different is the interpretation offered by Leslie Tentler, who accents the limited potential for organization among turn-of-the-century women workers.[4] Tentler argues that the subordination of women to men was more sharply defined at work than in any other aspect of life. In this view, the demographic characteristics of the female labor force and the prevailing division of labor so sharply constrained the potential for protest that work exercised a deeply conservative effect on the thought and action of working-class women.

Both these perspectives elide the crucial issues: the *conditions* under which women's participation in collective action will be more or less successful. Neither approach elucidates the variations in women workers' experiences – across industries or occupations, or over time. Those who, like Tentler, emphasize women's acquiescence in conditions of work, dismiss organization and militancy as epiphenomenal – but without providing any criteria for determining the relative importance of work and familial concerns, or for assessing differences in the organizability of women in various trades. On the other hand, those scholars highlighting the conflictual aspects of women's work experiences often presume an immanent tendency toward militancy, and fail to specify the structural opportunities for protest, or to acknowledge any constraints on organizing. And while Montgomery, in a critical response to Tentler, contends that historians should not see popular life-styles and leaders as mutually exclusive, his conception of studying the interaction between life-styles, struggles and organizational movements still neglects the social structure within which collective action necessarily takes place.[5]

This chapter attempts to specify the circumstances under which turn-of-the-century women workers engaged in successful collective action. Through a case study of the New York women's garment industry between 1900 and 1930, I argue that the trajectory of protest activity in the industry fundamentally diverged from the patterns associated with models of conflict or subordination. To be sure, the characteristics of the garment industry labor force and the antagonism of male unionists limited the potential for mass mobilization and for the institutionalization of women's interests within the trade union context. However, I will demonstrate that the ebb and flow of women's unionism in the garment trades was most closely linked to changes in the social technology of production and in the structure of the industry.

Though my evidence for this argument is drawn from the analysis of a single industry, the implications are of broader significance. The garment industry is a critical case for the analysis of women's labor-movement activity at the turn of the century, and has figured prominently on both sides of the debate about the capacities and limits of women's protest in this period.[6] Competitive in structure, offering employment conditions of little stability, and dominated by a youthful labor force, the garment industry exemplifies the social and economic conditions characteristic of women's labor at the time. In contrast to other women's industries – whether still more atomistic, as in the case of millinery or in the manufacture of artificial flowers, or more capital intensive, as with textiles or meatpacking – the garment industry also gave birth to a durable form of trade unionism in the early twentieth century. Consequently, it is possible to assess the strengths and limitations of women's trade union activity, as well as the various factors – both internal to the female labor force and generated by the wider environment – that affected the organizational outcomes of women's protest activities.

While conventional treatments of the role of women in the early garment industry focus on the dramatic events of 1909–10, this chapter includes analysis of the subsequent decades as well, adding a new dimension to our understanding of women's role in the development of needle trades unionism. Unionism among women garmentworkers went into sharp eclipse after World War I, which raises questions about the factors that precipitated the earlier and successful attempts at mobilization. Furthermore, the industry underwent important structural and demographic changes during the period examined here, and the resulting variations help to override the limits of a single case study.

Workforce characteristics and labor-market structure

The modern women's garment industry was a product of urbanization and the development of a national market. Still an item of household production in the 1880s, women's clothing rapidly became a factory-made good in the two decades that followed. As the demand for factory-made clothing grew, so did the industrial labor force: employing 39,000 workers in 1889, the industry grew to over 150,000 by 1905.

The upsurge of the American market coincided with large-scale immigration, first from Russia, and then from Italy. As a result, the industry grew up where the largest number of immigrants landed: New York City. In 1889, almost 65 percent of the fledgling industry's total output was produced in New York. By 1921, after thirty years of almost continuous growth, nearly three-quarters of national output was made in New York.

Although the emergent industry drew heavily on the rapidly expanding immigrant labor force, it incorporated male and female immigrants in different labor-market roles, largely in response to technological and market factors. The first items to be mass produced were coats and suits. The rapid growth of this branch of the industry in the 1880s and 1890s coincided with the influx of large numbers of male Jewish workers, who were drawn into the industry by the presence of German–Jewish employers and by common experience in tailoring prior to emigration from Europe. Though Jewish males crowded out female cutters and operators, male labor was generally restricted to jobs in the mechanized phases of production. In the remaining segments, operations were carried out by female handworkers. As output increased, the overall demand for handworkers in the complementary jobs grew as well.[7]

The uneven application of machinery in coats and suits and the emergence of markets for new products subsequently heightened the demand for semi-skilled female machine operators. New industries – the manufacture of dresses, shirtwaists, undergarments ('white-goods') and children's wear – developed after 1900. These were more heavily mechanized than coats and suits, fostering a different sexual division of labor: men filled only the relatively narrow tier of skilled jobs, while women were recruited for operating tasks, which had been deskilled, and for the traditional finishing jobs as well.[8]

Demand for female labor was further intensified by the seasonal character of the garment industry. The industry alternated between bursts of intense production, when demand strained even the amply available labor supply, and sharp declines that reduced peak employment by more than half. Because they were less skilled and often confined to jobs for which no training was required, women ideally fulfilled the industry's seasonal requirements, while their exclusion from the core jobs for which labor was relatively dear made them easily expendable in terms of slack demand.[9]

Women's clothing was only one of a group of closely related consumer goods industries in New York that relied on unskilled female labor. Although smaller, the men's clothing, artificial flower, tobacco and millinery trades all grew rapidly around the turn of the century, accounting for an increasingly large share of New York's swelling manufacturing labor force.[10] In 1910, these four industries employed 27 percent of New York's female blue-collar labor force, with women's garments accounting for a comparable share. Equally prone to seasonal variations and even more reliant on low-skilled handworkers, these industries contributed significantly to the increasing demand for female labor.[11]

At the turn of the century, young single workers furnished the bulk of the female labor force, greatly outnumbering married women with children. After 1890, the proportion of women workers aged 25–44 increased, but in manufacturing this barely changed the basic pattern. As late as 1920, almost 52 percent of the female operatives in manufacturing were under twenty-five years of age; by contrast, young workers comprised only 39 percent of females in all occupations.[12] Even more than other manufacturing, clothing was an industry of the young. Sixty-seven percent of the women workers surveyed in a 1908 US Bureau of Labor study of the men's clothing industry were under twenty-five, and workers aged seventeen and eighteen were the most numerous of all.[13] The Joint Board of Sanitary Control estimated that 50 percent of the women in the dress and waist industry were under twenty,[14] and the smaller garment and ancillary industries recruited even more heavily from the youth labor force.[15]

Female participation in the labor force reflected the income dynamics and life-cycle patterns of the immigrant family. The economic and physical vulnerability of the immigrant workingman impelled young immigrant women into the labor force; the large size of the immigrant family pushed them out shortly after marriage and no later than first childbirth. Jewish immigrant women remained homebound after marriage,[16] while among Italians, where family income was lower still and the pressures to work correspondingly greater, the burdens imposed by family-care and housework often permitted only intermittent employment.[17]

Frequently, married women immigrants adapted to the dual pressures of providing and homemaking by taking in work. Those who sewed at home did so to compensate for the low and unstable earnings of their mates. Over 48 percent of the home-sewers surveyed in the US Bureau of Labor study were married to men employed as day laborers in construction; 87 percent were married to men who had been jobless for part of the previous year.[18] As late as 1922, the situation of homeworkers and their husbands remained substantially unaltered. Fifty-five percent of the homeworkers surveyed that year by a special New York State Commission were married to unskilled workers, and their husbands had experienced an average of four months' unemployment in 1922.[19]

Given the seasonal, unstable nature of the industry, the virtual inexhaustibility of the labor supply and the short span of female working careers made for an unstructured labor market. The elasticity of supply offered employers no inducement to regularize production, and the pattern of female labor-force participation reinforced the resistance to rationalizing employment practices. In large measure, clothing was a casual labor market because it was a youth labor market. Girls typically began to work in early adolescence, generally starting at age fourteen. Fifty-nine percent of the Italian working women surveyed by Louise Odencrantz, for instance, had begun working at that age. Moreover, large numbers of girls were undeterred by child-labor laws and truancy codes, and under-age employment was common in the years between 1900 and 1920. One-fifth of the 252 millinery-workers surveyed by Mary Van Kleeck in 1913 had begun work at age thirteen, and one-sixth of the Italian working women questioned by Odencrantz had been similarly successful in evading mandatory schooling laws.[20] For the adolescent girls who thus entered the labor market, work was motivated by the prospect of immediate, short-term rewards. Envisaging limited career horizons, they sought work without regard to long-term earnings or employment possibilities.[21] Similarly, recurrent family crises conflicted with the burdens of family-care to create a pattern of intermittent employment among married women. For these workers, labor-force activity did not involve a process of occupational selection. Rather, as Katherine Anthony concluded in her study of women workers on New York's West Side, 'The mother who must earn . . . is willing to "take anything" from the start.'[22] Thus, the ties that bound immigrant women to their jobs were tenuous, at best. A committee of the New York State legislature investigating the garment industry in 1895 found that many women workers in small shops knew their employees only by sight, not by name, and that many employers did not even have records of their employees' names.[23]

The seasonal nature of work bore down heavily upon the immigrant workers. Busy seasons in women's clothing fell into two predictable, although all too short, periods: three to four months during the spring and another burst of between two and three months in late summer and fall. The intervening periods were characterized by month-long build-ups and declines, and four- to eight-week periods when virtually no work was available. Employment fluctuated wildly: during 1914, the workforce employed in the coat and suit industry swelled to 164 percent of its average size in

February, and sank to 50 percent in late May. In dress- and waist-manufacturing, the workforce employed during the active spring season of 1913 fell to 38 percent of its size during the inter-seasonal lull.[24] Consequently, relatively few women workers enjoyed a lengthy period of uninterrupted wage-earning. According to Odencrantz's study of Italian women workers, the minimum span of unemployment for those in the needle trades was eight to twelve weeks a year.[25]

Seasonality naturally produced overcrowding in the apparel labor market. In the absence of restrictions on the labor supply, the intensified demand for workers at seasonal peaks of production tended to retain surplus workers who might otherwise have been driven into other forms of employment. Variations in earnings, moreover, considerably exceeded the fluctuations in employment, so that many of the workers employed during the inter-seasonal period were in effect only working part-time. The reason was that firms used piecework as a device to retain workers during slack periods, thereby maintaining a capacity to respond instantaneously to sudden or momentary changes in demand.[26]

The multiple entries and withdrawals of young working women and their mothers combined with the churning effects of seasonality to make turnover levels extremely high. Under these conditions, firms had little to gain from insulating the workforce from the ebb and flow of demand. Indeed, employers kept overhead and training costs low by organizing production in ways that facilitated the integration of new unskilled workers. Yet most machine jobs retained a certain component of skill, and high levels of turnover and the shortness of seasons made employers reluctant to hire and train inexperienced workers. In addition, young girls were often inadequate sewers, and the constant variation in styles made it difficult to master a job. One solution was to take on new hires for the least-skilled jobs demanding no machine work, or for the simple and repetitive operations which could easily be learned. When employers did hire new workers, they were often forced to absorb the learning costs themselves. Young women were frequently hired as 'learners' or 'apprentices,' jobs for which they received substantially lower pay. In 1914, for example, over a quarter of the women workers in the New York waist and dress industry earned less than the union minimum because the employers claimed that they were learners.[27]

The presence of a large pool of untrained workers and potential homeworkers also retarded mechanization, thereby lessening the pressure to regularize production. Despite refinements in the basic single-needle sewing machine and the introduction of special machines for button-holing and other tasks, numerous operations – particularly those involved in finishing garments – proved resistant to mechanization until well into the 1920s. At least 33 percent of the 25,000 women workers employed in the waist and dress industry in 1913 were engaged in hand operations. A similar proportion of the 32,000 coat- and suit-workers were basting, lining and finishing garments by hand as late as 1921.[28] Reliance on handworkers was comparable in the men's clothing industry, and greater still in industries like millinery and artificial flower-making.[29] Since seasons tended to converge, demand for handworkers in the various trades peaked simultaneously and then bottomed-out abruptly, further enlarging the surplus labor pool.

Though operations requiring hand labor were frequently performed in the factory, there were few impediments to the removal of these jobs from the plant. The work could readily be done at home, and the articles were easily transportable from the factory to home and back again. Moreover, employing homeworkers was a technique for expanding production capacity during periods of peak activity: it rose and fell with the seasons, plummeting to near zero when the pace of factory activity declined. Thus, the availability of homeworkers further diminished the pressures to regularize employment – a pattern that remained unchanged from the turn of the century through the 1920s.[30]

Industrial change and the growth of the ILGWU

In contrast to other branches of manufacturing, the industrialization of the garment trades did not proceed by way of the centralized factory. Rather, clothing was principally made by home-sewers or by workers employed in small shops owned by contractors, who worked up goods for much larger distributors or manufacturers. The prevalence of contracting was a response to both market and organizational imperatives. While the demands of selling and distribution diverted potential manufacturers from production responsibilities, production could easily be expanded through contracting. In addition, contracting minimized and spread the risk, allowing manufacturers to react swiftly to each contraction or expansion of demand. Most importantly, contracting provided an ideal system of labor recruitment. Unlike the larger manufacturer – who, until 1914, was likely to be a first- or second-generation German–Jewish immigrant – the contractor shared religious, ethnic and home-town links with his Russian–Jewish and Italian employees.[31] These ties enabled the contractor to mobilize a workforce in response to seasonal swings in demand and – perhaps even more crucial – to maintain a grip on his labor force when intense seasonal activity sharpened the competition for labor.[32]

By 1900, however, changes in demand and marketing disrupted this set of arrangements. The new industries that developed shortly after the turn of the century – the manufacture of dresses, shirt-waists, white goods, children's wear, kimonos, wrappers – placed greater reliance on power-driven than on foot-driven machinery and employed less skilled labor.[33] At the same time, selling and buying practices altered: the rapid development of department stores and mail-order houses, both buying directly from manufacturers, undercut the role that wholesalers and distributors had played during the previous period.[34]

These developments impelled production back toward the factory as the number of contractors declined and establishment-size increased. The changes were particularly noticeable in the new industries that principally employed women. In 1913, for example, 56 percent of the dress- and waist-workers worked in factories with 75 or more employees, and 27 percent were in establishments of 100–200 workers.[35] Unlike the smaller coat factories and contracting shops where workers produced full garments, these factories fragmented garment-making into twenty or more operations performed by separate individuals.[36]

These changes in industrial structure provided fertile ground for successful organizing efforts. Larger units of production made for a more cohesive and concentrated workforce, mitigating the destabilizing effects of youth and compressed working careers. The emergence of large firms with relatively large capital investments also dampened competitive pressures. Most importantly, profits did not hinge on the primitive techniques of 'driving' or 'sweating' that prevailed among the contractors, so that the large firms had an interest in standardizing both employment conditions and wage rates.

Thus, collective action – initially episodic, isolated and unsuccessful – grew to industry-wide dimensions and enjoyed considerable success. Between 1906 and 1909, disputes over wage and piece-rate reductions, excessively strict discipline, and sexual harassment sparked walkouts among women white-goods-workers, waist-makers and wrapper-makers.[37] The strikes were largely spontaneous and the organizations shortlived. Typically, tentative stabs toward unionism emerged out of the specific grievances of individual work groups separated from one another by locality and trade: 'a group of girls working on wrappers somewhere in Brooklyn assembled in a room and began to discuss conditions . . . An idea came to their mind that it would be a mighty good thing to organize the workers into a union.'[38]

When earnings took a sustained fall in 1909, simmering discontent over arbitrary fines, discipline and requirements that workers pay for needle and thread boiled over into a series of spontaneous strikes among waist-makers that subsequently mushroomed into the famous 'Uprising of the 20,000.' The strike demonstrated that young, largely immigrant women possessed a tenacity and militancy that would keep thousands on the picket lines for several months. But the walkout culminated in a hollow victory, for the large manufacturers continued to resist organization. The waist-makers' union proved no more successful in developing mechanisms for standardizing rates among the plethora of small, independent shops or for enforcing the original agreement. Given the constant turnover of firms and the limited strength of the union, membership sank from 20,000 in 1910 to 7,000 a year later.[39]

Reorganization of the waist trade did not occur until 1913, and then under drastically different auspices. By this time the International Ladies' Garment Workers' Union had succeeded in organizing the male-dominated cloak and suit trade. In contrast to the previous waist strike, toward which the ILGWU leadership had assumed a rather distant stance, the union now sought to control organizing at the highest levels, divesting local officials of much responsibility. More importantly, the relationship that the ILGWU established with the employers in the cloak and suit trade –

embedded in the agreement known as the 'Protocols of Peace' – provided a framework for organizing the industry to which management was willing to assent. The large waist manufacturers, who had formed an association during the 1910 strike, revived their organization – this time not in order to quell unionization, but rather to develop a mechanism for bargaining with the ILGWU. By this time, the manufacturers wanted to stabilize the industry through the establishment and extension of standardized rates: in this way, they reasoned, competition from small producers with low overheads and more flexible labor arrangements could be controlled. Although the two sides came to terms after seven weeks' bargaining, the manufacturers withheld agreement, seeking instead to force the union into an industry-wide strike that would demonstrate the ILGWU's ability to organize the entire trade, including the small producers. What ensued was a successful strike from which the shops of the large, organized manufacturers were largely exempted. At its conclusion, a pre-arranged contract was presented to the largely female strikers who, in the words of the union's official historian, 'accepted [it] as a *fait accompli*, with some surprise, but without much animation.'[40]

Organizational resources and women's trade union roles

Though conditions proved conducive to unionism during the 1910s, the paucity of organizational resources dampened the potential for collective action and limited the autonomy of women's organizing efforts. In contrast to other unions, the ILGWU sought to organize women workers; shortly after its formation in 1910, it chartered locals in several of the women's trades. These fledgling locals, however, were shortlived, and the union proved unwilling to invest resources in organizing waist-makers or white-goods-workers. Instead, the ILGWU sought to enlist the Women's Trade Union League (WTUL) – to no avail in the case of the waist-makers, but successfully in the case of the white-goods-workers, where WTUL funds nurtured a small number of unionists through the difficult years of 1908–12.[41] Even after the organization of the cloak trade put the union on a sure footing, the ILGWU remained reluctant to involve itself fully in organizing the women's trades. Activity among the largely female waist-makers, wrapper- and kimono-makers, and white-goods-workers intensified in 1911, leading these locals to appeal for authorization for a general strike in November of that year. But the ILGWU withheld its sanction, not giving the go-ahead until 1913. At that time, as we have seen, control over organizing activity was withdrawn from local activists in the large waist and blouse trade. In the white-goods industry, where organizing was largely self-directed, the union leadership gave minimal assistance and almost withdrew endorsement on the eve of the general strike planned by locals in the white-goods industry.[42]

Resistance to organizing women in the garment trades stemmed from a variety of sources. According to Abraham Rosenberg, one of the early ILGWU presidents, most of the active male rank and file saw the women's 'locals as a drag on the International.'[43] Competition between male and female workers contributed to the indifference and antagonism that male unionists exhibited. When skirt firms, previously dependent on male operators, branched out into dresses and then recruited cheaper and apparently more tractable women dress-makers, the male skirt-makers sought to protect their jurisdiction, rather than organize the new group of women workers.[44] Even those male unionists who supported the organization of women were often ambivalent about the role of women in the industry, seeing them as a source of indirect competition. As one union official argued:

> so long as these women and girls work terribly long hours for incredibly low wages, they are sooner or later destined to leave their present employment and seek work in skirt or dress shops, or as finishers at cloaks, and thus still more increase the number of unemployed among our members.[45]

In addition, the male-dominated character of the union hampered the integration of female rank-and-file leaders. In the predominantly male cloak industry, it proved necessary to organize the 4,000 women cloak finishers into a separate, all-female local. 'We all know,' wrote Pauline Newman, commenting on this development, 'that girls feel more at home among themelves than among men. Then again, when they meet together with men, they hardly get a chance to express their opinions on questions that concern them.'[46] Though men also predominated in the children's cloak industry, 600 of the 2,700 union members in that trade were women. But male indifference to the concerns of their sisters left heavily female factories unorganized, and deterred women members from any form of participation in union affairs. 'It seems almost a tradition in the children's cloak local,' noted Catherine Denmark, 'that women are confined to the condition of "being organized." '[47] Women leaders coming out of organizing activities found little place for themselves in the union hierarchy. Rose Schneiderman, for example, did yeoman work organizing white-goods-workers on a virtually solo basis at a time when the ILGWU expressed little interest in this chiefly female trade. But when the fledgling white-goods local grew large enough to be embraced by the ILGWU, the union went outside the trade to install Samuel Shore at its head, a man whom Schneiderman later described as none 'too energetic, a bit pompous, and inclined to promise everything in the world.'[48] Some rank-and-file activists – Pauline Newman or Fannia Cohn, for instance – were absorbed into official positions, only to be sent on out-of-town organizing drives, rather than receiving leadership positions in the largely women's locals.[49] Others still – such as Clara Lemlich, a firebrand who ignited the 1909 waist-makers' strike – moved on to organizing for the WTUL and then drifted out of the trade altogether.[50] Thus, despite the emergence of large, female-dominated locals, women were excluded from positions of any importance. Between 1910 and 1920, the New York City ILGWU locals elected 450 delegates, of whom only twenty-five were women, to the six conventions held during that period. And of these twenty-five, few repeated the experience more than once: only one delegate attended as many as four conventions and four others were each elected to only two conventions.[51]

The size of the locals in the women's trades and the characteristics of the membership further limited the organizational resources available to women garment-workers. In contrast to the male-dominated sectors of the industry, where smaller locals were organized according to craft principles and then brought under the administrative umbrella of a large joint board, workers in the women's trades were combined into large, unwieldy units that brought together as many as 25,000 workers in a single local. Size was a source of considerable membership apathy, leading feminist and ILGWU leader Fannia Cohn to argue that 'the waistmakers need a better appreciation of the trade union movement.'[52] Problems of size were aggravated by the instability of the membership: almost a quarter of the Waistmakers' local's membership (Local 25) turned over each year. 'For girls,' complained the union's journal, 'the marriage license is an automatic withdrawal from the union.'⁵³ The constant churning in union ranks made it both necessary and difficult to reorganize the already organized firms. The *Ladies' Garment Worker* noted that the 'newcomers do not always realize their obligations to the union or to their sister workers – at any rate, not until the Union has gone to considerable expense of money and energy to impress union truths on them and get them into line.'⁵⁴

Such patterns of participation reflected family-income dynamics and cultural patterns, and these in turn worked quite differently among the two immigrant groups – Jews and Italians – that made up the union's base. Jewish women, rather than their Italian counterparts, provided the instigators and shock troops for the strikes of the period. They did so because the greater prosperity of Jewish immigrant families both permitted Jewish women temporarily to forgo wages and released them from time-consuming family responsibilities.⁵⁵ But Jewish women's militancy, if conducive to agitation and compatible with extensive stints on the picket line, flagged in the face of pressures for marriage and home. 'Girls will go to the limit to obtain better conditions,' noted Pauline Newman in the union's official journal, 'but as soon as the fight is over, [they] remain absolutely indifferent to the organization they so much fought for.'⁵⁶ And Newman voiced the same frustration in her private correspondence with Rose Schneiderman: 'Now you and I know that the [Jewish] East Side element is the hardest to work with, that is, hardest to keep . . . within the organization.'⁵⁷

The instability of individual work careers also hastened the process of ethnic succession. In the 1910s, union militancy emerged among young radical Jewish women, many of them veterans of revolutionary work in Russia or Poland.⁵⁸ But by the 1920s, young Jewish women were moving into white-collar occupations, while their Italian counterparts – among whom educational levels and family incomes were substantially lower – provided the main source of female labor.⁵⁹ Whether Jewish or Italian, many of these new recruits were native-born, in contrast to the male cloak- and suit-workers. The cloak and suit industry had ceased to grow after 1915, and stagnation deterred new entrants; at the same time, the declining industry retained experienced male workers for the remainder of their working lives. But in industries involved in the manufacture of dresses, blouses and waists, and white goods, the changes in the ethnic composition of the heavily female labor force distanced the women unionists from the radical, immigrant tradition that had provided both ideological and cultural support during the earlier phases of union activity. The Americanized workers proved less susceptible to ideological appeals. Repeatedly, ILGWU organizers complained that 'among the newer element of Italian–American and Jewish–American girls, it is hard to find the necessary leadership for the shop and the local.'[60] Mass organizing and spontaneous strike strategies, on which the union had previously relied, failed to evoke a positive response from the newer, more Americanized workforce that emerged among women in the 1920s.[61] Notwithstanding these difficulties, it was not until the late 1920s that the union's male leadership would look self-critically at its failure to develop women leaders and begin to consider the possibility of granting women greater internal autonomy.

Industrial change and organizational decline

The successful organizing drives that swept through the various garment trades – coats and suits, in 1911; waists, dresses, white-goods, and other miscellaneous trades, in 1913 – corresponded to the scale and technology of production activities at the time. The collective agreements secured by the ILGWU bound the union to the more established firms ensconced at the top of the market. The agreements embodied the desire of both labor and management to contain changes that would upset the dominance of the large producers and to curb cut-throat competition. But the position of the large firms weakened as the market for apparel altered after World War I. Until then, the garment industry had enjoyed extremely rapid growth as a result of the continuous substitution of ready-made for home- or custom-made clothes. During the second decade of the twentieth century, however, this process was completed, so that by the 1920s, the industry entered a new phase in which growth was determined by the normal changes in the demand and supply for apparel.[62] This transition into a cycle of slower growth altered the relationship between production and selling. Whereas in the period of rapid expansion, high demand insured an adequate level of profits, competition intensified under conditions of slower growth.[63]

Another major change in the industry in this period was the increased importance of fashion. In a sense, that development was the culmination of the trends that initially sparked the industrialization of clothing: urbanization, the widening of the market, and improved communication networks that created a mass public sensitive to changes in styles.[64] Structural relations within the industry underwent a significant change as marketing practices were transformed by the shift toward greater fashion consciousness. Wholesaling firms that could concentrate on selling and marketing were better positioned than the older manufacturers saddled with sizeable production facilities that demanded close attention. The squeeze on profits, moreover, encouraged a shift to a strategy that emphasized small unit profits on a large volume of sales. Given the investment in textiles and the overhead costs needed to maintain a sufficiently large inventory of styles, firms now strove to unburden themselves of fixed costs involved in plant and machinery.

The large firms began to substitute a plethora of small, outside contractors for their sizeable 'inside shops.' The locus of production decisively shifted out of the larger, more stable factories with the advent of the wholesaler-jobber. Decentralization proceeded expeditiously, because the existence of a large labor pool made small-scale, highly labor-intensive production methods economical – a matter of crucial importance for severely undercapitalized small contractors with high turnover rates. Dispersion also fitted neatly with the predilections of the workers. Conduct in the small shops was more relaxed and workers were not expected to conform to the rigid standards of attendance and punctuality that prevailed in the more established factories.[65] Tied by his experience and origins to the workers' social milieu, the contractor could also manipulate social and ethnic networks to secure a flexible workforce. 'Only comparatively recently [the contractor was] an employee in a shop,' noted a union leader. He 'lives in the district inhabited by the workers. He has friends and acquaintances among them, and he knows how to get help when needed.'[66] The smaller factories were also more apt to be located nearer to workers' homes, and as the immigrant neighborhoods branched out from the lower East Side, these locational aspects became increasingly important in the recruitment of women workers, for whom short-term stints of employment made it desirable to keep the costs of job-searching low. Small size also obviated the material-handling problems that tended to disrupt production flows in larger factories and consequently reduced piece-rate earnings. This in turn offered workers an opportunity to compensate for the lower prices paid per job.[67]

Shifts in product demand exercised a further destabilizing effect. By 1920, the shirtwaist had virtually disappeared as an item of consumer interest. In the white-goods industry – where almost 95 percent of the workforce was female and most had been employed in large factories – the industry moved from standardized muslin garments to fashion-oriented silk and rayon products better suited to small-scale production methods.[68]

Most importantly, the influence of fashion and marketing gave rise to a completely new industry, one less stable than all others and most accessible to new entrants – dress manufacture. 'With $2,500 a few customers, and a colossal amount of nerve, almost anyone can go into the dress business,' noted *Fortune* at the end of the 1930s.[69] Not a few entrepreneurs were so prompted. In 1929, 709 dress manufacturers began operations; the same year, 478 closed their doors. In 1931, more than one-third of all dress sales were made by firms that had opened within the previous four years; firms that had begun operations between 1923 and 1927 accounted for yet another third.[70] The transformation of the industrial situation undermined the rationale for union regulation.

In the 1920s, these shifts meant that bargaining relationships with the ILGWU were marked by continual attempts to evade the union controls exercised in the larger, more stable units and to relocate production to a welter of small, transient, contracting factories. The ILGWU consistently sought to maintain the importance of the inside shop. But moving as it did against the current of change in the marketplace, this stance proved ineffectual. Small contracting factories multiplied and remained unorganized. The number of factories was too large, the seasonal character of the industry was too accentuated, and the competitive habits of the workers were too strong for the union effectively to reassert control.[71]

Furthermore, decentralization sufficiently loosened the opportunity structure to lure large numbers of workers into business on their own in this period. 'My experience,' noted Benjamin Schlesinger, then president of the ILGWU, 'shows that a large number of petty bosses were at one time good union men.'[72] Small cooperatively run shops, jointly owned by a few workers and employing a very limited number of friends and relatives, reappeared after 1915. As conditions turned in favor of small-scale production during the 1920s, the number of such 'corporation shops' (a corruption of 'cooperation') multiplied rapidly.[73]

Under these circumstances, the potential for organizational maintenance and successful collective action diminished. In the dress industry, non-union and independent contracting shops mushroomed in the early 1920s, frustrating the union's repeated efforts to organize new entrants and control the flow of production from jobbers to contractors. In blouses and waists, the once-powerful waist-makers' local fell on hard times, having lost most of its firms and its former cadres to the burgeoning dress industry. Demand for blouses revived after 1922, but this time the industry remained non-unionized, impervious to the local's ineffectual attempts to organize the new, Americanized workers who had entered the trade. Similarly, union strength in the other women's trades found itself at low tide. In the white-goods industry, the large majority of firms were unorganized and the workers proved indifferent to the union's repeated overtures. And in the smaller, miscellaneous trades – all of which had earlier been fertile ground for ILGWU activists – the organizations spawned by the general strike of 1913 had virtually collapsed.[74]

Conclusion

The history of the women's garment-workers, treated in opposing accounts as an exemplar of either the militant potential or passive conservatism of women workers, involves a more complex trajectory. The demographic make-up of the workforce served as a limiting factor on the potential for mobilization. Dominated by young workers whose work careers were regulated by familial exigencies, the garment industry had an unstructured labor market. Under conditions of instability in the demand for women's clothing, employers responded to the virtual inexhaustibility of the female labor force in ways that weakened women's attachment to the job. Despite the volatility of the industry and the churning of workers among firms and in and out of the labor force, conditions in the garment trades triggered repeated bouts of strike activity. The outcomes of such protests, however, hinged on the overall structure of opportunities within the industry. When technology and market conditions favored the products of large-scale producers anxious to contain cut-throat competitive pressures, relative industrial stability facilitated collective activity. Durable organizational outcomes resulted from these circumstances. Subsequent changes in the structure of industrial activity eroded the competitive position of the larger, more stable producers, providing an environment supportive of small, informally organized firms. The destabilization of industrial conditions in the 1920s thus undermined the viability of trade union organization.

While the structure of the industry proved conducive to unionization between 1910 and 1920, the organizational resources available to women workers in the ILGWU limited their ability to institutionalize their interests within the union structure. Their putative external allies among the male unionists of the ILGWU were initially ambivalent about supporting organizing efforts. And, after organizing efforts proved successful, women activists found themselves excluded from positions of power and influence in the union, even though the sex-segregated nature of the industry created predominantly female locals in which women might easily have moved into leadership roles. Tendencies toward female activism were also limited by familial responsibilities and constraints (as in the case of Italian immigrants), or undercut (as with young Jewish unionists influenced by cultural norms emphasizing marriage and home). Most importantly, women's career patterns led to membership instability, increasing demands on the union's organizational resources and weakening the responsiveness of successive groups of women workers to organizing appeals.

Notes

1   Barbara Wertheimer, *We Were There*, New York, Pantheon, 1978.
2   Alice Kessler-Harris, *Out to Work*, New York, Oxford, 1981, pp. 160–1.
3   David Montgomery, 'To Study the People: The American Working Class,' *Labor History*, vol. 21, no. 4, p.496.
4   Leslie Tentler, *Wage-earning Women: Industrial Work and Family Life in the United States, 1900–1914*, New York, Oxford, 1979.
5   Montgomery, 'To Study the People.'
6   See, in addition to the works already cited, Meredith Tax, *The Rising of the Women*, New York, Monthly Review Press, 1980.
7   Mabel Willett, *Women in the Clothing Trade*, New York, Columbia University Studies in History, Economics and Public Law, 1902.
8   Helen Meiklejohn, 'Dresses – The Impact of Fashion on a Business,' in Walton Hamilton, ed., *Prices and Price Policies*, New York, McGraw-Hill, 1938; Joint Board of Sanitary Control, *Special Report on Sanitary Conditions in the Shops of the Waist and Dress Industry*, New York, Joint Board of Sanitary Control, 1913; Joint of Board of Sanitary Control, *Six Years of Progress: An Experiment in Industrial Self-Management*, New York, Joint Board of Sanitary Control, 1916.
9   Gertrude Greig, *Seasonality in Women's Clothing*, New York, Columbia University Press, 1949.
10   Mary Van Kleeck, *Artificial Flower Makers*, New York, Russell Sage Foundation, 1913; Mary Van Kleeck, *A Seasonal Industry*, New York, Russell Sage Foundation, 1917.
11   United States, Bureau of the Census, *Census of Population*, Washington, DC, Government Printing Office, 1890, 1900, 1910, 1920.
12   Joseph Hill, *Women in Gainful Occupations*, Census Monograph, vol. 9, Washington, DC, Government Printing Office, 1929.
13   United States Senate, *Report on Conditions of Women and Child Wage-earners: Men's Ready-made Clothing*, vol. 2, Washington, DC, Government Printing Office, 1911, pp.36–42, 66–70.
14   Joint Board of Sanitary Control, *Special Report*, pp.7–19.
15   Van Kleeck, *Artificial Flower Makers* and *A Seasonal Industry*; 'The Stress of the Seasons,' *Survey*, March 8, 1913, p.806.
16   Thomas Kessner, *The Golden Door*, New York, Oxford University Press, 1977.
17   Louise Odencrantz, *Italian Women in Industry*, New York, Russell Sage Foundation, 1919, p.21.
18   United States Senate, *Report on Conditions*, pp.238–305, 369–84.
19   State of New York, Commission to Investigate Laws Relating to Child Welfare, *Third Annual Report*, Albany, 1924; Jean M. Heer, 'Industrial Homework in New York City,' MA dissertation, Columbia University, 1924.

20 Odencrantz, *Italian Women*, p.248; Van Kleeck, *A Seasonal Industry*, p.150.
21 Tentler, *Wage-earning Women*.
22 Katherine Anthony, *Women Who Must Earn*, Russell Sage Foundation, 1914, p.84.
23 Robert Smuts, *Women and Work in America*, New York, Schocken, 1971.
24 United States Department of Labor, *Wages and Regularity of Employment and Standardization of Piece Rates in the Dress and Waist Industries*, Bulletin no. 146, Washington, DC, Government Printing Office, pp.18–23.
25 Odencrantz, *Italian Women*, pp.122–6.
26 United States Department of Labor, *Wages and Regularity*.
27 State of New York, Factory Investigations Commission, *Fourth Report of the Factory Investigating Commission*, vol. 2, Albany, 1915, pp.521–79.
28 Louis Levine, *The Women's Garment Workers*, New York, Huebsch, 1924.
29 Van Kleeck, *Artificial Flower Makers* and *A Seasonal Industry*.
30 State of New York, Commission to Investigate Laws, *Third Annual Report*, pp.41–52.
31 Moses Rischin, *The Promised City*, Cambridge, Harvard University Press, 1962.
32 United States Senate, *Report on Conditions*, pp.415–25; Jesse E. Pope, *The Clothing Industry of New York*, Columbia, University of Missouri Press, 1902, pp.62–7.
33 Axel Josephson, 'The Manufacture of Clothing,' in *United States Census of Manufactures*, Washington, DC, Government Printing Office, 1902.
34 Levine, *The Women's Garment Workers*.
35 United States Bureau of the Census, *Census of Population*, 1908, 1914, Washington, DC, Government Printing Office.
36 United States Department of Labor, *Wages and Regularity*.
37 Nancy Schrom Dye, *As Equals and as Sisters: Feminism, the Labor Movement and the Women's Trade Union League of New York*, Columbia, University of Missouri Press, 1980.
38 'Progress of the Kimono and House Dress Workers,' *Ladies' Garment Worker*, April 1918. For an account of quite similar trade union origins in the children's dress trade, see 'Two Women Workers' Local,' *Ladies' Garment Worker*, May 1918.
39 Levine, *The Women's Garment Workers*; Melvyn Dubofsky, *When Workers Organize*, Amherst, University of Massachusetts Press, 1968.
40 Levine, *The Women's Garment Workers*, p.226.
41 Dye, *As Equals*.
42 Harry Lang, *'60': Biography of a Union*, New York, Local 60, 1940.
43 'President Rosenberg's Report to the Toronto Convention,' *Ladies'*

Garment Worker, June 1912, p.15.
44 ILGWU, *Proceedings of the Convention*, 1912, p.55.
45 *Ibid.*, p.12.
46 Pauline Newman, 'Our Women Workers,' *Ladies' Garment Worker*, May 1913, p.18.
47 Catherine Denmark, 'Our Women Workers,' *Ladies' Garment Worker*, August 1914, p.24.
48 Rose Schneiderman with Lucy Goldthwaite, *All for One*, New York, Paul S. Erickson, 1967.
49 Dye, *As Equals*; Alice Kessler-Harris, 'Organizing the Unorganizable: Three Jewish Women and their Union,' *Labor History*, vol. 17, winter 1976, pp.14–28.
50 Paula Scheier, 'Clara Lemlich Shavelson,' *Jewish Life*, vol. 8, November 1954.
51 ILGWU, *Proceedings of the Convention*, 1910–20.
52 Fannia Cohn, 'The Biggest Local of the International,' *Ladies' Garment Worker*, February 1918, p.17.
53 'New Activities in the Waistmakers' Union, Local 25,' *Ladies' Garment Worker*, October 1918, p.27.
54 'A Few Stirring Events: In the Waist and Dress Trade,' *Ladies' Garment Worker*, September 1915, p.12.
55 Miriam Cohen, 'From Workshop to Office: Italian Women and Family Strategies in New York City,' PhD dissertation, University of Michigan, 1978.
56 Newman, 'Our Women Workers,' p.21.
57 Quoted in Dye, *As Equals*, p.115.
58 Charlotte Brown, Paula Hyman and Sonya Michel, *The Jewish Woman in America*, New York, NAL, 1977.
59 Ronald Bayor, *Neighbors in Conflict*, Baltimore, John Hopkins Press, 1978.
60 ILGWU, *Report of the General Executive Board*, 1928, p.242.
61 *Ibid.*, 1925.
62 Meiklejohn, 'Dresses – The Impact of Fashion on a Business,' pp.343–7.
63 Levine, *The Women's Garment Workers*.
64 Paul Nystrom, *The Economics of Fashion*, New York, The Ronald Press, 1928; Florence Richards, *The Ready-to-wear Industry*, New York, Fairchild, 1951.
65 Jesse Carpenter, *Competition and Collective Bargaining in the Needle Trades*, Ithaca, New York State School of Industrial Relations 1972, p.105.
66 Benjamin Schlesinger, 'What the Workers in the Sub-factories Have to Endure,' *Ladies' Garment Worker*, March 1915, pp.22–3.
67 Benjamin Schlesinger, 'Earnings in the Shops of the Sub-manufacturers,' *Ladies' Garment Worker*, February 1915.
68 ILGWU, *Report of the General Executive Board*, 1928.
69 'America Comes to Seventh Avenue,' *Fortune*, July 1939.

70 National Credit Office, *The Development of the Dress Industry*, New York, National Credit Office, 1931.

71 Levine, *The Women's Garment Workers*; Carpenter, *Competition and Collective Bargaining*.

72 Benjamin Schlesinger, 'Our Recent Struggle and its Results,' *Ladies' Garment Worker*, September 1915.

73 Margaret Gadsby, 'Trade Agreements in the New York Garment Industry,' *Monthly Labor Review*, vol. 16, no. 6, 1923.

74 ILGWU, *Report of the General Executive Board*, 1920–30.

6

Problems of coalition-building: Women and trade unions in the 1920s

Alice Kessler-Harris

Commentators on women's labor history have repeatedly remarked upon the many tensions between women workers and trade unions. Here, Alice Kessler-Harris ventures beyond description of that problematic relationship, and offers an explanation for it, with particular reference to the 1920s. She explores both the institutional characteristics of unions and the cultural self-conception of wage-earning women, and suggests a structural basis for the tension between the two in the period following World War I. On the basis of the influx of women into the labor movement in the 1910s, and of the suffrage victory, the postwar decade seemed to offer auspicious opportunities for developing a solid relationship between women workers and the unions. Instead, however, as Kessler-Harris shows, male trade union leaders continued to regard women with suspicion, ultimately contributing to the decline of union strength in the 1920s.

The focus here is once again on the case of the garment-workers, but unlike Waldinger, who stresses the shifting structure of the garment industry in his account of the ILGWU's decline in the 1920s, Kessler-Harris's argument rests on an analysis of the internal politics of the labor movement itself. The embattled group mentality of the unions – intensified in the 1920s by the external attacks on labor – led male trade union leaders to a perception of women workers as not only 'different' but also as weak and unreliable allies. In industries like garment manufacture, the labor force was female-dominated, and women had to be admitted to union membership. However, efforts to build woman-centered organizational forms within the existing union structure were viewed with suspicion and actively discouraged, while women were excluded from the inner leadership circles as well. Thus, the promise of fruitful coalition between men and women in the labor movement confronted formidable obstacles in the 1920s and, in the end, the opportunity to build on the gains made in the century's second decade was lost.

How do we, who are feminists and committed to the labor movement, come to terms with the failures of organized labor with regard to women? How do we explain the persistent failure of women to make their way to positions of power inside trade unions? In a path-breaking essay, Ruth Milkman has argued that contemporary feminists who neglect the labor movement (with all its faults) risk perpetual weakness, just as a labor movement that fails to come to terms with wage-earning women risks continuing stagnation.[1] In the end, Milkman laid the absence of common goals at the door of an exclusionary and male-oriented trade union movement, and pleaded with feminists not to turn their backs on it. But her description of organized labor's years of neglect of women and their concerns yields no source for optimism, and her argument offers few hints of any possibility of change. Whether the trade union movement can ever become a vehicle for non-sexist activity on behalf of all its members is still a major question for women. The need to develop a strategy in that direction remains one of the pressing issues of the contemporary period.

This chapter addresses the unresolved tension between trade unions and women from the perspective of the past. Drawing upon a relatively brief moment in their relationship, it attempts to make sense of seemingly paradoxical behavior on both sides. It does so around two central questions. What can we say about the nature of trade unions that will help us to understand how organized labor treats its female members? And what can we say about women's culture (especially the culture of wage-earning women) that will help us to understand women's sense of themselves inside the trade union movement?[2] I want to focus on the quality of relationships between men and women inside trade unions – on the sources of tension and agreement. This approach tends to emphasize the problems or paradoxes in coalition-building at the expense of illustrations of harmony. But because it juxtaposes women's needs against the purposes of trade unions, it holds the promise of some useful political lessons for the present.

Tensions between women and men in trade unions were not new in the 1920s. A hundred years earlier, organized men had complained that wage-earning women deprived breadwinners of jobs, reduced wages and lowered standards. Repeatedly in the nineteenth century, they debated the efficacy of organizing women as opposed to excluding them from their trades, and they appealed to the state to regulate women's work lest their own efforts to raise standards be hindered.[3] But I have chosen the 1920s as the focus for exploration and illustration for several reasons. It was a decade when issues posed by the spread of waged work, especially for married women, were the subject of national debate.[4] Trade unions not only participated in the debate, but accepted women for the first time as a permanent factor in the labor force. Women had, after all, just won the vote – a circumstance many thought would move them quickly toward economic equality. Moreover, the decade followed a period of rapid and heady organization by women, such that in 1920 nearly 400,000 women (6.6 percent of all non-agricultural wage-earning women, and 18 percent of all women in industry) belonged to trade unions.[5] Although these figures may seem tiny by present standards, they reflect a quintupling of the absolute numbers of women in trade unions over the preceding ten years, and that alone should have laid to rest prevailing skepticism about the possibility of organizing wage-earning women. Indeed, one can argue that by this time most trade unionists involved in female-employing industries had stopped asking whether to organize women and started wondering which women. Given the corporate assault on trade unions in general and an unsympathetic national mood, the possibility for a successful coalition between men and women existed. That this did not occur certainly contributed to (though it by no means explains) declining trade union membership nationwide and the labor movement's relative weakness throughout the decade.

Despite incentives, male trade union leaders failed to create fruitful alliances with the women in their organizations. In an embattled period, one expects little effective organizing activity of men or women, but the record shows a pattern of treatment of women that can be described at best as an uneasy truce. Trade union leaders paid little attention to the methods needed to organize or service their female members. The labor movement as a whole (the rhetoric of American Federation of Labor presidents Gompers and Green notwithstanding) welcomed women no more than in the period before they had demonstrated their effectiveness. Even in the face of the great garment and textile strikes with their militant demonstrations of female commitment and leadership, women remained on the periphery of trade union structures. They were recruited, sometimes reluctantly, as dues-paying members, tolerated as shop-level leaders, and occasionally advanced to become business agents and local and international officers. But incentives or inducements designed to create a loyal and effective female membership were virtually non-existent.[6]

Instead, we find the opposite. Where it could have fostered harmony, cooperation and a sense of belonging, the trade union movement persistently mistrusted its female members. It created friction, resentment and defensiveness among them, reducing their value and undermining their ability to do good work. Why would a labor movement aware of, and articulate about, the problems posed by female members, consciously perpetuate divisions between these workers and others?

Let us begin with an initial discussion of how women entered the trade union movement in the second decade of this century. In 1920, about 40 percent of unionized women (169,000) were garment-workers in the International Ladies' Garment Workers' Union (ILGWU), the Amalgamated Clothing Workers of America (ACW) and the United Garment Workers (UGW). Eighty percent of these women had been recruited since 1910 and, given the high turnover rate in the garment industry, probably less than 5 percent had been union members for ten years. Another 15 percent of the nation's unionized women were textile-workers, close to 90 percent of whom were new recruits. About 30,000 shoe-workers were organized into three unions. Most of the remaining unionized women were railway clerks, food-workers, printers, department-store clerks and school teachers.[7] The weight of numbers makes it necessary to speak primarily of garment-workers, though I think the conclusions are valid generally.

Everything we know about trade union organizing between 1910 and 1920 points to the fervor with which women entered the process. From the 1909–10 garment strike in which the 'spirit' of the 'girl' strikers captured the heart of the public and formed the backbone of the ILGWU, down to battles against discrimination on the job fought by telephone operators, railway clerks and printers in 1920, women appealed to the community's sense of morality.[8] Observers described them as idealistic, self-sacrificing, willing to suffer, and committed. Bread-and-butter issues were never unimportant, but as James Oppenheimer successfully conveyed in his 1912 poem about the Lawrence strike, they were accompanied by a demand for 'roses' as well. Dignity, honor, right and justice had their place. The strength of these battles lay in the appeal wage-earning women made to the discrepancy between their wages and conditions at work and their ability to be virtuous and pure – potential mothers of the race. From the perspective of wage-earning women themselves, this rhetoric is probably best understood as a demand for time to attend to family and personal needs: to launder, to cook, to help out at home, to go to night school; and for sufficient wages to live decently, without dependence on family or men. In contrast to the perceptions of skilled male workers, dignity involved not so much the practice of one's craft, as the capacity to retain one's sense of place while earning a living. Mary Anderson put it this way in 1911:

> If the women who labor could only realize that the union movement . . . means better wages and shorter hours. Better wages means a home – a real home, and shorter hours mean family life, a life where father, mother and children have time to be with one another and learn together and play together.[9]

Around this set of perceptions, wage-earning women allied with middle-class women prepared to legitimize and give voice to their struggle.

Lacking economic power or political voice, and with meager trade union support, wage-earnng women relied on tactics of moral suasion to achieve their goals. In contrast to the 1930s, the big women's battles of twenty years before were won not so much by denying employers needed services or by exerting economic pressure, as by relying on public support, indignation and protest. Resort to moral suasion created a sense of what anthropologist Victor Turner calls 'communitas.'[10] Women drew together out of a need for companionship, for bonding, in their effort to attain a larger goal. Without developed leadership or a formal organizational structure, women's shared sense of violation of accepted norms provided the warmth behind cross-class alliances and sustained them. For, as women organizers were fond of pointing out, individual women remained in the labor force only briefly, and when they struggled, they fought for the women who would follow them.[11]

The tactics of struggle reflected the knowledge that moral outrage, not economic pressure, was their trump card. Women repeatedly put themselves in positions where they forced the authorities to violate convention, as when they were beaten up or thrown into jail with prostitutes, or when a pregnant striker at Lawrence, Massachusetts, was shot by city police. By such extreme measures, women dramatized the injustices of their daily treatment in the shop and factory. Addressing a nation committed to the rhetoric of chivalry, motherhood and the ideal of 'the weaker sex,' they demonstrated the brutal treatment which daily violated ideas about womanhood – inside as well as outside the workplace. Their actions called attention to the discrepancy between what society thought women ought to be and what working life made possible for them. They affirmed the reality of women's accusations of shopfloor abuse, lending legitimacy to their demands for decent pay, shorter hours and reasonable sanitation.

Such demonstrations rested squarely on the notion that women were 'different' from men: not that they were unequal, but that their actual or potential motherhood gave them special claims to a woman's sphere. Wage-earning women, like their middle-class allies, accepted and relied upon their special place as the moral basis of their demands for better workplace conditions. As Agnes Nestor, then a lining-maker and organizer for the International Glove Workers' Union, wrote of her trade union struggles in 1902, 'we shall keep our womanly dignity through it all.'[12]

Male trade union leaders, at first skeptical of this mode of organization, soon recognized its advantages, and began admitting women to their organizations as weaker members in need of protection. Thus, John Mitchell, president of the United Mine Workers, told a garment-workers' convention in 1913 that there was 'no one more anxious that women should be queen of the home than the working man.' He would, he added, 'be happy indeed if our industrial conditions were such that every woman in America could have the protection of a home.'[13] Since that was not possible, Mitchell conceded that 'chivalry' ought to be carried into the factory, where organized women could be protected by organized men. Expectations became practice. Women entered unions with lower initiation fees and dues that, as economist Theresa Wolfson eloquently pointed out in 1926, justified paying women lower strike, sickness and death benefits, as well as paying less attention to their wage negotiations. 'In many instances,' Wolfson noted, leaders 'naively explained the difference in wages by the fact that women's dues in the union were less than men's.' The lesser commitment represented by the lower dues placed each woman in the continuing 'status of an apprentice.'[14]

After World War I, a series of events undermined assurances about the differences between men and women, and reduced the effect of appeals to women's sphere in the public mind. Unions therefore lost some of their incentive to admit women as a matter of chivalry or protection. Probably most important among these developments in the 1920s was women's new sense of place, including the public perception that many women worked out of choice, not necessity – a perception reinforced by the image of the flapper. The newly acquired vote was thought to offer political options to women, providing them with the same possibilities as men to redress grievances, and opening to them formerly closed paths to labor-force equality. This idea was buttressed by the creation of a Women's Bureau within the Department of Labor – an agency meant to provide a voice for all wage-earning women. As political structures opened to women, middle-class allies who had been drawn by the appeal of community drifted away from providing organizing aid and publicity and moved instead into the battle to maintain pro-tective labor legislation – a battle that would utilize women's new political clout even as it preserved women's traditional place. A startling number of female trade union activists moved into government jobs and paid administrative positions, where they hovered around the edges of legislative action. Mary Anderson, Elizabeth Christman, Emma Steghagen and Rose Schneiderman are among them.

As the political realm altered, so women's relationships to trade unions changed. Women had won the protective arm of organized labor on the grounds that they were different. Primarily out of self-interested fear of female competition, reinforced by their perception of the male role, trade union leaders had taken advantage of women's need for protection. Now women threatened to take jobs away from organized men. Bitter postwar struggles by women to defend places they had earned during the war effort raised questions about whether women would utilize trade unions to serve their own ends in ways that violated societal norms. In an environment in which political access had reduced the value of moral arguments, leaving economic clout as the only viable weapon to win strikes and improve the position of workers, how were trade unions to treat women? From the male trade union perspective, the demands of women for continued protection as future mothers, on the one hand, and their insistence on equality in the competition for jobs, on the other, seemed irreconcilable. The editor of *Advance*, the official journal of the ACW, put it this way:

> the social inferiority of women . . . is a sequence of tens of thousands of years of recorded history and development. In a world based upon fierce individual competition, . . . there is no escape from the truth that if women want an improvement of their status, *they must fight for the improvement of their status, not appeal to men.*[15]

In the new environment of the 1920s, protection would come from legislation, while trade unions would reduce competition for jobs by organizing those women who competed directly with their male members. Women inside unions would continue to be treated as 'different' but now not because they required protection, but because they lacked economic power.

From the perspective of the female trade unionist, in contrast, membership was an invitation to struggle for equal pay and access to good jobs. Believing that their new political voice could be translated into economic power, women expected to participate fully in union activities. They abandoned the tactics of moral suasion as well as the security of their own 'communitas,' hoping to join trade union structures as full-fledged political participants. Yet the continuing belief in women's special place, coupled with the realities of discrimination, led trade union women to resist attempts to dismantle the hard-won privileges of legislative protection – a solution that yielded divided loyalties. Where wage-earning women were concerned, the trade union was only one avenue for increasing well-being. The other, which was heir to the higher morality of the pre-war period, was protective labor legislation. Their ambiguity about the relationship between equality and difference left women who were inside the trade union movement vulnerable in struggles for power and, because ambiguity provided an alternative means for regulating job competition, encouraged male trade unionists to treat women as 'outsiders.'

Women's own perceptions of the work experience explain how easily that happened. I want here to adopt what some anthropologists have called an emic stance – to ask how the female wage-earner, and especially the female trade union member, saw herself in the period before and after World War I. The work of economist Charles Sabel is helpful. In *Work and Politics*, Sabel suggests that different groups of workers enter the workplace with different worldviews which condition their notions of 'ambition,' 'dignity,' or 'social honor' as well as their ideas about 'which jobs are disgraces and which are accomplishments.'[16] We recognize this phenomenon in American history in the so-called 'bird of passage' – the immigrant who came to the USA to make his fortune, hoping to return home with sufficient funds to buy land and marry. Such a person was willing to work at jobs other workers would not take, under conditions that would have created revolt among his fellows. His 'dignity' or 'honor' were not tied to the job so much as to the potential rewards his sacrifice would provide when he returned to the Old World. Since every worker lives in a family, comes out of a tradition or culture, and is at a particular place in his or her life-cycle, workers have a variety of (sometimes competing) worldviews and act on those that are dominant at a given moment. Herbert Gutman offers a parallel notion when he argues that to understand how immigrants from different racial/ethnic groups and rural/urban traditions approach their jobs, we need to examine their traditional values and customs.[17]

Social scientists have just begun to develop the notion of culture to understand women's special place. Instead of a pattern imposed by a dominant male society, woman's culture is now understood as the way women perceive and impose social order, construct family relationships, act out their own roles, socialize one another, and acknowledge meaning in their lives.[18] In this context, we need to ask questions about how women approach the world of work: how they create what Charles Sabel calls 'careers at work.' I want to argue that women, as a group, bring to the work experience a socialization, a set of values, roots in home and family – in short, a *culture* – that shares class, ethnic and racial characteristics with their menfolk, but that differs in terms of gender. While workers with similar traditions and roots share many work values, the 'cultural baggage' associated with gender enters into a woman's sense of 'dignity' or 'honor' at work, ordering her perceptions of what she is willing to tolerate, and what violates her sense of dignity. How women acted on that sense of honor or dignity accounts for much of the strength of their organizing campaigns between 1910 and 1920, and the power of moral suasion in that decade. Their failure to pay attention to these aspects of difference accounts for women's relative weakness in the labor movement of the 1920s. For just as allegiance to trade union discipline among men addresses the cultural factors unique to them, so organizing among women and maintaining their loyalty to the trade union require special attention to the cultural factors unique to wage-earning women.

In the period before World War I, wage-earning women supported by an expanding women's movement successfully incorporated their perspective into the labor movement. To organized labor they brought notions of self-sacrifice for the future, a recognition of women's particular needs, and special attention to sanitation and cleanliness as well as traditional demands for higher wages and shorter hours. These perspectives are captured in the unique ways in which women related to their unions in this period: ILGWU officials called it 'spirit,' and women organizers developed it by meeting the social needs of young women through dances, social hours, education and entertainments. Fannia Cohn put it this way: 'I do not see how we can get girls to sacrifice themselves unless we discuss something besides trade matters . . . There must be something more than the economic question, there must be idealism.'[19] Mary Anderson spoke of undertaking the burden of additional preparation and clean-up in order to create a 'homelike atmosphere and a social get-together now and then for shoe workers.'[20] Together, these issues add up to what we earlier called 'communitas' and what some contemporaries referred to as 'soul.' They seem to have been as effective at galvanizing loyalty and discipline among women as appeals to bread-and-butter issues were among men.

But while such tactics had the advantage of developing unity and strength among women, they carried new risks. To represent a female constituency effectively – to draw on women's own sense of honor – required women to stimulate and lead the kinds of activities that male unionists labeled irrelevant in periods of quiescence and perceived as a challenge to their leadership in periods when they felt threatened. Allegiance to women and their modes of organization could be of itself subversive because it risked creating dual loyalties. And in reducing the strength of a militant organization, it could undermine the trade union itself.

The assertion of a separate culture that served women so well in organizational campaigns of 1910–20 ran foul of the internal politics of the trade union movement in the 1920s, which adopted a more pessimistic outlook and perceived a heightened need for loyalty. Best captured by Robert Michels's notion of an embattled group, loyalty to which transcends its members' original idealistic purposes, the trade union movement had already developed oligarchic characteristics by 1920. Craft-oriented, protective of special interests, concerned more for its membership than for the whole class of workers, by 1920 the AFL (with which 80 percent of all organized workers were affiliated) had developed a primary commitment to job security and bread-and-butter gains. With the dismemberment of the Industrial Workers of the World in World War I, and the intense divisions within the American left that resulted from the Russian Revolution, unions with a social agenda found themselves operating defensively. In 1920, only 20 percent of US workers belonged to trade unions, and that number was declining. Survival of the institution was key. Battling communism, one side, and the 'American System,' on the other, the AFL and its international affiliates drew the wagons into a tight circle.

By 1920, most US trade unionists had become what they have remained since: agents of 'social closure,' to use Frank Parkin's felicitous phrase. Seeing their major task as preserving or extending the socio-economic position of their members, they operated primarily to increase (or usurp) authority and social place from those above them. Any union's capacity to provide increasing benefits depended on the loyalty of its members, and membership loyalty, conversely, rested on the degree to which leadership came through for them. Leaders had to insure that they could control a job and had the economic resources to sustain lengthy strikes. Weak or potentially weak members were unwelcome, except when leaving such people out might increase labor-market competition and lead to the loss of job control. Then, when closing the doors to membership threatened the possibilities for increased usurpation, trade unions accepted new recruits.[21] Parkin calls this phenomenon 'dual closure.' The trade union's primary gain comes from utilizing the economic power of a strong and united constituency to gain more benefits for its members. A secondary gain derives from keeping out those whose presence would tend to weaken the organization's bargaining power – that is, those who are readily replaceable in the workforce.

Applied to male-dominated trade unions in the 1920s, the concept of dual closure illuminates the persistent tension between the labor movement and wage-earning women. To engage in activities calculated to usurp, the trade union movement required a tight political structure and loyalty on which it could rely. But women as wage-earners were perceived as different – a perception of which women themselves had taken advantage of in the past, and which they were still reluctant to abandon. Could they then be relied upon for the solidarity necessary for successful usurpationary activities? In industries where jobs were largely male-defined, unions preferred simply to exclude them. In other industries, where women competed directly with male members for jobs, unions admitted them to membership and then protected usurpationary struggles by relegating women to special places justified in the same language of difference that women used to protect themselves. To rally women to membership in such female-employing industries as those manufacturing garments, textiles and shoes, unions appealed to shared notions of social justice. In male-dominated industries and crafts, these appeals were unnecessary and unions sought solidarity through exclusion. The conception of woman as outsider served both kinds of unions well. AFL president William Green testified to its continuing value in a 1929 *American Federationist* editorial. 'When there were hand industries in the home,' Green argued, 'women were definitely a part of production undertakings. But when industries left homes to go into factories, men were the first to follow. They made the factory their job before women entered to any appreciable extent.'[22]

If male trade unionists, fearing that women would reduce internal strength or loyalty, could divest themselves of the responsibility of chivalry, they could not so easily shed the burden of a potentially competitive female labor force. The notion of dual closure illuminates some of the discrepancies between the rhetoric of the AFL regarding women and the actions of its constituent members. For while an exclusionary demand relies on the integrity of the group as it already exists, usurpation often involves appeals to some higher authority and morality, such as to the principle of justice or to the right to a living wage.[23] Exclusion calls for internal unity and cohesion against an unwitting Trojan horse; usurpation requires solidarity in the cause of right, and must appear at least to represent all workers. The AFL, representing the labor movement as a whole, could and did take strong moral positions in favor of organizing and integrating women. Not to do so would drive away the support of friendly social reform groups such as the League of Women Voters, the National Consumers' League and the Women's Trade Union League. Introduction and passage of the AFL's well-known resolution and program for organizing women in 1925 must be seen in this light. Cognizant of competition, as well as of the permanent place of women in industry, the AFL asked its affiliates to support an extensive organizing campaign among them. But the campaign foundered, scuttled by local resistance. For, as Theresa Wolfson noted in her classic volume on women workers in the trade unions, the AFL 'has had a far more liberal and far-sighted official attitude than the unions which it depended on for carrying into operation its official attitude.'[24]

The constituent members responsible for carrying out the program had their own protective interests in mind. In their capacity as agents of exclusion, unions in such male-dominated industries as iron-molding continued to refuse to admit women to membership, using legalistic tactics whenever possible and reverting to moral arguments about propriety and a woman's place when it was not. When employers tried to substitute women for male workers, unions too weak to resist the change were forced to confront the issue of solidarity. The Journeymen Barbers' Union provides a good example. Young women began to 'bob' their hair after the war, and barber shops added women to their staff. The union refused to admit 'lady barbers' under a constitutional provision that denied females the right to membership. As shop after shop became 'open' and then moved out of union hands altogether, the union realized it had a problem. Theresa Wolfson records the 1924 convention debate which ranged from questions about whether women's sense of honor from a pecuniary standpoint 'would be as strong as a man's' to whether the presence of several 'ladies in a shop of ten or twelve chairs would be conducive to good discipline.' But the nub of the matter seems to have been whether an attractive woman would 'not have a tendency to create discord among the men, who, up to the time of her admittance to membership, were real working brothers.' Women, in other words, would disrupt the solidarity of male members, interfering with the smooth running of the organization to become, in the end, 'nothing but a blithering liability.'[25] The Brotherhood of Electrical Workers solved this problem by isolating a strong union of female telephone operators into a separate local, where they were relegated to second-class status. Other internationals relied on their ability to control access to the job, or, like the railway clerks and printers, appealed directly to the state to declare their jobs off limits to women.

One notes in passing that such instances of exclusion often relied on state legislatures to do the job that the unions could not themselves undertake.[26] Appeals to the state were rationalized by male trade unionists on the grounds that women's potential motherhood required protection; within the labor movement, recourse to the state was justified by trade unionism's self-perception as an embattled force that would inevitably be weakened by the admission of workers who could not be counted upon. There was enough truth in both perceptions in the 1920s to legitimize them.

More complicated issues arose within female-dominated industries where women were of necessity inside the unions. There, the same sense of women's place that excluded women from other unions blinded labor leaders, eager to close ranks in the service of a militant fighting force, to the desirability of community for women. Indeed, they often insisted that women accede to the prevailing male methods and goals, and interpreted women's attempts to find new paths to loyalty and participation as subversive. The ILGWU leadership offers repeated examples. Its women leaders insisted, and some of its male vice-presidents recognized, that who organized and the manner of organization had consequences. But the union's General Executive Board (GEB) persisted in attributing failure and success to the character of women, rather than to union policy. So, for example, in 1921, the board decided to suspend 'out of town organization work in the waist and dress industry' because 'to attempt to organize largely gentile girls in the small towns would, under the present conditions, be a waste of money and energy.'[27] This sort of sexism could inhibit a union's growth, for, as one vice-president who successfully organized gentile girls reported, 'Most of them are married which makes them independent and full of fighting spirit. The girls in the little cities, it seems, are the best element.'[28] In 1917, President Benjamin Schlesinger recommended reducing the union's involvement in Toronto because the majority of workers in the industry there were 'women, and largely Gentile, and consequently not an organizable element.'[29] Not everyone agreed with him. When the predictable stagnation happened, the leaders of three Toronto locals chastised the GEB. They asked for an English-speaking woman organizer because 'men organizers appointed by the union failed to achieve satisfactory results . . . and only women organizers can have access to this unorganized element.'[30] Repeatedly, the ILGWU ignored requests such as the one for 'a girl organizer' to go to St Louis; or, in one case, for fifteen unemployed Philadelphia union girls to go to Baltimore where organizer Hortense Powdermaker was sure they could successfully recruit the most difficult American-born women.[31]

ILGWU policies came not out of a failure to understand the need to recruit women for the union's own protection, but rather out of a conviction that women did not constitute a 'fighting force.' Incredibly, this view persisted despite the ILGWU's own history of militant female activity. Seven short years after 'inexperienced' girl strikers successfully rebuilt the union in 1909, a vice-president commented on a hard-fought Chicago strike:

> I must say here that I never expected that the girls, being out for the first time on strike would understand and be so devoted and active and ready to sacrifice and to listen and take orders and do everything and more than we could possibly expect from strikers.[32]

Another vice-president recalled the willingness with which a group of young anarchist women responded to union requests. 'When the union asked them to be on the picket line at 7 o'clock in the morning, they were there . . . Every morning I saw the girls there.' And yet, he insisted that these women were so argumentative and divided that they 'needed the men to keep peace between them.'[33]

Suspicion and doubt about female commitment to unionization undermined women's efforts to make their own demands. It meant that women would spend enormous energies simply convincing men that they belonged in a common struggle. Men resented what Ann Washington Craton called women's 'optimism, and freshness as well as the way they upset traditional routines.'[34] And even their successes required apology. Fannia Cohn, reporting to the ILGWU membership on a victorious strike of women noted that

> they never were willing to accept better conditions unless their brothers who were working with them were also included. Our women members realized long ago, as did the International, that there must be no such thing as sex division in the trade unions.[35]

Being part of, and yet not part of – this was the dilemma of the woman trade unionist of the 1920s. In 1924, at the ILGWU's biennial convention, Cohn introduced a motion instructing the union's delegates to the forthcoming AFL meeting to 'introduce resolutions and work for the adoption [of] . . . a plan of organization of workingwomen that shall include an educational campaign among women directly and through organized men indirectly.' The committee to which the resolution was referred rejected it reprovingly. 'It can be stated without contradiction,' the committee noted, 'that as yet no successful methods of organizing women workers have been found.' And then it went on to argue that the union's delegates 'possess a quite satisfactory acquaintance with the principles, policies and methods of our International Union and can be fully relied upon to carry out such policies during conventions of the AFL without any specific instructions to do so.'[36]

Female rank and filers who failed to support women implicitly acknowledged the real power structure and simultaneously protected their own interests. Women who supported male leadership faced fewer accusations of disloyalty. And since female trade union officials did not speak for women or to their particular issues, and had minimal voice in the union as whole, women members reasonably felt they deserved better representation than that offered by women. This explains the seeming paradox of Jennie Silverman. An ILGWU business agent, she was rejected by a women's shop as its representative. A manager of the local recalled that the shop refused to be persuaded by the argument that 'you are all women. Jennie is a woman . . . She and you will work together.' The workers simply replied, 'never mind this, we want a man.'[37] Here, workers acknowledged the power of the formal political structure as they did in a similar instance recorded by the New York *World* in 1922. Before women got the vote, a Massachusetts shoe-workers' local had consistently selected a woman to be their manager. Afterward, they repeatedly chose men. A woman stitcher explained why: 'The business man,' she said, 'is getting so he doesn't pay as much attention to the requests of women as he did before we were given the franchise.'[38]

The practical manifestation of this set of dilemmas was the extraordinarily awkward place in which women in the labor movement found themselves. Ann Washington Craton, after she had left her position as organizer with the ACW, despaired of the situation. In an article written for the *Nation* in 1927, she noted that in order to maintain even minor official positions in the trade union movement, women 'have discreetly learned to play the union game as men play it . . . On the theory that a poor union is better than no union, they steadily refused to embarrass labor officials by a vigorous protest at the discriminations and inequalities to which women have been subjected in the unions.' The result, as she correctly observed, was that 'they have been unable to achieve any outstanding leadership among the rank and file of trade-union women.'[39]

Perhaps no single union so successfully illustrates the way a woman's worldview could translate into disloyalty as Local 25, the waist- and dress-makers' local of the ILGWU, in the immediate postwar period. Familiarly known as 'the girls' local,' its size and strength had come from the great organizing strikes of the 1909–12 period. Though it had gone through ups and downs since its organization, by 1919 Local 25 had 30,000 members and was by far the largest single local in the ILGWU, with nearly 25 percent of the international's total membership. Shop chairladies were virtually all female; local officers, all male. Despite political disputes among the leadership, which ranged from anarchist and socialist to 'American-born gentiles,' the local managed to maintain a loyal and active membership as the result of its unique educational program started in 1915 by Barnard instructor Juliet Stuart Poyntz. With the support of a core of young women, including Cohn, Pauline Newman and Rose Schneiderman, Poyntz initiated a program that touched the spirit of Local 25's members. Classes in history, politics, physical fitness and art, as well as concerts, plays and discussion groups, appealed to the idealism of rank and filers and drew them in huge numbers into borrowed school buildings known as Unity Centers. The local went on to purchase a large country house where members could take vacations together. In 1919, it counted 10,000 members in its various classes and an additional 7,000 in attendance at concerts and plays. Other women's locals in Philadelphia and Chicago followed the example of Local 25. Unorthodox activity produced traditional results. Despite a membership that turned over entirely every three years, members managed to achieve some of the best wage and hour gains among semi-skilled workers. In a lengthy and spirited 1919 strike, the waist- and dress-makers won a forty-four hour week.[40]

By 1919, fired by the idealism the local had nurtured, young women began to agitate for a greater voice in union affairs. The shop-delegate system they proposed threatened the international's GEB, whose sole female member – Fannia Cohn – retreated under the attack. Sometime after 1920, shop delegates organized into leagues which seem to have been taken over by communists, providing added incentive to the male leadership's decision to break them up. This they did, first splitting Local 25 into three constituent locals, under the supervision of a Dress and Waistmakers' Joint Board, and then combining that board with one of male cloak-makers. Simultaneously, the GEB passed a rule denying anyone with less than two years' membership in the union the right to hold office.

The result was as devastating for the ILGWU as for Local 25. In vain, women protested the two-year rule, declaring they would find no one eligible for office. In a period when membership was declining because shops were shifting from urban areas to small towns and from north to south, and the trade was changing in character, female membership dropped disproportionately – falling from 75 percent of the total in 1920 to 38.7 percent in 1924.[41] Women, as organizer Jennie Matyas recalls, simply 'ran away. If I couldn't go with these idiots and I couldn't fight them, I would just go to school. And a lot of my colleagues who felt as I did went out. Some got married, some went into some or another little business. They couldn't stay in the union and not be on one side.'[42]

Without debating the justice of the international's post-1921 acts, it seems clear that a union that could meet the needs of female members could expect to hold and keep their loyalty to the organization. Moreover, the ILGWU accepted their activity until women, building on their own sense of priorities, began to demand democratic participation, or insider status. At that point, as early as 1919, before any discussion of communist infiltration, and while the local was engaged in what the GEB acknowledged to be an 'energetic campaign' to recruit dress-makers in which 'thousands of new members enrolled,' the ILGWU began to accuse Local 25 of in-efficiency and of not paying attention to union business.[43] In 1919, an outsider was hired to take over Local 25's educational program and, in 1920, the international appointed a supervisor for education who would work with the vice-presidents.

Fannia Cohn got caught on the firing line. Having initially sup-ported – indeed, having helped to create – Local 25's activism, she did not quickly abandon the young women when they came under attack. But she moved away, turning back to her primary interest in education and insisting that, under trade union control, education made good unionists. She did not move quickly enough. Her loyalty remained in question, leading Israel Weinzweig to warn Cohn's friend Theresa Wolfson in the spring of 1922 about the strong possibility of Cohn 'being dropped by the administration forces as a candidate for vice president.' She had not, according to Weinzweig, been among the 'deserving followers' who had participated effectively 'in the attack on the left wingers.'[44] With her capacity for creative activity on behalf of women crippled, and lacking the female support that had sustained her spirit as well as theirs, Cohn retained her precarious, sometimes humiliating position until she was removed from the vice-presidency in 1926 and denied even the directorship of the education program she had created.[45]

But neither Cohn nor the ILGWU women who withdrew from the struggle fully understood that in moving from tactics that relied on a spirit of social unity to develop strength, they had also moved from expressions of solidarity to alter the union in their image. Local 25's representatives to the 1922 convention recorded their goals quite clearly. The movement for a shop-delegate system 'aimed to weld together all workers of an industry into a strongly organized representative unit with many workers participating in the making of decisions rather than leaving it to officers, executive boards and a small group of active members who are responsible to no one but themselves.'[46] Their plea that this process had 'stimulated thought and awakened a healthy progressive interest in our union,' as well as winning 'the support of a number of our local officers' produced an entirely negative reaction. For, in challenging leadership, they subjected themselves to the full fury of an embattled and oligarchic political machine, opposition to which was described by President Schlesinger in a *Justice* editorial as a 'veritable treason.'[47]

While trade union leaders insisted on what the ILGWU male leadership called 'unity, discipline, faithfulness,'[48] the female rank and file searched for community, idealism and spirit. But when spirit brought loyalty into question, it became too costly for the male leadership to risk. Labeling women leftists and communists was not so much an indication of their political position (although some were surely communists) as an acknowledgment of their potential power and a fear that oppositional politics of whatever kind would breed disloyalty in a fighting organization. On the other hand, to toe the line, as Cohn did, was to neglect the needs of women members in the interests of organizational loyalty. Cohn watched helplessly as Local 25 was first split asunder and then shriveled into what one vice-president described 'as a very small local with little influence to do any extensive organizing work and to build up a strong union.'[49] Although she clung, still, to the notion that education would unify members and revive their spirit, she ran into a leadership determined in the 1920s to direct education to its own ends. She never again had charge of education for the ILGWU.

Conflict in organizational and leadership styles also appeared in the ACW – the second-largest concentration of unionized women in the 1920s. There, as in the ILGWU, women raised the issue of how they wanted to participate in their union. In the fall of 1926, the female leaders of a women's local in Chicago challenged the male leadership to acknowledge the separate needs of women. The

Executive Board of Local 275 asked, in a letter to *Advance*,

> What means do our leaders employ to combat the idea that
> women are not temporarily in industry? What methods do our
> officials use to promote greater activities among women
> workers since they have become a permanent factor in industry?
> What has become of the Women's Bureau for which the women
> have so long struggled?

The editor responded predictably that it was up to the women to
rectify their complaints:

> Leadership in the union is a prize to those who know how to win
> it. Leaders of unions are not likely to leave their positions of
> vantage in favor of women, any more than women would in
> favor of men. The battle for mastery is a human trait, a very
> human trait too. The nature of this battle remains the same
> regardless of whether men or women are found on one side of
> the fence or the other. It is up to women to fight their way to the
> front.[50]

A member from Rochester replied almost immediately:

> 'No, Mr Editor, it is not leadership or power that we want, but
> special attention given our women so that they may have an
> opportunity to develop as intelligent members. You will
> probably say, 'Why Special Attention . . . why not adopt the
> same methods as the men?' No thank you, Mr Editor, we will
> not take your advice. We hope that we'll never learn to adopt
> the same methods as some of the men use to come to the front.[51]

There followed an exchange of letters over several months, most
of them charging the ACW with failure to offer adequate support to
its female members. But the editor would not budge. 'Do we,' he
asked, 'want to build up a "Solid South" of women or anti-women in
the Amalgamated?' Instead of criticizing the union, women, he
repeated, should ally with men to organize other women. 'Those
who want to climb the stairs which lead to the top must first come
down to what is the basis of distinction – strength. They will have to
match power with power, and prove that they are stronger.'[52]

The difficulty with following this advice and accepting the ACW's
invitation to become like men was that female unionists felt them-

selves to be different. As one member wrote, 'I'm sure you will agree with me that, historically woman is a product of the kitchen. Though she has been coming out of it in the last twenty-five years, mentally she is still in the kitchen and hopes to remain there.'[53] For the ACW women, this difference was a strength upon which they hoped their union would build. For Cohn, by 1927, it had become a weakness:

> Just as soon as women can reasonably dissociate their personal feelings from the job they must do, just as soon as they can deliberate coolly and decide a case on its merits and not on the prejudices aroused by their excessive emotions, so soon will they find that they have very much in common with men.[54]

If struggling for difference within unions invited defeat, women would have to accept the challenge to become like men. Cohn suggested that women could contribute 'persistence, endurance, devotion and all of the other traits women have developed as the mothers of the race' to the trade union movement. They could add 'their enthusiasm, freshness and vigor' and thus 'exert a great influence on men in the movement and on the movement itself, from the infusion of their qualities into the work.' She did not suggest that these qualities would enable women to become leaders. But they would allow women to function within the trade union movement in ways that provided satisfaction and material gains while they sporadically protested the evident discrimination against them. Women who continued to see themselves as a community would have to be satisfied with only a peripheral relationship to power in the larger organization.

Activities that continued to develop community, such as women's summer schools, women's locals, the Women's Bureau, and the Women's Trade Union League, persisted on the edge of the trade union structure. As a way of channeling women's aims, they worked well. As a way of 'catching up' with men, women's locals seemed to many the ideal alternative. Agnes Nestor put it this way: 'where the women have locals of their own, greater interest is shown because they have full responsibility for their own affairs. In these unions, women leaders have developed because they were forced to assume responsibilities and develop leadership.'[55] Women in one New Jersey local decided to organize separate monthly meetings because 'they felt that the men were further advanced in organization work and were rather timid about speaking.' The result was a 'friendly spirit, which has drawn the girls together and kept them in touch with one another's working conditions.'[56] A hosiery-worker noted that her 'girls' meetings' had taught '[us to] conduct our own business, get women speakers, and try to solve our own problems.' Like its New Jersey counterpart, this local engaged extensively in social activities – forming a basketball team, sending children to summer camp, and sponsoring parties, picnics, banquets and dances, all of which united members into 'one big family and that's what we want.'[57] Here was community without a threat to power.

Ironically, the struggle against the 1923 Equal Rights Amendment (ERA) – called the 'Blanket Amendment' by trade union women – provides the most successful example of the resuscitation of the spirit of community that prevailed in the pre-war period. The labor movement's unmitigated antagonism to this first ERA illustrates the remaining strength of moral suasion. For here was an amendment that proclaimed the equality of men and women – an equality that trade union women knew had no economic reality but which, if it were asserted, would threaten even their limited organizational position. Eager to affirm their sense that women still required the special protection offered by labor laws, women labor leaders joined with middle-class allies and the Women's Bureau to renew once again the spirit of struggle. Acting now as a community of women seeking not to usurp the prerogatives of men but to acknowledge their own special place, they drew on trade union support to bring the ERA to a standstill. Male trade union leaders, of course, understood protective labor legislation as a way of restraining women's demands for admission into their organization, and opposed the amendment all too willingly.

Self-definition as outsiders and the development of a notion of community without a politics of its own enabled individual women to continue to function within the trade union movement, extracting some benefits from it. Those who became spokespeople won more social and economic mobility for themselves than most working women could hope to achieve. With the Women's Bureau as their vehicle, they were able to bring public attention to many of the problems facing women wage-earners, and they succeeded in gaining the tacit support of the male-dominated trade unions for issues that concerned women. But the trade union movement offered women no access to the power structure and insisted that women in its ranks accept male assumptions about their role and place. It thus undermined whatever female leadership developed within the movement, leaving women like Rose Pesotta, who rebeled, without support (labeled 'unstable') and those like Cohn, Newman and O'Connor, who conformed, without power.

What then of the power of difference? The material presented here suggests that two intersecting factors have to be acknowledged if we are to understand the past and present relationships of women to trade unions. Between 1910 and 1920, a sense of women's culture was joined with the more open stance of some trade unions to create successful alliances. By the 1920s, the alliance had broken down on two fronts. Some elements of the feminist coalition looked to a new equality with men to transcend women's confined place. And the labor movement, no longer convinced that appeals to women's place worked as well as economic struggle, and itself battling to survive, perceived women as a source of weakness better taken care of by the state. Ambivalent about an equality that seemed illusory, and now without the organized feminist support that had sustained the struggle for difference, trade union women floundered or, as Jennie Matyas put it, 'ran away.'

Failure was not so much a result of bad faith as of conflicting perceptions. For women to come to terms with the changing social values of the 1920s, to integrate their worldview with the decade's new realities, was a difficult task. To do so in the context of a defensive and harassed trade union movement might have been impossible. At the same time, to expect an embattled trade union movement to recognize women's cultural space seems equally difficult. But such were the conflicts of the 1920s.

They give us cause to hope that the dual purposes of feminism and trade unionism are not irreconcilable. In the contemporary period, when socio-economic forces have confronted wage-earning women with profound challenges to their perceptions of themselves as wage-earners, and when trade unions are beginning to recognize the workforce shifts that demand organization of new groups of women workers, the culture of women might yet find a place in the politics of unions.

Notes

1   Ruth Milkman, 'Organizing the Sexual Division of Labor: Historical Perspectives on "Women's Work" and the American Labor Movement,' *Socialist Review*, vol. 10, January–February 1980, pp.95–150.

2   I am here moving away from the question of organizability – partly because I am convinced that how and why trade unions recruit women is a function of some of the other phenomena I will discuss, and partly because recent scholarship has provided a fairly clear sense of the social and industrial factors that inhibit and encourage women's organizing efforts. These include factors such as occupational segregation, the kinds of industries organized, the historically high turnover rates of women, and especially sex-role socialization which often instills in women a sense of deference to men, involves them in time-consuming household commitments, and suggests an alternative set of roles to those offered by waged work. For access to this literature, see Alice Kessler-Harris, 'Where Are the Organized Women Workers?', *Feminist Studies*, vol. 3, fall 1975, pp.92–110; Heidi Hartmann, 'Capitalism, Patriarchy and Job Segregation by Sex,' in Martha Blaxall and Barbara Regan, eds, *Women and the Workplace: The Implications of Occupational Segregation*, University of Chicago Press, 1976, pp.137–69; as well as Milkman, 'Organizing the Sexual Division of Labor.'

3   Helen Sumner, *History of Women in Industry in the United Sates*, New York, Arno Press, 1974 (first published 1910), is probably still the best summary of the nineteenth-century experience. But see also Barbara Wertheimer, *We Were There: The Story of Working Women in America*, New York, Pantheon, 1977, and Philip Foner, *Women and the American Labor Movement: From Colonial Times to the Eve of World War I*, New York, Free Press, 1979.

4   It was not the total number of women who worked for wages which was at issue. The proportion of such women expanded only modestly during the decade. But the kinds of women who worked (native-born, married) caused concern, as did the seemingly more permanent nature of their jobs.

5   Leo Wolman, *Growth of American Trade Unions, 1880–1923*, New York, National Bureau of Economic Research, 1924, pp.97–8. By 1924, the number of organized women had dropped to 250,000, and the figure increased only slightly over the rest of the decade. Theresa Wolfson estimated that the number of organized women was only one-thirty-fourth of all women then earning wages. See 'Trade Union Activities of Women,' *Annals of the American Academy of Political and Social Science*, vol. 143, May 1929, p.120.

6   Incentives mentioned in the 1920s, but only rarely employed, included women organizers, discussion groups and social occasions, women's bureaus within unions, and vacation houses.

7 Wolman, *Growth of American Trade Unions*, pp.98–9, 107, estimates that one-quarter of all organized women in 1920 were in New York State.

8 See the account of the 1919 New England telephone operators' strike in Maurine Greenwald, *Women, War and Work: The Impact of World War I on Women Workers in the United States*, Westport, Connecticut, Greenwood Press, 1980, pp.218–22.

9 Anderson was thirty-eight years old and single when she wrote this, quoted from Mary Anderson, *Women at Work* as told to Mary N. Winslow, Westport, Greenwood Press, 1973 (first published 1951), p.46.

10 Victor Turner, *Dramas, Fields and Metaphors: Symbolic Action in Human Society*, Ithaca, Cornell University Press, 1974, pp.45–7. For a sense of how this worked in practice, see Nancy Schrom Dye, *As Equals and as Sisters: Feminism, Unionism, and the Women's Trade Union League of New York*, Columbia, University of Missouri Press, 1980, chapters 2 and 4.

11 Rose Schneiderman, for example, commented on high turnover rates among women, 'I wish they would realize that joining the union would bring untold benefits during the five years they are in trade, not to mention how it would help the girls who come after them.' Zoe Beckley, 'Finds Hard Job Unionizing Girls Whose Aim is to Wed,' New York, *Telegram and Sun*, June 18, 1924, p.4.

12 Agnes Nestor, 'The Experiences of a Pioneer Woman Trade Unionist,' *American Federationist*, vol. 36, August 1929, p.926.

13 GEB Minutes, May 1, 1913, p.39, International Ladies' Garment Workers' Union Archives (hereafter: ILGWU Archives). See Kessler-Harris, 'Where Are the Organized Women Workers?' for additional examples.

14 Theresa Wolfson, *The Woman Worker and the Trade Unions*, New York, International Publishers, 1926, pp.81, 86–7.

15 Italics in original. 'Yes, Women Are Discontented, But What of It?', *Advance*, May 6, 1927, p.6.

16 Charles F. Sabel, *Work and Politics: The Division of Labor in Industry*, Cambridge University Press, 1982, p.80.

17 Herbert Gutman, *Work, Culture and Society in Industrializing America: Essays in American Working-class and Social History*, New York, Alfred A. Knopf, 1976, chapter 1.

18 See especially Nancy Chodorow, *The Reproduction of Mothering: Psychoanalysis and the Sociology of Gender*, Berkeley, University of California Press, 1979, chapters 2 and 11. I would here explicitly disagree with those formulations of women's work which measure self-experience in terms of ties to family or community of origin. The prime example is Louise Tilly and Joan Scott, *Women, Work and Family*, New York, Holt, Rinehart & Winston, 1978.

19 As quoted in W. Elliot Brownlee and Mary M. Brownlee, eds, *Women in*

the *American Economy: A Documentary History, 1675–1929*, New Haven, Yale University Press, 1976, p.223.

20 Mary Anderson, *Women at Work*, p.66. The technique could be used by both sides. Organizer Sarah Shapiro reported to the general strike committee of Local 25 that she had almost won a lengthy strike of Italian girls when 'the bosses finally succeeded in getting them back by giving them an increase in wages, and in some cases shortening the hours, and giving them parties and dances in the shops.' February 21, 1919, Benjamin Schlesinger Collection, Box 3, File 16, ILGWU Archives.

21 Frank Parkin, *Marxism and Class Theory: A Bourgeois Critique*, New York, Columbia University Press, 1979, pp.44–6, 74.

22 *American Federationist*, vol. 36, August 1929, p.914.

23 Parkin, *Marxism and Class Theory*, p.98.

24 Wolfson, *The Woman Worker*, p.73.

25 *Ibid.*, pp.77–8.

26 This process was successfully used by professional organizations like the American Medical Association and the American Bar Association as well.

27 Baroff report in GEB Minutes, September 26, 1921, p.1,523, ILGWU Archives.

28 Sigman in GEB Minutes, October 17, 1923, p.1,825; and see also Halprin in GEB Minutes, March 26, 1923, p.1,736, ILGWU Archives.

29 GEB Minutes, April 24, 1917, p.641 (see also comments of John Pierce on p.655), ILGWU Archives.

30 ILGWU, *Report and Proceedings of the 15th Biennial Convention*, 1920, p.90; see also GEB Minutes, September 26, 1921, p.1,552, ILGWU Archives.

31 GEB Minutes, June 11, 1923, p.1,800, and September 26, 1921, p.1,552, ILGWU Archives.

32 Report of Vice-President Seidman, in GEB Minutes, April 24, 1917, p.675, ILGWU Archives.

33 Transcript of interview with Israel Breslow conducted by Henoch Mendelsund on March 2, 1982, pp.5, 14, ILGWU Archives.

34 Ann Washington Craton, 'Working the Women Workers,' *Nation*, vol. 124, March 1927, p.312.

35 *Justice*, February 16, 1923, p.4.

36 ILGWU, *Report and Proceedings of the 17th Biennial Convention*, 1924, pp.226–7.

37 Breslow interview, p.25.

38 'Women's Union Decides that Men Must Conduct their Affairs,' *New York World*, January 29, 1922, p.4.

39 Craton, 'Working the Women Workers,' p.312.

40 Some of these activities were summarized in a 1922 pamphlet published by Local 25. See *Report of the Ladies' Waistmakers' Union Local 25 to the 16th Convention of the International Ladies' Garment Workers' Union*, Cleveland, May 1922, pp.3–5. The pattern was followed by

Philadelphia's Local 15, described in 1920 by the GEB as a 'banner local.'
See *Report and Proceedings to the 15th Biennial Convention*, 1920,
p.29.
41 Louis Levine, *The Women's Garment Workers*, New York, B. W.
Huebsch, 1924, p.431.
42 Quoted in Brownlee and Brownlee, *Women in the American Economy*,
pp.239–40.
43 *Report and Proceedings*, 1920, p.29.
44 I. Weinzweig to Theresa Wolfson, May 9, 1922, in the possession of
Peggy Frank. Quoted by permission.
45 A remarkable example of Cohn's humiliation exists in the following GEB
comment which is here quoted from the GEB Minutes, June 11, 1923,
p.1,796, in its entirety:

> The trip to Europe made last year by Miss Fannia Cohn at the advice of
> her physician, the financial loss of which she had to bear herself, has
> made it impossible for her to straighten out her financial situation and
> she asked therefore to be reimbursed four weeks' pay. It was decided to
> grant this request and in the future on occasions of that kind, requests
> are to be made prior to the taking of vacations. While in Europe, Miss
> Cohn attended the First International Conference on Workers'
> Education as the delegate of the Workers' Education Bureau.

The effect of such treatment on the morale of female members of the
ILGWU is illustrated by Rose Pesotta's outburst in an undated letter to
David Dubinsky (David Dubinsky Collection, Box 134, File 2, ILGWU
Archives):

> Fannia Cohn's service to our organization is only recognized by those
> on the outside who can dispasssionately evaluate such unselfish efforts
> on the part of one person, for the cause of workers' education. But
> most of the credit is now the heritage of a director who has entered the
> field after the thorns were weeded out, the marshes dried and all other
> obstacles removed. She remains a tragic figure amidst her own fellow
> workers, whom she helped to gain prestige with the outside
> educational world. Were she a man, it would have been entirely
> different.

46 *Report of the Ladies' Waistmakers' Union*, p.7. The pamphlet was
signed by four delegates to the convention from Local 25. They were
Miriam Levine, Lena Goodman, Ida Rothstein and Rose Pasatta (sic).
Only Ida Rothstein was an avowed communist. Pesotta was an anarchist
and both she and Levine opposed communist attempts to undermine the
ILGWU. I have no information on Lena Goodman.
47 *Justice*, October 8, 1920, p.2. Schlesinger continued, 'We hope there are
no such spirits in the Waist and Dressmakers Union. But should there
appear any, we assure them that the International will know how to
combat them.'

48 *Report and Proceedings to the 16th Convention*, 1922, p.114.
49 Abraham Baroff in the GEB Minutes, Ocober 17, 1923, p.1,833, ILGWU Archives.
50 *Advance*, September 3, 1926, p.1.
51 *Ibid.*, October 8, 1926, p.6.
52 *Ibid.*, May 6, 1927, pp.6, 7.
53 *Ibid.*, October 8, 1926, p.6.
54 Fannia M. Cohn, 'Do Sex Quarrels Help?', *Justice*, October 14, 1927, p.186.
55 Nestor, 'Experiences of a Pioneer Woman Trade Unionist,' p.932.
56 Helen Hamilton, 'Women's Locals,' *American Federationist*, vol. 36, September 1929, p.1,061.
57 *Ibid.*, p.1,060; Belle Trouland, 'The Woman's Local,' in *ibid.*, p.970.

7

Survival strategies among African–American women workers: A continuing process[1]

Rosalyn Terborg-Penn

For most of the twentieth century, black women were far more likely to be in the waged labor force than their white counterparts. Most were confined to domestic work and other poorly paid, marginal jobs. The obstacles to union organizing were enormous, particularly in domestic work, where employment was highly unstable and decentralized. In addition, until the 1930s, most unions took little interest in the plight of black women, who were subject to both race and sex prejudice within the labor movement as well as in society. Yet, as Rosalyn Terborg-Penn shows in this chapter, black women workers continually attempted to organize themselves into unions and union-like associations. Drawing upon traditional African mutual aid and collective survival strategies, black women built labor associations even in the most 'unorganizable' of occupations, although many of these efforts proved shortlived. Terborg-Penn sheds new light on this history with her emphasis on the threads of continuity between ancestral African female traditions of mutual support and the self-organization of black women in the twentieth-century USA.

Since slavery ended in the USA, the majority of African–American women wage-earners have worked in low-paying, low-status jobs. Paid work was essential to their survival and to that of their families. Hostility engendered by racism and sexism required that black women develop collective organizational forms to sustain their communities during the many hard times. Organization among African–American women took a distinct form, contrasting with labor union development among other groups within the working class. The occupational ghettoization of black women, on the one hand, and racial prejudice against blacks in mainstream labor unions, especially before the rise of the Congress of Industrial Organizations (CIO) in the 1930s, on the other, promoted organizational forms involving networks of mutual support and aid rooted in African traditions. Even during the twentieth century, black women workers have continued to rely upon those networks.

The majority of African–American women workers in the USA are descended from slaves brought to America from African societies, where women had a long tradition of self-organization for mutual support in relation to most life activities, including work. Labor was an essential female role and responsibility in traditional Africa, and indeed, women's labor output generally far surpassed that of men. In most communally owned, subsistence economies in the slave-trading era, Africans assigned equal value to male and female labor, and women enjoyed considerable decision-making power, especially in relation to agricultural production.[2]

As African women were brought to the New World, Western cultural concepts of women as workers clashed with those of Africa. Although white women in industrializing America labored in a variety of ways, their endeavors were rarely viewed by the society as valuable, and women's work was considered inferior work. Unlike African women, who considered work a continuous function in life, white women workers hoped for the day when they could be totally relieved of the burdens of labor.

White Americans profited greatly from the African concept that women not only should work, but could labor as well and as hard as men. Since slavery, African–American women have been expected to toil by those in the mainstream society as well as those in their own subculture. And, unfortunately, their passage from traditional African societies, through slavery, to waged work has left women of African descent in the USA at the bottom of the economic ladder – even during the twentieth century.

During the first half of the twentieth century, the economic survival of black women and many black families was precarious.

Black women workers were overwhelmingly concentrated in menial, unskilled jobs throughout this period. In 1910, among over one million black women in the workforce, 52 percent were farm laborers and 28 percent were cooks or washerwomen.[3] By 1930, the number of gainfully employed black women in the US was double the 1910 figure, but their position had not improved: 90 percent were engaged in farm labor or domestic work. Jean Collier Brown of the US Women's Bureau, and future organizer of a domestic workers' labor union, observed in 1938:

> Though women in general have been discriminated against and exploited through limitations of their opportunities for employment, through long hours, low wages, and harmful working conditions, such hardships have fallen upon Negro women with double harshness.[4]

As late as 1960, 50 percent of the more than two million domestic workers in the nation were black women, and this occupation still accounted for over 30 percent of the more than three million employed African—American women.[5]

Consigned as they were to poorly paid, marginal jobs, African—American women workers formed networks from the earliest period to ease their plight, in keeping with traditional African survival strategies. As early as the period immediately after the American Revolution, free black women organized mutual aid and benevolent societies to help themselves and the needy in their communities. By the late nineteenth century, this tradition was carried on by the volunteer spirit of the Women's Club Movement. Within their own communities, white as well as black women in the movement sought to uplift the female victims of a developing industrial society.

Domestic workers and their organizations

In the twentieth century, as black women migrated from rural to urban areas, they moved from farm labor to domestic labor (and, to a lesser extent, to factory labor). In the period from 1930 to 1960, the growth of domestic work as a black female occupation was especially dramatic. Even under slavery, African—American women had been the backbone of the household workforce, north and

south, as they worked without pay to keep white households going –
washing, cleaning, cooking, nursing the young and the sick, weaving
and sewing.[6] In the twentieth century, many were hired to do 'day's
work,' which involved general household cleaning, with cooking,
child-care and production of household goods left to others. In many
cases, however, total housekeeping chores were still left to black
women by their employers under this system.

Conditions under which black domestic workers labored were
appalling during the first four decades of the century. In 1912, an
anonymous African–American woman described her life as a tread-
mill. She had worked as a domestic servant for white families from
the time she was ten years of age. As late as 1935, black women
performed housework and laundry for three dollars a week and
washerwomen, who took work home, did a week's wash for seventy-
five cents. Journalist Louise Mitchell wrote about the 'slave markets'
in New York City, where every morning African–American women
stood on selected street corners in the Bronx and in Brooklyn,
waiting to be hired by white employers for 'day's work.'[7]

In response to the exploitation and degradation of African–
American women domestics, black women like Victoria Earle
Matthews and such organizations as the Women's Loyal Union,
New York City, offered remedies in keeping with traditional African
survival strategies. As early as 1897, Matthews organized the more
affluent black women of the city, who provided the resources and the
time needed for the development of the White Rose Industrial
Association. Along with the association, the White Rose Working
Girls' Home was established to protect female domestics from the
exploitative city employment bureaus that preyed upon black
women who had recently migrated from the south. Matthews had
been born a slave in Georgia shortly after the start of the Civil War.
Her family migrated to New York City in 1870, where she attended
the public school for black children. She readily identified with the
plight of her southern black sisters migrating to the north.[8]

Matthews, who was known in literary circles as Victoria Earle, not
only championed the rights of poor black women, but identified
strongly with her African heritage. During the early 1890s, she wrote
several primers for youth to 'trace the history of the African and to
show that he and his descendants have been prominently identified
with every phase of this country's history.'[9] Matthews carried this

race pride into the White Rose curriculum, which combined academic and vocational education. Classes provided training in domestic work, cooking, sewing and art. Lectures were provided by noted African–American literary figures such as Paul Laurence Dunbar and his future wife, Alice Ruth Moore, who also taught kindergarten classes for children of working mothers at the White Rose Home.[10]

This multifaceted approach to providing services for black women workers, although unique to black urban communities, had its roots in traditional Africa, where older women were responsible for socializing and training groups of younger women. The White Rose Association continued to serve black Harlem women well into the twentieth century, even after Matthews's death in 1907, and it served as a model for future network-based associations.

Frances Kellor, a white philanthropist, founded the Inter-municipal Committee on Household Research in 1905 to develop associations in Philadelphia and New York City. Here again, the aim was to protect black women migrating from the south. Blacks were quite active in these organizations, called Associations for the Protection of Negro Women. Agents from Richmond to Boston attempted to place black women in lodging-houses, to provide education, and to locate jobs. By 1909, the National League for the Protection of Colored Women (an outgrowth of Kellor's organization) had established associations in New York, Philadelphia, Memphis, Baltimore, the District of Columbia, and Norfolk. S. Willie Layten, a black woman from Philadelphia, replaced Kellor as the general secretary of the league and in 1911, the organization joined with three others to form the National Urban League.[11]

The establishment of support networks continued as more black women in urban centers took the lead. Nannie Helen Burroughs, a dynamic leader of the black National Baptist Women's Convention, despite the reluctance of the male leadership in the National Baptist Convention, recruited the women's support for a training school for black females. Burroughs began her campaign in 1901 at the first annual conference of this Baptist women's organization. By 1907 the National Baptist Training School for Women and Girls was a reality, occupying a six-acre tract of land in the Lincoln Heights section of the District of Columbia. The school trained black women to become missionaries, Sunday school teachers, stenographers, bookkeepers, musicians, cooks, laundresses and housemaids. Burroughs managed to remove the word 'Baptist' from the school's name so it could be a non-sectarian institution emphasizing industrial education. The board of trustees, all black and all female, reflected African tradition, as a network of women providing support and guidance for one another. This inevitably alienated male factions in the Baptist Convention. None the less, the school flourished, gaining most of its financial support from black resources outside the convention. It had only thirty-one students when it opened officially in the fall of 1909, but by 1934, enrollment had grown to more than 2,000 students, many of whom boarded at the institution. Although missionary work was included in the curriculum, domestic science was the major emphasis. Burroughs argued for this early in the school's history, predicting that 58 percent of black women workers would be employed as domestics. Her aim was to train them as professionals in domestic science.[12]

Organizing what some of them called 'unions' was another strategy black women domestics developed on the eve of the US entry into World War I. One of several such groups around the nation was the Association of Women Wage-earners, based in Washington, DC. Association president Jeannette Carter described the group as an effort to help black women become more self-reliant. Women's organizations throughout the country were urged to cooperate with the association, which also sought to assess the conditions and wages of wage-earning black women, most of whom were domestics. In a keynote address delivered at its Founding convention, Carter discussed the association's goals, some of which paralleled those of the White Rose Association and its successors: to provide a home where domestic science would be taught and where employers could find workers. However, the organization also promised to serve as an agent between employers and employees in order to develop better relations among the two and to improve working conditions for domestics. The Association of Women Wage-earners never accomplished its goals, for it did not have the national impact its leaders hoped for, and soon disappeared from the scene.[13]

After the war, there were some other attempts to organize black domestics into unions. In 1920, there were ten locals of black domestic workers in southern cities affiliated with the Hotel and Restaurant Employees' Union of the American Federation of Labor.

However, most black women worked as domestics in private homes rather than in hotels and restaurants. Furthermore, the AFL record of discriminatory treatment of black workers was well known in the 1920s, and blacks could not count upon union officials to work on their behalf. T. Arnold Hill, writing in an Urban League publication in 1928, advised blacks to look to groups such as the Young Women's Christian Association (YWCA), the American Workers' Communist Party and the Trade Union Committee for Organizing Negro Workers, rather than to the AFL. 'Heretofore the Negro worker has had the choice of two loyalties – organized labor and the employing groups,' Hill wrote. 'To this is now added a third – the radical wing of the labor movement.'[14]

African–American women domestic workers did not flock to the radical groups during the 1920s and the 1930s, however. Instead, they attempted to organize themselves independently. In 1936, a domestic workers' union was organized in Washington, DC. The 100 members succeeded in raising the prevailing weekly wage for domestics from three dollars to ten dollars. A year later, the Domestic Workers' Association was founded in New York City, and similar groups sprang up in other cities as well.

Most of these organizations proved shortlived, however. One reason was that black women simply lacked the power to have labor rules and agreements enforced by law. Another reason was the large oversupply of domestic workers, which made it difficult to raise wage rates, especially during the Great Depression. The net result was that black domestics remained on the fringe of the labor movement.[15] Some efforts to assist domestic workers were made by the US Women's Bureau in the 1920s and by the US Department of Labor during the New Deal. But these government programs were so ineffective that they merely underlined the need for black women to rely upon themselves for mutual aid.

The plight of black domestics did not improve until the 1940s, when US entry into World War II led to severe labor shortages and a sharp increase in the market for domestics, who could now demand improvements. In response to these developments, Jean Collier Brown left the Women's Bureau to organize the United Domestic Workers' Local Industrial Union 1283, affiliated with the CIO, in Baltimore in 1942. As the union's organizer, Brown wrote to all the employers who had hired the local's members. She promised that

Local 1283 would be accountable to employers and would place only satisfactory household-workers in jobs. In exchange for reliable help, employers agreed not to discriminate against workers and to pay the union wage scale of three dollars a day, or one dollar and seventy cents for a half a day. The union also reduced the time domestic workers spent on the job, which traditionally had often ranged from eleven to twelve hours a day. Local 1283 established a full day as nine hours with one hour for lunch. A week's salary was fifteen dollars and fifty cents for five-and-a-half days' work, over five times the prevailing weekly rate for domestic workers in the 1930s.[16]

This CIO local was a labor organization more in keeping with mainstream American standards of the time than with the tradition of African women's associations. Unlike the voluntary associations of the past, the United Domestic Workers provided no lodging and offered no classes in culture and skill development; instead, it functioned as a bargaining agency. The local maintained an office with a small full-time staff. Along with Brown, there was Bertha Wilson, the employment director. It was Wilson who responded to a critical letter in the Baltimore *Sun* in 1942, which portrayed black domestics as untrained and less than reliable, and questioned why they should not be expected to stay overnight at employers' homes. Wilson replied:

> We ask that employers pay workers for the amount of work they do and that they may return to their homes like any other industrial workers because, after all, a domestic worker is just as skilled in her line of work as any other kind of worker.[17]

Apparently, the Baltimore public did not accept the argument, and Local 1283 continued to try to persuade employers that domestic workers were entitled to the same benefits as union members in other industries. By 1944, Susie Taylor was the president of Local 1283 and Malinda McFadden had replaced Bertha Wilson. That year, the union executive board voted to include sick leave and vacation pay as benefits for union members employed full-time for a period of six months or more. The extent to which this policy was successful is not known, but by the end of World War II, the United Domestic Workers' Union had ceased to be a viable bargaining agency, a casualty of the postwar era, when the shortages of black domestic workers were no longer acute.[18]

A new national organization of domestic workers, the National Committee on Household Employment, was formed in 1979, with Carolyn Reed as the founder. A former domestic worker, Reed attempted to unite household-workers with the women's movement in New York City during the 1960s. Unsuccessful because of race and class biases among white feminists, Reed turned to the National Urban League, and the Household Employment Project was established under the league's umbrella as a federation of black and hispanic household-workers' organizations.[19]

Black women factory-workers and the unions

Although domestic work was the fastest-growing wage-earning field among African–American women during the first half of the twentieth century, factory work in the garment industry and in laundries was also available to some. Factory work was less racially segregated than domestic work, bringing workers of various racial groups together. However, work assignments were often racially defined, and in some factories only black workers were hired. Even in those factories where blacks and whites worked together, racism limited the potential for effective unionization.

From 1910 to 1930, there was an increase of 33,000 in the number of African–American women employed in manufacturing, and by 1930 there were an estimated 101,000 of them. In comparison, there were 600,000 black women domestic workers employed in private homes. These US Labor Department statistics did not include the unknown number of black women who 'passed' as whites, mostly Caribbean-born immigrants, employed in the New York City garment industry. If the statistics understate the extent of African–American women's employment in manufacturing, there were also forces at work limiting the factory jobs available to them. Technological changes in industry, beginning in 1920, eliminated many low-skilled positions – the jobs previously held by the majority of African–American women in industry. Jean Collier Brown noted in 1938 that most of the black women employed in industry were hired to sweep and to clean, while others did general labor in factories. Only a few ran machines or held positions of responsibility. Not surprisingly, the largest category of black women in manufacturing was the 20,000 dress-makers employed outside of factories.[20]

Prejudice against African–American women in the garment industry had become institutionalized very early, despite the fact that slave women had provided invaluable services as dress-makers throughout the pre-Civil War era. As early as 1869, Frances Ellen Watkins Harper testified at a women's rights meeting that, in New England, white women in factories refused to work alongside black women.[21] And, from the earliest period, garment industry unions discouraged black members. None the less, by the turn of the century, efforts to organize African–American women in the industry were under way. One of the pioneers was Mary Watson Webster, who attempted to establish a branch of the Needle Work Guild among black women in Washington, DC, in 1900. The national president of the guild advised Webster to form a 'colored section' of a white branch of the union, because an independent branch of black women was against guild policy. Offended, Webster established the National Sewing Council, a black organization open to both men and women. A self-help association, which remained local in membership, the council provided clothing for the needy, organized a sewing school for young girls, and raised funds for an old folks' home, later called the Webster Home. The survival strategies developed by the women (most of them black) in this Anacostia-based network reflected traditional African values. Like the early domestic workers' organizations, the National Sewing Council was not a collective bargaining agency, nor did it aim to elevate the status of black women *vis-à-vis* management.[22]

Few attempts seem to have been made to include black women, let alone to elevate their position in the early-twentieth-century garment industry. African–American women garment-workers were paid less than white women for performing the same tasks. Double standards in hiring, in community aid, and in union support of labor could be found in the industry throughout the nation. A 1929 YWCA survey of black female workers in Indianapolis found that very few held skilled positions in the garment industry there. Of nearly 1,500 black women employed in the city in 1929, only 338 worked in garment industry factories, making gloves, coats, jackets and uniforms, for average weekly salaries of twelve to fifteen dollars. While there is no evidence of union activity among these workers, in 1930 the black-operated Phillis Wheatley YWCA provided an employment bureau, which monitored salaries for black women and refused to send out full-time workers for less than ten dollars a week. May B. Belcher was the program's executive secretary and Mrs F. B. Ransome chaired the Committee of Management. Like African–American women throughout the nation, they attempted to fill the void in community services available to black women. The Wheatley Association had begun independently of the YWCA in 1922, under the auspices of the Volunteer Workers' Group. Like the Women's Loyal Union of New York, the Wheatley Association offered a variety of 'racial uplift' programs as well as lodging for black girls. In 1923, the association became part of the YWCA,[23] and thereafter was called 'the Wheatley Branch' by the people in the community.

The Indianapolis Phillis Wheatley YWCA was but one of several Phillis Wheatley Associations founded in the south and the midwest during the early twentieth century, providing support systems for black female workers in such cities as Nashville, Washington and Cleveland. The association in Cleveland, for example, was founded by Jane Hunter in 1913, because at the time the YWCA in Cleveland discriminated against blacks. The Wheatley House, as it was called, made lodging available for black girls while they were working or seeking employment. It also served as a center where whites could come to hire servants. In 1918, the association was accepted as a member of the Cleveland Welfare Federation, which enabled the organization to receive public aid. In the mid-1920s the association established an employment department to locate jobs for black women. In 1928 alone, the department placed over 1,000 women in various domestic and industrial positions in Cleveland.[24]

By the 1930s, YWCA agencies throughout the north had accepted some responsibility for black women's concerns. In 1936, the Chicago branch surveyed the black women working in the cotton-garment industry, which employed more blacks than any other industry in the city. The report noted that although the National Recovery Act minimum rate for experienced workers had been thirteen dollars a week, of the nine African–American women surveyed who had experience, five earned less than ten dollars weekly (after the NRA ceased to function). Another Chicago YWCA study investigated black women working in the needle trades. Only thirteen of the forty-eight firms surveyed employed African–American women, and eleven of these made low-priced house-dresses and aprons. Even within this modest industry, opportunities for black women were distinctly limited. Several of the companies employed blacks only on presses, work that required unusual strength and endurance. Officials justified hiring blacks exclusively for these tasks on the ground that 'the Negro can stand heat better than a white girl.' Few companies employed both white and black workers on power machines, and those firms that did employ large numbers of African–American workers hired virtually no white workers.[25] Here again, black women received lower salaries and fewer opportunities than whites, and trade unionism afforded no support on their behalf.

Although racism defined the position of black women factory-workers in New York City, the situation there among garment- and laundry-workers was somewhat unique between the world wars. In New York, Caribbean immigrant women were recruited into the industry rather than southern black women. Many of the black women who found responsible jobs as dress-makers in factories had arrived in the United States with special skills in needlework, and they were often assumed to be white by their employers. The survival strategies these immigrant women developed conflicted with traditional African values, for they were forced to reject their heritage on the job site, in 'passing' as whites. Here, trade unionism played a more important role than in other areas of the country.

The testimony of friends and relatives of Delia Bierman Terborg, a draper in the New York City garment industry from the post-World War I years until she retired in the mid-1950s, illustrates this. Terborg's employers did not take her for black. A mulatto from Suriname, she spoke with an accent like most of her co-workers. She kept to herself and worked very hard. As a result of her skill and early union affiliation, Terborg rose quickly in the industry, earning the union rate for drapers of twenty-seven dollars weekly as early as the late 1920s. It was at this time that she recruited a young friend, Mabel Greaves Lake, who was hired as her assistant at the non-union rate of eighteen dollars weekly. Lake was a Barbados native, educated in the Brooklyn public schools. A graduate of Girls' High School, she was a mulatto, who passed as Spanish. Lake recalls that by the mid-1930s, the International Ladies' Garment Workers' Union was not encouraging new membership, because so many of their members were unemployed due to the Depression. None the less, in 1936 Lake obtained a union card thus assuring her skilled position as a draper. She now finally received the union rate and could no longer be assigned to machine work. Both Lake and Terborg worked for a firm where better dresses were manufactured for exclusive New York stores such as Bergdorf Goodman. Employment in such a company was not only prestigious, but earned workers good salaries. The majority of the skilled workers in the workforce of this company were Italians. Some blacks may have worked in the factory area, but Mabel Lake recalls that she saw very few blacks employed in any capacity until the 1940s.[26]

One important motive for black workers in the garment industry to pass as whites was the access to union protection this offered them. Until the late 1920s, few efforts were made by the garment industry union to include African–Americans. In 1929, the ILGWU, representing 45,000 white dress-makers, did launch a special effort to unionize the 4,000 black women working in New York City dress shops. At this time, black women earned from eight to twelve dollars a week, while union workers received from twenty-six to forty-four dollars a week. Why was there this sudden interest in black workers? Perhaps the anti-racist commitment of the Communist Party faction in the ILGWU during the 1920s stimulated black recruitment. Perhaps the sudden move to recruit blacks was inspired by the union's fear that African–American women would continue to work after union workers went on strike. Whatever the reason, the following year a strike occurred and black dress-makers were again encouraged to join. The union recruitment drive apparently did not succeed, however, for only a few hundred of them joined.[27]

Trade unionism was more successful in the laundry industry in New York. The United Laundry Workers' Local 300 of the Amalgamated Clothing Workers of America, representing primarily black women who laundered towels and uniforms, won a union contract in the mid-1930s limiting weekly hours to forty-five, providing a minimum wage of fifteen dollars and seventy-five cents, a week's vacation and three days' sick leave after one year of service, and seven fixed holidays with pay.[28] The success of this union was based upon the fact that almost all of the workers were black, in contrast to the situation in the dress-making shops in New York.

With the rise of the CIO in the late 1930s, interest in organizing black women into unions grew significantly. But, as union organizer

Sabrina Martinez remarked in 1941, many black women were reluctant to join unions even then. Martinez noted that anti-labor management propaganda, and the legacy of the old 'Jim Crow' policies of the AFL, made it difficult for the CIO to organize black women. None the less, she observed, by 1941 unionization had made inroads among African–American women in laundries, cleaning and dying establishments, textile factories, and among teachers and domestics.[29]

Even with these gains, prejudice among union officials was still evident during the 1940s and 1950s, creating new barriers for black women. Florence Rice, an ILGWU chairlady during the 1950s, felt the union was the 'greatest thing' for blacks in the industry. However, in time she learned that union officials discriminated against minority workers. She recalls:

> Many of the black workers never felt that the union really represented them. What you always found out was that the Union man would say something in front of your face and would go back to the boss and it would be completely different.
>
> I would say that all the white girls was making exceptional good pay. Regardless. It was seen that they made good pay. White folks was always supposed to make more money than black folks. It was done in mostly all the shops.[30]

Black women in the garment industry, even when they were unionized, thus continued to rely upon their own survival strategies.

Epilog and conclusion

Historically, institutionalized racism and sexism have defined blacks as fit only to carry the burden of hard labor, and women as inferior workers not worthy of the monetary compensation given to men's work. For African–American women workers, the burden of prejudice was a double one. Black women's protective associations, Phillis Wheatley Associations and similar networks aided many women who had to work under oppressive conditions for substandard wages during the pre-World War II years. If the traditional African value system which permitted women to form these support systems had not been preserved, the very survival of black families would have been jeopardized.

Since World War II, there have been two major changes in the status of African–American women workers. One is in their occupational position. While racial prejudice and racially defined work persist within the female labor market, there has been a marked decline, especially since the 1960s, of domestic work as an occupation, as black women have been incorporated into clerical and service jobs. As a result, the wage gap between black and white women wage-earners has narrowed significantly. None the less, black females continue to rank fourth in earnings when compared to white males, black males and white females.[31]

It is in the context of African–American female survival strategies that the second major change in the status of black women workers may be understood. In recent years, there has been a reversal in the roles of black and white women in relation to involvement in organized labor. As of 1980, 24 percent of black women workers were members of labor organizations, while only 15 percent of white women workers were members.[32] Interestingly, this has occurred during a period when the strength of organized labor has been declining. Black women are moving against the mainstream trend here, in what may constitute a new adaptation of their ancestral tradition of providing mutual support through collective networks.

Notes

1 I would like to thank JoAnn Ooiman Robinson, Sharon Harley and Ruth Milkman for sharing resources, reading this manuscript and making helpful suggestions. Some of the research for this paper was made possible by a grant from the Faculty Research Committee and Board of Morgan State University Press.

2 See Filomina Chioma Steady, ed., *The Black Woman Cross-culturally*, Cambridge, Schenkman Publishing, 1981, pp.9–11; Niara Sudarkasa, 'Female Employment and Family Organization in West Africa,' in *The Black Woman Cross-culturally*, pp.53–5.

3 Benjamin Brawley, *Women of Achievement: Written for the Fireside Schools*, Nashville, Woman's American Baptist Home Mission Society, 1919, pp.16–17.

4 Jean Collier Brown, *The Negro Woman Worker*, Bulletin of the US Women's Bureau, no. 165, Washington, DC, US Government Printing Office, 1938, p.1.

5 US Department of Commerce, *Statistical Abstract*, Washington, DC, US Government Printing Office, 1981, p.381.

6 Sojourner Truth, *Narrative of the Life of Sojourner Truth: A Bondwoman of Olden Time*, Chicago, Johnson Publishing, 1970, pp.14–22.

7 Louise Mitchell, 'Slave Markets Typify Exploitation of Domestics,' in Gerda Lerner, ed., *Black Women in White America: A Documentary History*, New York, Random House, 1972, pp.229–31.

8 Gilbert Osofsky, *Harlem: The Making of a Ghetto, Negro New York, 1890–1930*, New York, Harper & Row, 1966, pp.56–7.

9 *The Woman's Era*, vol. 1, May 1894, p.1.

10 Hallie Q. Brown, *Homespun Heroines and Other Women of Distinction*, Xenia, Ohio, Aldine Publishing, 1926, pp.210–12.

11 Carolyn Reed, 'Household Workers and the Urban League: An Historical Connection,' *Household Employment News*, fall 1981, pp.1–4.

12 Evelyn Brooks Barnett, 'Nannie Burroughs and the Education of Black Women,' in Sharon Harley and Rosalyn Terborg-Penn, eds, *The Afro–American Woman: Struggles and Images*, Port Washington, New York, Kennikat Press, 1978, pp.98–101.

13 *The New York Age*, 29 March 1917.

14 T. Arnold Hill, 'Labor,' *Opportunity: A Journal of Negro Life*, vol.6, October 1928, p.311; Brown, *The Negro Woman Worker*, p.3.

15 Elizabeth Ross Haynes, 'Negroes in Domestic Service in the United States,' *Journal of Negro History*, vol. 8, October 1923, pp.395 and 414.

16 Jean Collier Brown to employers, 31 December, 1942, in Vertical File, United Domestic Workers, Enoch Pratt Free Library, Baltimore.

17 The Baltimore *Sun*, 2 July, 1943, in Vertical File, Enoch Pratt Free Library.

18 Susie Taylor to employers, 7 February, 1944, in Vertical File, Enoch Pratt Free Library.

19 See *Household Employment News*, fall 1981, pp.1–8.

20 Brown, *The Negro Woman Worker*, pp.2 and 8.

21 Elizabeth Cady Stanton *et al.*, eds, *History of Woman Suffrage, 1861–1876*, New York, Arno Press and The New York Times, 1969, p.392.

22 Louise Daniel Hutchinson, *The Anacostia Story: 1608–1930*, Washington, Smithsonian Institution Press, 1977, pp.132–5. (Anacostia is a community in Washington, DC.)

23 *The Crisis*, vol. 37, June 1930, pp.189–91.

24 *The Crisis*, vol. 36, December 1929, pp.411–12.

25 Brown, *The Negro Woman Worker*, pp.10–11.

26 Mabel Greaves Lake, Jamaica, New York, interviewed by Rosalyn Terborg-Penn, 27 November, 1982; Jeanne K. Terborg, Jamaica, New York, interviewed by Rosalyn Terborg-Penn, 26 November, 1982.

27 *The Crisis*, vol. 36, November 1929, p.380; *The Crisis*, vol.37, January 1930, p.21.

28 Brown, *The Negro Woman Worker*, p.15.
29 'Negro Women in Organizations – Labor,' in Lerner, *Black Women in White America*, p.263.
30 Florence Rice, New York City, interview with with Gerda Lerner, 23 September, 1970, in *Black Women in White America*, pp.278–80. Punctuation, etc., as original.
31 US Department of Commerce, Bureau of Census, *Statistical Abstract of the US, 1981*, p.444; US Department of Commerce, Bureau of Census, *Current Population Report*, Bulletin nos 1–60, p.129; Michael Reich, *Racial Inequality: A Political-Economic Analysis*, Princeton University Press, 1981, Table 2.3, p.32.
32 US Department of Labor, *Earnings and Other Characteristics of Organized Workers, May 1980*, Bulletin no. 2,105, Washington, DC, US Government Printing Office, 1980, pp.5–7.

8

'I know which side I'm on': Southern women in the labor movement in the twentieth century

Mary Frederickson

Southern women workers, black and white, have always had a special relationship to the US labor movement, by virtue of the region's distinctive economic and political characteristics. Historically, a relatively small proportion of women workers in the south were employed in manufacturing jobs, and industrial production was highly dispersed geographically, so that militancy was often localized in isolated 'company towns.' The biracial workforce and a highly repressive political system further add to the complexities of organizing in the region. Indeed, southern women workers, even more than their sisters elsewhere in the nation, have faced enormous obstacles when they attempted to unionize. In this chapter, Mary Frederickson analyzes the factors which have shaped women's labor history in the region, and documents the tradition of activism and militancy among southern women workers over the course of the twentieth century.

Throughout the twentieth century, black and white women in the southern United States have led spontaneous walkouts, become militant labor activists, organized community resources and solicited national support during prolonged strikes. The courage of women workers in the south has matched that of women anywhere, and yet the number of southern women in trade unions has remained small. The episodic history of the labor movement in the south has been marked by a discontented, mobile labor force, intense and frequently successful organizing drives, and deeply entrenched, sometimes violent, opposition. Many southern women have struggled to advance the cause of unionism and have bequeathed a union heritage to their children. Yet their gains have often been eroded by economic hard times and the tenacious resistance of employers.[1]

The low level of sustained union participation by southern women workers is the product of economic and political factors distinctive to the south; these have hampered organizing efforts and compounded the difficulties of maintaining union membership. An abundant biracial female workforce, the high concentration of women workers in non-manufacturing jobs, rurally based industries far from urban labor centers, a manufacturing base largely controlled from outside the region, and a repressive political system – all have functioned as barriers to union participation. Nevertheless, organized labor has been a consistent presence in the south, enticed by the large numbers of unorganized workers and coerced by the threat unorganized workers posed to the labor movement in the north. Since World War II, the movement of black workers into jobs previously reserved for whites has changed the character of the southern workforce and of the region's labor movement. Today, as in earlier decades, southern women remain in the forefront of labor struggle.

Barriers to unionization

The primary impediment to industrial organization among women workers in the south in the twentieth century was the relatively small fraction of the female workforce holding manufacturing jobs. The occupational distribution of women workers has varied dramatically between the north and the south. In the south, as late as 1950, fewer than 18 percent of the region's women workers worked in manufacturing, the segment of the workforce most likely to become unionized, while 34 percent of the northern female workforce was concentrated in manufacturing. In 1910, 83 percent of the southern female workforce was in agriculture and domestic service, compared to 33 percent in the north. By 1940 agriculture and service jobs, which received little attention from organized labor, occupied 46 percent of women wage-earners in the south as against 24 percent in the north. Southern women in these sectors, and especially in agriculture, constituted a large pool of workers waiting to 'move up' to manufacturing work. This labor surplus reduced the job security of female industrial workers and increased the leverage manufacturers had over them.[2]

The margin of survival for southern women workers always has been much thinner than for their northern sisters. Before 1940, southern wages were substantially lower than the national average, while the cost of living in the south was only 5 percent lower than in other regions. In textiles, for example, New England workers earned 64 percent more than workers in the south in the 1920s. This differential dropped to less than 20 percent in 1933–4 and increased to 39 percent four years later. In 1946, southerners made up 25 percent of the nation's population, but received only 8 percent of the national income. Because wage rates were low for all workers, southern families often depended on the wages of two or more family members, and women's wages were more critical to the family economy than in the north. Women working in cotton textiles typically provided 30–40 percent of the family income. The limited resources of most southern families also made sustaining a strike or taking other action against employers more difficult.[3]

Child labor was another factor which hampered the organization of southern women workers. The low standard of living of southern families and the lack of legislative restrictions on manufacturers in the region perpetuated the use of child labor long after it had disappeared in New England. Between 1880 and 1900, the number of children in mills and factories in the southern industrial piedmont quadrupled. The proportion of adult women workers declined from 47 to 33 percent, while jobs held by children under sixteen increased to 26 percent of the total.[4] This had serious effects on the prospects for organizing. 'Unionism is a signal failure in textile work, as cotton mills employ too many children,' the secretary of a textile union reported in 1911. In Texas, she noted, 'About one-third or more of the hands are children, most of them too small to take into a union.'[5]

Because of the detrimental impact of child labor on adult jobs, wages and organizing efforts, the Knights of Labor, the American Federation of Labor, local textile affiliates and state federations concentrated on eliminating children from southern factories. In

1901, child labor bills were introduced in the region's four leading textile states, the Carolinas, Georgia and Alabama.[6]

Such protective legislation met with opposition not only from mill-owners, but also from unorganized mill-workers, for whom the issue was fraught with contradictions. It was very difficult for un-organized workers, the overwhelming majority of the southern workforce, to risk losing the immediate wages of their working children on the chance that this might eventually lead to financial gains for the adult workers within the family. In large families, the role of the woman as household manager and caretaker of small children was essential, and the family economy benefited more if children, rather than mothers, went out to work for wages. The issue of child labor not only diverted organized labor from the task of organizing unorganized southerners, but also placed the unions in a position antagonistic to the majority of southern workers. Not until World War I brought increased production and speed-ups to the mills did this divisive issue diminish in importance as the number of employed children declined.[7]

The biracial composition of the female workforce in the south was another difficulty the labor movement had to confront. Sixty percent of the southern female workforce was black in 1910, and the figure was 40 percent as late as 1940. Until the 1960s, black women were completely excluded from operative positions in the textile mills and were restricted to seasonal handwork in tobacco factories. This exclusion was partially at the insistence of white workers, who at times went out on strike to protest against the hiring of black workers. In Macon, Georgia, in 1919, a rumor that black workers were going to be hired precipitated mob attacks on black women, resulting in two deaths. White women employed in Danville, Virginia, during World War II, successfully struck to obtain the dismissal of recently hired black women workers.[8]

Occupational segregation by race was staunchly defended by southern white workers, not only as a reflection of their racism, but also because they feared being replaced by black workers. Despite the willingness of manufacturers to acquiesce to white employees' demands that black workers should not be hired, managers re-peatedly threatened to hire black workers in the place of white employees. Operative positions in southern mills were not open to black women until the 1960s, when management cited federal civil rights legislation to explain its sudden abandonment of exclusionary hiring. In fact, however, employers were forced to hire black workers not because of the legislation, but because full employment in textile mills and the expansion of other industries in the south had created a scarcity of white workers.[9]

One of the most difficult problems unions have had to confront in the south involved organizing black and white workers together. Unity among southern women workers could never be achieved as long as black and white women remained segregated both on the job and in the labor movement. But not until the independent Congress of Industrial Organizations entered the region would black and white southern women join the same local unions, and even then the system of occupational segregation which banned black women from most industrial jobs precluded the widespread integration of black and white women in southern locals until after 1965.

Still other characteristics of the southern industrial economy made the task of unionization difficult. The manufacturing sector is highly dispersed across a 1,000-mile stretch of piedmont from the Appalachian mountains to the eastern coastal plain. Long distances between factories and mills made it difficult for workers to communicate and arduous for organizers to cover their assigned territories. Located in agricultural areas, away from urban centers of skilled workers, many southern factories provided the only waged work available for miles around, so that while many workers competed for a few jobs, few factories had to compete for workers. When southern industrial workers organized, they generally did so in isolation. The assistance of nearby farmers who supplied food during southern strikes could not take the place of sympathetic unionists in an urban environment who would honor a picket line or strike in support of fellow-workers.

Moreover, southern industries frequently operated within incorporated company towns where workers had no political autonomy, and minimal personal independence. Edith Kowski, a New York City garment-worker and Amalgamated Clothing Workers of America (ACWA) member, visited one of these towns in 1928. The mill in West Durham, North Carolina, employed 1,100 workers and provided housing, a community center complete with gym, bowling alleys, library, movies, night high school classes, and clubs for everyone from baby to grandmother. Kowski found the workers' lives 'so absolutely entrenched in the village life that there is no leaving it and Mr Erwin, the owner, reigns as "God Almighty." '[10] This pattern of paternalistic control was duplicated throughout the south as manufacturers created an extensive institutional infrastructure of houses, schools, stores and churches to control the lives of their workers. Patriarchial control in the mill village mirrored paternalistic management inside the mill, where an elaborate hierarchy of male employees controlled the large unskilled female workforce, denied access to higher-paying skilled or supervisory positions.

The other major type of southern industrialist was the absentee owner. Beginning in the last quarter of the nineteenth century, northern manufacturers invested heavily in southern industry to create a regional colonial economy, supplying raw materials and labor for northern-based businesses. Profits were skimmed and reinvested far from southern mill communities. This system of absentee ownership allowed manufacturers intransigently to oppose the demands of workers with whom they had no direct contact and in whose community they had only an economic interest. While absentee owners and paternalistic mill barons had very different philosophies of social organization and control, they were united in their inflexible opposition to all efforts to unionize 'their people.'[11]

Religion has served as one of the most useful control mechanisms in southern society; within the region's industrial communities, church attendance has typically been encouraged, if not required. Churches were often directly subsidized by industrialists who hired ministers, determined sermon topics, and set the moral tone for the community. Southern women who attended churches run by the factories in which they worked were bound by a worldview which dictated dependence, subservience and quiet obedience. Women strikers in North Carolina in the 1920s were dismissed from their churches for joining the union, and CIO organizers in the 1930s constantly encountered 'the prostitution of religion by paid revivalists who put up tents in the mill villages and poured out a constant stream of propaganda against the CIO.'[12]

Lack of personal autonomy within the church coincided with the absence of political control by workers within industrial communities. Social services either came directly from management, or did not exist. Prior to World War II, white southern workers could vote, if their poll taxes were paid up, but they were often escorted to the polls by management and 'encouraged' to support a specific slate. Like the churches, public schools in southern mill communities were often subsidized by management, which hired and fired school-teachers, approved textbooks and changed the school schedule to meet the exigencies of mill production.[13]

Like southern blacks who faced economic, social and political segregation, most southern white industrial workers lived in communities set apart from the larger white population. A 1944 study of a cotton mill community near High Point, North Carolina, conducted by the Textile Workers' Union of America (TWUA), emphasized the isolation of the seventy homes surrounding one mill. Workers lived outside the city corporation limits of High Point, away from public schools and shopping facilities. There was no postal delivery, streets were unpaved, drainage ditches open, and there were no playgrounds. Women working in the mill had to make an expensive and difficult journey to the city to obtain any ordinary household necessity, with the exception of groceries. Workers' families had little contact with people outside the village and depended on each other and the mill management for all their needs.[14]

In creating and nurturing isolated industrial communities throughout the south, southern state and local governments have provided multifaceted assistance to manufacturers. Exemption from taxes, low utility rates, cheap land, available workers and state-supported technical education programs have comprised the basic incentives. Most importantly, however, the south has been billed as a haven from organized labor, and state and local governments throughout the region have worked hard to maintain both the image and reality of a union-free south. From the beginning of the century, southern states have provided manufacturers with military assistance in strikes. Local government authorities have routinely routed union organizers from their communities, often at gunpoint. After 1947, 'right to work' laws banning closed union shops were passed in many southern states, and, fearing the competition of union labor, manufacturers in non-union strongholds within the region have used their political influence to prevent unionized firms from moving into the area.[15]

Southern women and labor militancy

Despite all these factors impeding the ability of organized labor to unionize the southern workforce, women workers in the region have been engaged in labor struggles for decades and have made substantial gains in wages as well as working and living conditions. From the late nineteenth century on, southern women workers' labor activism has been tied to the strategies they used to control their working lives within the mills. The local, spontaneous collective actions which established the limits of behavior women were willing to accept from management, often expanded into formal labor protests or formed the germ of union organizing efforts.

Black domestic workers were among the first southern women to participate in organized resistance to existing working conditions. Their locally organized and self-financed efforts were modest in scale, rarely involving an entire community or municipal area. In 1880, for example, black washerwomen in Atlanta organized an association in a black church; a year later, 3,000 washerwomen, cooks, servants and child-nurses struck for higher wages. A high city licensing fee was levied against the association and the women were threatened with rent increases. The strikers held out and sent the mayor a letter warning him that 'We mean business this week or no washing.' In the end, the police broke the movement by arresting eight strike leaders and fining them for 'disorderly conduct and quarreling.' For each publicized protest of this type, there were no doubt hundreds of similar, even smaller efforts of which no record has survived.[16]

Keeping a lower profile, domestic workers in one Alabama town in 1905 were reported as having 'something like an organization' through which they collected regular dues and agreed not to work in homes where another worker had been fired. Townspeople argued that 'an incipient strike is going on nearly all the time,' and women workers in 1905 were proposing an organized strike, a 'general quitten' in order to demonstrate their employers' dependence on them. In 1968 when Dorothy Bolden began to organize domestic workers in Atlanta, she followed this same pattern of locally based self-organization. Women workers met in a church in the black community and individual self-employed women were taught how to negotiate with private employers to achieve wage increases that they had collectively established.[17]

Women employed in the textile and tobacco mills across the south also organized themselves, but relied on tactics distinctive to an industrial setting. Women unfairly reprimanded by supervisors retaliated by contacting relatives in supervisory positions or by organizing their work to inconvenience management. For example, in the early 1920s, when a woman worker in a small North Carolina spinning mill became involved in a dispute with her foreman about how she wound her bobbins, she reported the incident to her uncle, a supervisor in the mill. The uncle 'said something to the other one,' and, as she recalled, 'he [the foreman] never did say another word to me about my work as long as I worked down there, and he never did measure my cones.' To further impress her point upon the foreman, this woman, with the help of a cousin who came into the mill off-shift, ran her spinning frame 'so hard trying to keep every end going' in order to give her foreman 'a doff at six o'clock' which she knew would make him 'have to stay there until after we quit.' She had decided it was worth the extra work 'after he treated me like he did.'[18]

This type of individual protest, often executed with the help of a co-worker, could easily escalate to involve a roomful of workers, or the workforce of an entire mill or factory. Such spontaneous collective action was characteristic of the famous wave of strikes in the southern textile industry in 1929. The first strike began in Elizabethton, Tennessee, led by Margaret Bowen, a worker in the inspection department. Demoted from her position as section head when she asked for a raise from the $10.64 she earned for a fifty-six-hour week, Bowen organized the workers in her section. At the appointed hour, 533 out of 550 women left the mill. Within a week, 5,000 workers were out and the two large rayon plants in town were shut down. Like the 'turn-outs' organized by New England mill women in the 1840s, the Elizabethton strike involved women responding collectively to the treatment of an individual worker and adding to the original grievance broader workplace issues affecting all of the workers in the community.[19]

Spontaneous action by a group of southern women workers frequently provided the impetus for organized labor to move into the region, or to begin organizing in a specific area within the south. In other cases, southern workers on strike have called in a union to assist them. In Elizabethton, once Margaret Bowen had led over 500 women from the Glazstoff mill and workers in the nearby Bemberg plant had come out in support, a mass meeting of strikers sent an appeal to the AFL in March 1929 to send organizers into what was ironically called the 'Happy Valley.' The United Textile Workers (UTW–AFL) came into town with the strike 'boiling all over the place' and 4,653 of the 5,500 strikers became new union members. Three-quarters of them were women. A few months later, in Marion, North Carolina, 650 workers, half of them women, walked out of the Baldwin Manufacturing Company to protest the addition of twenty minutes to their twelve-hour shift. The Marion workers had heard of the strike and union in Elizabethton, and sent a small delegation the seventy-five miles through the mountains to bring back an organizer.[20]

The militancy of women in the Gastonia, North Carolina, strike, which also took place in March 1929, prompted the National Textile Workers' Union to send a delegation of women organizers to North Carolina. There, northern women like Vera Buch Weisbord met southern women activists, who were 'in the front ranks at all the meetings.' Women ran the relief headquarters during the five-month strike, mobilized a picket line of women and children, faced attacks by police, deputy-sheriffs and state national guard troops, and served time in jail.[21]

Women played an equally crucial supportive role in organizing coal miners, especially in Appalachia. The militancy of miners' wives is eloquently depicted in the true story of a mountain woman represented by the fictional character Dolly Hawkins in Myra Page's novel *Daughter of the Hills*. Hawkins's miner father led a ten-year fight against the use of convict labor in the mines. She married a miner who left the pit permanently maimed, and reared a son who, out of necessity, followed his father's trade. Hawkins became a leader in her mountain hollow. She spoke for the miners and their families, argued for safer conditions in the mines and better facilities in the camp. Like Florence Reece, author of the ballad 'Which Side Are You On?' Hawkins's heritage as a miner's daughter included her firm allegiance to the union and a deep understanding of the struggle between workers and management in the south. She knew which side she was on.[22]

Labor militancy by southern women in coal, textiles and domestic work, in the pre-war years was easily matched by the activism of women tobacco-workers in North Carolina and Virginia during World War II. As more operative positions opened for southern black women due to the wartime labor shortage, during World War II organizing efforts in the tobacco industry increased. Black women took the lead in these drives, while the white workforce reluctantly followed suit. For example, in July 1943, in Winston-Salem, North Carolina, 10,000 predominantly black and female workers went out on strike. With help from United Cannery Agricultural Packinghouse and Allied Workers of America (UCAPAWA–CIO) organizers who had worked with agricultural workers in the south and southwest, these black workers in Winston-Salem had formed the Tobacco Workers' Organizing Committee (TWOC). After the committee had held some meetings, the dismissal of a woman who had become so ill she could not work led to a spontaneous sit-down at the R. J. Reynolds Tobacco Company. The day after the firing, 1,500 women reported to the factory but did not work.[23]

These women workers soon gained the support of black male employees in the factory who, upon hearing that the women had not started their machines for the day, cut off their machines and refused to work under existing conditions. As one leader told a company vice-president: 'I think it's wrong for me to be working in # 64 with my wife over in # 60 trying to better her condition with all those other people.' Reynolds workers won a National Labor Relations Board (NLRB) election in December 1943, and signed a contract in April 1944. Like the workforce, the union had a majority of black members, but white workers did join. As one black woman leader put it: 'I told them they had nothing to be afraid of. Because we had stood together, the company couldn't do anything to us. I told them if they stood together, they could make the company listen to them.'[24]

If standing together was not always successful in obtaining or sustaining a union, the solidarity of female workers did make employers listen to workers' grievances and improved the living and working conditions of southern workers. Organizing drives often pressured employers to raise wages or repair mill housing in an effort to defuse worker dissatisfaction and thereby defeat the union. A striker from Marion, North Carolina, recalled that the 1929 organizing drive 'got the . . . managers . . . busy. They underpinned and cleaned up the houses. They put bathrooms in the houses, and tried to do that to keep the union out, which it did; I mean, the people went for that.'[25]

Similarly, hard-won pay raises in unionized plants were often passed on to non-union factories to lessen the attractiveness of the union to unorganized workers. For example, in the 1940s when the TWUA had won a minimum wage of sixty-five cents and substantial across-the-board increases in numerous mills throughout the south, the CIO reported that 'quick reaction came in the major unorganized mills, with the big Cannon Mills Company announcing a 10 cent increase and a 65 cent hourly minimum for its 18,000 employees.' The gains realized by a 'lost' union campaign or a successful drive at a distant mill were rarely credited to the union. But if these indirect gains are taken into account, the achievements of the southern labor movement loom far greater than the level of union membership in the south would suggest.[26]

Labor looks south

Since the 1880s, the south has been swept by wave after wave of organizing campaigns mounted by virtually every branch of the US labor movement. The Knights of Labor was the first group to recognize the strategic importance of organizing in the south. Then, in the 1900s, the AFL looked to 'The Awakening of the South,' promising to enter the region 'like a solid wedge against the injustice and wrong of child labor and overlong hours.' Throughout the 1920s, unionists from the northeast sought to organize southern workers in order to stabilize industry and save their unions, especially in cotton textiles, garments and hosiery. The independent CIO also launched intensive drives to organize southern workers from the late 1930s until the early 1950s. In the 1960s, black women began to take the lead in organizing in the garment, tobacco and textile industries. And today, as women workers throughout the region cling to ever-more scarce jobs in manufacturing and take new jobs in the service and clerical sectors, the south is again the potential target of efforts by national unions to organize the unorganized.[27]

The most successful nineteenth-century labor organization in the southern region was the Knights of Labor. The Knights' national policy of including women and black workers in its membership ranks was particularly important in the south. In 1889, there were already over fifty women's local assemblies in the region. Established between 1884 and 1886, southern women's locals comprised 30 percent of the Knights' women's assemblies in the United States. Black women organized one-fifth of the women's assemblies in the south. By 1890, however, the Knights began to wane nationally, and labor organization among southern workers reached a nadir. After local orders of the Knights had dissolved and the cotton textile industry in the south had grown sufficiently to challenge New England's supremacy in the production of coarse-cotton goods, the AFL-affiliated National Union of Textile Workers (NUTW) began to organize in southern mills. A craft union, the NUTW organized only the skilled male operatives, and by 1900 it had only 5,000 members out of the 90,000 textile-workers in the south. Not until a generation later would southern women textile-workers organize on a large scale.[28]

In the 1920s, unions were enticed into the region by pleas of spontaneously militant workers, and by the potential for vast union gains in the south. The attention of the labor movement was also commanded by the south's growing importance within the national industrial economy. As Edith Kowski put it after spending the summer of 1928 in the south, it was necessary to 'worry about the south . . . if for no other reason than to save our own union hides from an onslaught of company unionism and open shop drives.'[29]

Labor activity in the south in the late 1920s centered on the Full-Fashioned Hosiery Workers, a Philadelphia knitters' union determined to organize southern workers in order to protect the jobs and wage levels of hosiery workers throughout the east. Union organizer Alfred Hoffman established the Piedmont Organizing Council in 1927, and invited the AFL to assist with general organizing work in the south. Southern delegates at the AFL's 1928 convention in New Orleans mapped out a plan for organizing the south, but the federation actually put few organizers in the region and offered local organizing drives little monetary support. Its backing of southern textile strikes in 1929–30 was minimal, and women strikers received more support from middle-class reform groups within the region than from the AFL.[30]

Women's organizations and southern women workers

Throughout the 1920s, the plight of women workers in the south drew the attention of the Young Women's Christian Association (YWCA), the National Women's Trade Union League (NWTUL) and the Southern Summer School – all of whom recognized the unwillingness of AFL trade unions to deal with the problems facing southern women workers. By emphasizing the importance of organizing all of the workers within a given industry, by focusing on the unmet needs of the thousands of southern women workers, and by providing direct assistance to striking southern workers, these groups provided a crucial transitional form of organizing which went beyond the limited goals of the AFL and which later facilitated the emergence of the CIO in the south.[31]

The YWCA reached more working women in the south than any other organization. Thousands of women workers, both black and white, attended meetings of YWCA industrial clubs and became familiar with the principles of collective bargaining and the issues of industrial reform. Many women union members in the region acknowledged the importance of the YWCA in awakening and supporting their activism. Labor unions and workers' education programs recognized the involvement of the industrial department with working women and used it to communicate at the grassroots level with women workers, as well as for recruiting, fund-raising and strike support.[32]

From the outset, YWCA work in the southern region involved confronting difficult economic and social issues. Depending on middle-class financing, but committed to promoting the unionization of southern workers, YWCA leaders found themselves in a 'ticklish business.' In southern mill villages, the YWCA had to depend on mill-owners for support and facilities; in larger towns where networks of women's organizations supported YWCA programs, manufacturers fought any effort to help workers bargain for higher wages, shorter hours or better working conditions. Employers frequently sent representatives to meetings of the industrial clubs and occasionally women lost their jobs for active participation in the YWCA. Still, as one of the few organized groups accessible to women workers in the south, the YWCA Industrial Department often provided the only forum in which southern women could discuss workplace issues, even in communities with viable central labor organizations.[33]

Although the YWCA Industrial Department reached larger numbers of women workers, the NWTUL, founded in Boston in 1903, also had a substantial impact on the lives of working women in the south. The league began organizing work in the upper south as early as 1916, by assisting striking hosiery- and silk-mill-workers in Maryland. In the early 1920s, several southern women workers attended the league's National Training School in Chicago, promising to return south as organizers. In 1923, Matilda Lindsay, a native of Maryland with family in Virginia, joined the NWTUL staff as field representative and gradually expanded the league's work south of the Mason-Dixon line. By 1925, a local league had been organized in Birmingham, and the next year delegates at the annual NWTUL convention launched a 'Southern Campaign' with the goal of organizing the growing number of women workers in the expanding southern textile industry.[34]

In focusing on unorganized women workers in the south during the 1920s, league members sought to rekindle the spirit of their earlier efforts to support spontaneous strikes by women workers in northern cities. The southern campaign, described by one league member as 'the stiffest piece of work undertaken in some time,' offered a perfect opportunity to pump new life into the league, and the campaign plans expanded accordingly.[35] As Elisabeth Christman, NWTUL secretary-treasurer, later wrote, 'Each time we talked over the Southern program, it seemed to take on greater proportions.' In 1927, the league hired a permanent organizer, prepared leaflets, raised money and established a southern head-quarters in Richmond.

In 1929, the Philadelphia league launched a national campaign to help 'Organize the South.' The league sold small lapel-pins to raise money for the UTW–AFL's organization drive in southern mill towns. Cast in the shape of a shield, with the inscription 'Organize the South,' the pins had a tiny spinning wheel in the upper half to remind the wearer of 'Gandhi's stupendous effort to free the wage slaves of India.' Elisabeth Christman urged league members to 'Sell the pins now' on behalf of 'the young people whose youth is being blighted in the great plants of the south.'[36]

Because of their inexperience in the region and their task, which 'loomed up as a giant,' league members relied on the assistance of women from other organizations who were already active in the south. Those who helped included UTW–AFL organizer Sara Conboy, NWTUL field representative Matilda Lindsay, and Louise Leonard and Lois MacDonald, two women with experience in the YWCA Industrial Department who were designing a workers' education program specifically for southern workers. Already established in the south, Leonard and McDonald welcomed the arrival of the NWTUL in the region. Both women had grown tired of the slow, cautious pace at which social change could be promoted within the YWCA.[37]

As the NWTUL expanded its contacts in the south, Leonard and MacDonald were establishing the Southern Summer School for Women Workers in Industry, a workers' education program modeled on the Bryn Mawr Summer School and Brookwood Labor College, but adapted for women in the southern region. Women workers were recruited from over twenty southern communities to come to the school. Avoiding the 'middle-class atmosphere' of a college campus, the Southern Summer School convened in the 'more simple environment' of a rented camp school in the mountains of North Carolina. At the school, southern women workers took a six-week course in labor history and economics, read 'literature of social progress,' attended sessions on organizing tactics, and learned how to run a cooperative store. The school's students had access to union organizers and met regional labor leaders. In 1928, the Southern Summer School sponsored the first interstate labor conference held in the southeast, and the next year students and faculty traveled to nearby Marion, North Carolina, to attend strike meetings, organize union parades and help with relief efforts. Over a dozen women strikers from Marion, Elizabethton, Gastonia and communities in South Carolina attended the school in the late 1920s. The fact that so many southern women workers became involved in protests, walkouts or strikes during this period convinced students at the school that they had an important role to play in the ongoing efforts to organize workers across the region. After attending the school, one Virginia woman wrote: 'I feel a responsibility now, to all my southern sisters in industry. I learned that our problems were common, and this more than anything else brought us closer together.'[38]

Southern women workers who became active in the YWCA, joined the NWTUL, or attended sessions at the Southern Summer School formed a generation of women trained in the principles of industry-wide union organization. They shared a commitment to bringing southern workers in large, unorganized industries – furniture, tobacco and cotton, for example – into the ranks of organized labor. To these women, the AFL and its emphasis on craft organization could not provide the leadership so desperately needed in the south. Accordingly, they became a natural base for the CIO drives of the 1930s and 1940s.

In 1937, the clothing unions joined with the Textile Workers' Organizing Committee (TWOC) to launch the CIO's first major campaign in the south. Women organizers, especially native southerners, were now hired to work in the south. The CIO looked to the Southern Summer School to provide women leaders, and at least ten former students became organizers in the TWOC campaign. Initial exposure to the concept of industrial organization in the YWCA, and subsequent work with the Southern Summer School prior to being hired by the CIO, was the background shared by middle-class women like Lucy Randolph Mason, the CIO's southern public relations representative; Mary Lawrence, hired from the Highlander Folk School staff to work with TWUA; and Pat Knight, who led education programs for the TWUA. Southern women workers who had followed the same path included Hilda Cobb (ACWA), organizer of a campaign in Richmond, Virginia, in 1936; Polly Robkin (TWOC), sent to organize workers in a small south Georgia community; and Jennie Spencer (TWOC), organizer at the American Viscose plant in Roanoke, Virginia.[39]

Organizing southern women workers after World War II

After World War II, the CIO launched a far more intensive drive to organize southern workers than that of the 1930s. Called 'Operation Dixie,' its goal was to sign up one million workers in twelve southern states. The CIO sent 200 organizers to the south and spent one million dollars on the effort during the first year (1946); optimism ran high. The effort focused on the textile industry, which the CIO believed was the key to organizing the south. At that time, 75 percent of the nation's organized textile-workers were in the north, while almost three-quarters of the nation's textile industry was employed in the south, where 15–20 percent were organized.[40]

Women workers made up over 50 percent of the industry's work-force in most southern states and the 'Operation Dixie' campaign focused specifically on union benefits for women workers. A 1946 pamphlet prepared by TWUA promised 'that women get whatever men get' in a union drive, and concluded 'THAT'S WHY ALMOST HALF OF TWUA'S 400,000 MEMBERS ARE WOMEN.' Specific efforts to attract southern women to the CIO were quite successful. Of the 400,000 new union members recruited between 1946 and 1948, at least half were women. But the CIO campaign was arduous. Bitter conflicts between the AFL and the CIO in the south impeded organization. Aided by local law-enforcement officials and the national guard, employers met the drive with armed violence and refusal to employ activists. In addition, the work of local organizers, especially women, was often slowed by union administrators. Women organizers were usually hired on a temporary basis for one-half to two-thirds of the salary paid to men doing the same work. Despite planning and strategy mistakes, when the CIO southern organizing campaign terminated officially in 1953 industrial unions had made substantial gains in a variety of sectors – textiles, auto, steel, rubber and communications.[41]

Organizing in the south, as elsewhere in the nation, proved in-creasingly difficult in the 1950s and 1960s. State, federal and municipal anti-labor legislation, combined with strike defeats and declining membership, forced unions to abandon massive region-wide campaigns like 'Operation Dixie,' and to concentrate on local organizing efforts. White southern women, still the overwhelming majority of the female industrial workforce, played important roles in these drives. For example, in the 1958 strike in Henderson, North Carolina, and in the campaign against J. P. Stevens in Roanoke Rapids, North Carolina, which began the same year, women cam-paigned actively for the union, picketed, arranged strike relief and travelled north to raise money.[42]

More recently, however, the leadership in southern union organizing efforts has come increasingly from black women. Brought up in opposition to white authority and trained in the civil rights movement, in many southern mills black women have been the workers most responsive to seeking cooperative solutions to work situations. Previously excluded from production jobs, black women now hold over 50 percent of the operative positions in many southern plants. Many black women have entered textiles after having worked in domestic service; unlike their fathers and brothers, they have come into the mills without previous industrial experience, and often without having worked outside the region. Yet they have brought with them to the mills a firm commitment to improving their lives by working together, the way their mothers worked within the church.[43]

The difficult process of uniting black and white southern women within the union has been repeated throughout the region. Since 1965, in garment factories across the south the relationship between black and white women workers has become a critical factor in whether union elections are won or lost. As the number of black women in southern mills began to increase in the late 1960s and early 1970s, the number of successful union elections also multiplied. Black women took the lead in contacting unions, getting cards signed, fighting management's legal obstacles, and participating in contract negotiations. A majority of black women workers within a plant could usually convince younger white women to join them in supporting the union; with this interracial coalition, an election could be won.[44]

Both management and the unions have been fully cognizant of the correlation between a majority of black workers and a viable union. After 1964, when black women were hired at the Oneita Knitting Mills in Andrews, South Carolina, the configuration of the work-force changed and so did the union's chance for success. By 1971, 75 percent of the workers were black, 85 percent of whom were women, and the union easily won an election for bargaining rights. In the 1969 Charleston, South Carolina, hospital workers' strike, a small group of black women led their co-workers, almost all black women, through the four-month ordeal.[45]

Today, the leadership of southern black women is critical not only in industrial organizing, but also in the clerical sector. In Atlanta, one of the region's fastest-expanding urban areas, clerical work became the largest occupational sector for black women in the late 1970s. Established in 1980, Atlanta Working Women affiliated with the national '9 to 5' organization in 1982. A rapidly growing group, 9 to

5 in Atlanta has more black members than white, and relies heavily on the support of black women who, because of their previous work in either the church or the civil rights movement, have more leadership experience than most of their white co-workers, and have quickly gained expertise in issues affecting clerical workers – including office automation, health hazards and pay equity.[46]

Conclusion

For generations, lost strikes and failed organizing drives among southern women workers have obscured a history of consistent labor activism and unswerving union loyalty. Much of this history is embedded in family sagas and in the collective past of workers' communities. Nineteenth-century southern women active in the Knights of Labor bequeathed a union heritage to their children and grandchildren; daughters of unionized railroad-workers and coal miners struggled to establish early-twentieth-century textile, tobacco and garment union locals; and the children of women textile strikers in the 1920s joined the CIO's 'Operation Dixie' in the 1940s. In the 1960s, the momentum of the civil rights and women's movements, together with full employment in textiles, led to renewed efforts to unionize the south's largest industry.

In the 1980s, advances made in the previous two decades have been eroded by a deep recession in the south's basic industries – textiles, tobacco, furniture and steel. Today, however, the labor movement is once again looking to southern workers, as unions attempt to bolster declining rosters in the northeast and the industrial midwest, and try to deal with the continuing problem of runaway shops. Current efforts to unionize southern workers parallel earlier organizing attempts in a region still plagued by an oversupply of workers, low wages, powerful manufacturers, and compliant state and local governments. Women are entering the southern workforce at earlier ages, staying at work for longer periods, and looking toward the labor movement to solve collectively the problems they face as workers in a changing economy.

Notes

I would like to thank Jennifer Wooddell, Mary Walter, Jane Sherwin and Clint Joiner for their assistance in the preparation of this chapter.

1   For an overview of southern labor history, see F. R. Marshall, *Labor in the South*, Cambridge, Mass., Harvard University Press, 1967; G. Mitchell, *Textile Unionism and the South*, Chapel Hill, University of North Carolina Press, 1931; T. Tippett, *When Southern Labor Stirs*, New York, Jonathan Cape & Harrison Smith, 1931; M. Miller, ed., *Working Lives: The Southern Exposure History of Labor in the South*, New York, Pantheon Books, 1980. Works dealing specifically with twentieth-century southern women workers include US Department of Labor, Women's Bureau, *Women's Place in Industry in Ten Southern States*, by Mary Anderson, Washington, DC, Government Printing Office, 1931; E. Otey, 'Women and Children in Southern Industry,' *Annals of the American Academy of Political and Social Science*, vol. 153, 1931, pp.163–9; D. Janiewski, 'Sisters Under Their Skins: Southern Working Women, 1880–1950,' in Joanne V. Hawks and Sheila L. Skemp, eds, *Sex, Race and the Role of Women in the South*, Jackson, University of Mississippi Press, 1983.

2   US Department of Commerce, Bureau of the Census, *Thirteenth Census of the United States*, 1910, vol. 4, pp.48–9; *Sixteenth Census of the United States*, 1940, vol. 2, pp.94, 96, 230–1; *Seventeenth Census of the United States*, 1950, vol. 1, pp.399–411, vol. 8, p.22, vol. 9, p.19, vol. 20, p.33, vol. 36, p.42.

3   Wage-differential figures from H. J. Lahne, *The Cotton Mill Worker*, New York, Farrar & Rinehart, 1944, pp.165–6; G. Baldanzi, 'The South Is 32 Million Americans,' *Labor and Nation*, vol. 1, 1946, p.43. Figures on women's contribution to family income available in Lahne, *Cotton Mill Worker*, pp.134–5 and in TWUA, *Southern Textile Conference Notes*, Atlanta, Georgia, January 25, 1941, p.12.

4   E. H. Davidson, *Child Labor Legislation in the Southern Textile States*, Chapel Hill, University of North Carolina Press, 1939, p.11. Figures on women workers from Lahne, *Cotton Mill Worker*, p.290, and sixty-first Congress, second Session 1909–10, Senate Documents, *Women and Child Wage-earners*, vol. 1: *Cotton Textile Industry*, Washington, DC, Government Printing Office, 1911, p.29.

5   Sixty-first Congress, second Session, Senate Document no. 645, *Report on Condition of Woman and Child Wage-earners in the United States*, vol. 10: *History of Women in Trade Unions*, by John B. Andrews and W. D. P. Bliss, Washington, DC, Government Printing Office, 1911, p.177.

6   Davidson, *Child Labor Legislation*, pp.18–122.

7   Lahne, *Cotton Mill Worker*, p.124; Davidson, *Child Labor Legislation*, pp.52–68.

8 US Department of Commerce, Bureau of the Census, *Thirteenth Census*, vol. 1; *Sixteenth Census*, vol. 1, Table 23. For detailed information about the exclusion of black women from southern industry, see J. Blackwelder, 'Women in the Work Force: Atlanta, New Orleans, and San Antonio, 1930 to 1940,' *Journal of Urban History*, vol. 4, 1978, pp.331–58, and D. E. Janiewski, 'From Field to Factory: Race, Class, Sex, and the Woman Worker in Durham, 1880–1940,' PhD dissertation, Duke University, 1979. Racial incidents among women workers in Macon and Danville described in Janiewski, 'Sisters Under Their Skins,' p.26.

9 M. Frederickson, 'Four Decades of Change: Black Workers in Southern Textiles, 1941–1981,' in J. Green, ed., *Workers' Struggles, Past and Present: A 'Radical America' Reader*, Philadelphia, Temple University Press, 1983, pp.62–82.

10 E. Kowski to A. J. Muste, September 8, 1928, Box 52, Folder 16, Brookwood Labor College Papers, Archives of Labor History and Urban Affairs, Wayne State University, Detroit, Michigan. For additional material on patriarchal control, see L. Frankel, 'Paternalism and Protest in a Southern Mill Community,' in Karen Sacks and Dorothy Remy, eds, *My Troubles are Going to Have Trouble With Me: Everyday Trials and Triumphs of Women Workers*, New Brunswick, New Jersey, Rutgers University Press, 1984.

11 For a discussion of northern investment in the south and its effects see C. V. Woodward, *The Origins of the New South, 1877–1913*, Baton Rouge, Louisiana State University Press, 1971, pp.291–320, and G. B. Tindall, *The Emergence of the New South, 1913–1945*, Baton Rouge, Louisiana State University Press, 1967, pp.433–72.

12 See L. Pope, *Millhands and Preachers: A Study of Gastonia*, New Haven, Yale University Press, 1942; D. Newman, 'Work and Community Life in a Southern Town,' *Labor History*, vol. 19, 1980, pp.204–25; *Documentary History, ACWA: 1936–1938*, 'Report of the General Executive Board and Proceedings of the Twelfth Biennial Convention of The Amalgamated Clothing Workers of America, May 9–17, 1938,' Atlantic City, New Jersey, New York, Allied Printing Trades' Council, p.412.

13 A detailed description of social control in a southern mill village is provided in Newman, 'Work and Community Life,' pp.204–25.

14 Textile Workers' Union of America, Research Department, 'Housing Study #1,' September 1944, pp.4–5.

15 Marshall, *Labor in the South*, pp.241–2.

16 D. Katzman, *Seven Days a Week: Women and Domestic Service in Industrializing America*, New York, Oxford University Press, 1978, p.196.

17 W. L. Fleming, 'The Servant Problem in a Black Belt Village,' *The*

Sewanee Review Quarterly, vol. 13, 1905, p.15; G. Lerner, ed., *Black Women in White America: A Documentary History*, New York, Vintage Books, 1972, pp.234–8.

18 Interview by the author with Louise Jones, Bynum, North Carolina, October 13, 1976.

19 The 1929 southern textile strikes are documented in Tippett, *When Southern Labor Stirs*, pp.54–172; Marshall, *Labor in the South*, pp.101–20; P. Foner, *Women and the American Labor Movement from World War I to the Present*, New York, The Free Press, 1980, pp.225–43.

20 Tippett, *When Southern Labor Stirs*, p.69; Foner, *Women and the American Labor Movement*, pp.228–9; Marshall, *Labor in the South*, pp.105–7.

21 V. B. Weisbord, *A Radical Life*, Bloomington, Indiana University Press, 1977, p.185.

22 M. Page, *Daughter of the Hills: A Woman's Part in the Coal Miners' Struggle*, New York, Persea Books, 1977; F. Reece, *Against the Current*, Knoxville, Tennessee, Keith Press, 1981, p.2. Material on coal-mining women in K. Kahn, *Hillbilly Women*, New York, Avon Books, 1974 and Foner, *Women and the American Labor Movement*, pp.244–55.

23 B. Korstadt, 'Those Who Were Not Afraid: Winston-Salem, 1943,' in Miller, *Working Lives*, pp.184–99.

24 *Ibid.*, pp.192 and 194.

25 Interview by the author with V. Finley, Marion, North Carolina, July 22, 1975.

26 A. S. Haywood, 'We Propose to Unionize Labor in the South,' *Labor and Nation*, vol. 1, 1946, p.35.

27 'The Awakening of the South,' *American Federationist*, vol. 8, 1901, p.167; G. S. Mitchell, *Textile Unionism in the South*, Chapel Hill, University of North Carolina Press, 1931; Marshall, *Labor in the South*, pp.182–201; C. Ashbaugh and D. McCurry, 'On the Line at Oneita,' in Miller, *Working Lives*, pp.205–14; L. Fink, 'Union Power, Soul Power: The Story of 1199B and Labor's Search for A Southern Strategy,' *Southern Changes*, vol. 5, 1983, pp.9–20.

28 For the history of the Knights of Labor in the south see Andrews and Bliss, *History of Women in Trade Unions*, vol, 10, chapter 4; M. A. McLaurin, *Paternalism and Protest: Southern Cotton Mill Workers and Organised Labor, 1875–1905*, Westport, Connecticut, Greenwood Publishing, 1971, pp.68–119; and L. Fink, *Workingmen's Democracy: The Knights of Labor and American Politics*, Urbana: University of Illinois Press, 1983, pp.149–77. The United Garment Workers (UGW) did organize in the south in the early twentieth century. Of its 96 locals with a 90 percent or more female membership, 18 were located in the south. The UGW sold labels to manufacturers of ready-made clothing. UGW women's locals included 3,200 women members in 1902; 600 of these women were in the south. See Mabel Hurd Willet, *The Employment of Women*

in the Clothing Trade, New York, Columbia University Studies in History, Economics and Public Law, 1902, pp.168–89.

29 Kowski to Muste, September 8, 1928.

30 Marshall, *Labor in the South*, pp.102–5; A. Shields, 'Organizing the South: How Labor Movement Can Do this Job,' *Labor Age*, vol. 17, 1928, pp.4–7.

31 The YWCA in the south is discussed in M. Frederickson, 'Citizens for Democracy: The Industrial Programs of the YWCA,' in J.L. Kornbluh and M. Frederickson, eds, *Sisterhood and Solidarity: Workers' Education for Women, 1914–1984*, Philadelphia, Temple University Press, 1984; the NWTUL's southern work is documented in G. Boone, *The Women's Trade Union League in Great Britain and the United States of America*, New York, Columbia University Press, 1942, pp.64–110; the Southern Summer School is described in M. Frederickson, 'A Place to Speak Our Minds,' in Miller, *Working Lives*, pp.155–65.

32 Frederickson, 'Citizens for Democracy.'

33 Louise Leonard Reports, Industrial Department, 1922–6, YWCA National Board Archives, New York City.

34 Boone, *The Women's Trade Union League*, pp.163–4.

35 E. Christman, 'Summary of Activities,' March 1, 1927 to February 1, 1928 (Reel 4), National Women's Trade Union League Papers, Library of Congress, Washington, DC.

36 Christman to Members of the Executive Board, June 29, 1927, p.1 (Reel 4); Christman to the Presidents and Secretaries of Local Leagues and Committees, September 19, 1929 (Reel 5).

37 Christman to Members of the Executive Board, June 29, 1927, p.4.

38 Frederickson, 'A Place to Speak Our Minds'; quotation from Mary Jordon, Norfolk, Virginia, Southern Summer School Scrapbook, 1927, Southern School Papers, American Labor Education Service Records, 1927–62, Labor-Management Documentation Center, Cornell University, Ithaca, New York.

39 L. R. Mason, 'The CIO in the South,' *The South and World Affairs*, vol. 6, 1944. Interviews by the author with: P. Knight, Greensboro, North Carolina, March 19, 1980; P. H. Robkin, New York City, November 2, 1974; J. Spencer Pedigo, Charlotte, North Carolina, July 25, 1975.

40 Marshall, *Labor in the South*, pp.246–69; 'Labor Drives South,' *Fortune*, vol. 34, 1946, p.138.

41 Textile Workers of America, 'What Every Woman Should Know,' New York, 1946. See 'Operation Dixie: The CIO Organizing Committee Papers, 1946–1953,' New York, Microfilming Corporation of America, 1980, especially Series IV, 'Virginia, 1937–1953' (Reel 55), pp.1,150–92.

42 Marshall, *Labor in the South*, pp.270–82. The Henderson strike is analyzed in Frankel, 'Paternalism and Protest.' The J. P. Stevens campaign in Roanoke Rapids is documented in M. Conway, *Rise, Gonna, Rise*, New York, Anchor Press, 1979.

43 Frederickson, 'Four Decades of Change,' p.78.

44 P. McLendon, 'Sarah Boykin: "I'm Still Here," ' *Facing South*, Chapel Hill, Institute of Southern Studies, 1980.
45 Ashbaugh and McCurry, 'On the Line at Oneita,' pp.205–14; S. Hoffius, 'Charleston Hospital Workers' Strike, 1969,' in Miller, *Working Lives*, pp.244–58; Fink, *Workingmen's Democracy*, pp.9–20.
46 Telephone interview by the author with C. Cameron, Director, Atlanta 9 to 5, January 18, 1984.

9

'Where I was a person': The Ladies' Auxiliary in the 1934 Minneapolis Teamsters' strikes[1]

Marjorie Penn Lasky

Women's role in the organized labor movement has never been limited to their participation as workers in unions. As the preceding chapters by Hyman, Cameron and Long all attest, women's labor activism, much more than men's, extends outside of the workplace and into the larger community. One classic form of female community activity on behalf of the labor movement is that of the women's auxiliaries, which played a particularly important role in the massive organizational strikes of the 1930s. In this chapter, Marjorie Penn Lasky analyzes the history of the Ladies' Auxiliary in the 1934 Minneapolis Teamsters' strikes, drawing on previously unexplored sources and oral histories. Lasky uses this case study as a means to look at some of the broader issues relating to the auxiliary as an organizational form. Auxiliaries performed highly stereotypical 'women's work' within the labor movement – preparing food, administering first aid and performing union office work during strikes, for example – all on behalf of auxiliary members' husbands. Sometimes, however, auxiliary activities spilled beyond the boundaries of conventional female roles, especially during strikes, when women often assumed quasi-military responsibilities. Under these circumstances, auxiliaries could transform the consciousness of their members in ways which threatened to undermine the existing structure of female subordination in the family and in society. Lasky suggests, however, that this potential for female radicalization within auxiliaries was severely constrained, both ideologically, in that women's militancy was explicitly defined as an extension of their domestic roles and responsibilities, and politically, in that male union leaders remained in authority over the activities of auxiliaries.

On July 2, 1934, the newspaper of Minneapolis Teamsters, Local 574, carried the following appeal for women's support:

> The Ladies' Auxiliary to Local 574 was formed during the heat of battle in the May [1934] strike and has enjoyed a healthy growth through the efforts of a small group of militant women who served so faithfully during the strike . . . You, too, must realize that, in this struggle for a decent living, for the right to educate your children and give them a fair chance to continue to live decently after you have passed on, you must take your place beside your husband. His struggle is your struggle. His wages are your livelihood. Stand shoulder to shoulder with him and fight. What can you do? Attend the Auxiliary meetings the second and fourth Mondays of each month. Take an active part in the work of the organization. Help to further the cause for which your husband is fighting.[2]

Locked in a bitter struggle against the city's Employers' Association, the local relied on traditional gender ideology to mobilize women in the public sphere. Among trade unionists, this technique was not new. At the turn of the century, for example, the Western Federation of Miners attempted to organize working-class women in Cripple Creek, Colorado, by appealing to their 'moral and domestic concerns.'[3] And, in 1916, the famous Mother Jones highlighted women's supportive role when she urged the wives of striking streetcarmen in El Paso, Texas, to 'organize if you want your men to earn a decent wage.' Exhorting these women to 'think of your babies and their future,' Jones contended that 'it is the women who must organize to help the men.'[4]

Auxiliary activities also reflected traditional ideas about gender. As Local 574's newspaper appeal said, auxiliary members developed a 'faith and understanding . . . of the role women are destined to play in the movement . . . through their experiences in the first aid station, in the commissary, and in the office at strike headquarters, and through their observations of grim reality on the picket lines.'[5]

Although ambiguous about women's participation as pickets, this message clearly revealed that auxiliaries performed 'women's work' within the labor movement. Organizationally, auxiliaries appeared as public extensions of domesticity, recreating women's separate sphere and reinforcing gender stereotypes.

In practice, however, these organizations often embodied liberating potential. During strikes, when auxiliaries emerged most vigorously, women's behavior continually threatened to spill beyond the bounds of traditional roles. Particularly when family needs went unmet or when authorities refused to yield, women willingly 'bashed in' heads, served as pickets, or otherwise engaged in life-endangering activities. Moreover, exhilarated by their public roles, auxiliary members often became increasingly aware of their own abilities and dissatisfied with domestic responsibilities. In this respect, auxiliaries harbored a rudimentary feminism – a willingness to confront male authority along with an unarticulated acknowledgment of life beyond domesticity.[6] Given an opportunity, auxiliary participants might have evolved into self-conscious opponents of male domination.

Auxiliary members, however, were mobilized precisely because they could be counted upon to do women's work in the public sphere. As conventional females, they accepted the idea of women's proper place, and, although willing to confront unjust authorities, they had little incentive to challenge male supremacy. Even when a feminist movement existed alongside auxiliaries, working-class housewives were rarely touched by feminist ideas. Rather, these women were constrained by the conservative nature of the very ideology that had enabled them to organize.

Male union members also inhibited an auxiliary's liberating potential. As adherents of traditional gender ideology, men, too, acted to reinforce conventional roles. Moreover, they usually required that women accede to union authority; otherwise, unions might withdraw support, leaving auxiliary members with little reason or motivation to persist. Women's obeisance, however, did not guarantee an auxiliary's permanence. Most auxiliaries were born during crises, when unions needed women's help, and they generally died when that need ended. As a consequence, auxiliary members had little time to consider the potential impact of their growing autonomy, even if they were so inclined.

While auxiliaries did not foster a self-conscious feminism, they inevitably loosened some traditional bonds, and, for a few women, produced longer-lasting changes. Participating in labor struggles narrowed the differences in the experiences and worldviews of women and men, as both became more class conscious and less attached to the political and economic status quo. Auxiliary activity did not permanently transform gender roles, but it permitted and sometimes even encouraged women's radicalization along class lines – a transformation more compatible with their own experiences, and probably more permissible in male eyes. Such radicalization was especially likely in the auxiliary of Teamsters' Local 574 since, at the time of the Minneapolis conflict, a handful of Trotskyists and their supporters controlled both the union's strike committee and the auxiliary.[7] Examining the development and dissolution of Local 574's auxiliary, therefore, makes it possible to explore both the dynamic interplay between traditional gender ideology and unconventional female behavior, and the potential for radicalization within auxiliaries.

Several factors contributed to the Minneapolis upheaval.[8] Significant among these were the city's depressed economy, the anti-union policies of the Citizens' Alliance, 'a mysterious organization [of bankers and business executives] with no known membership but immense power and resources,' and the oppressive conditions within the city's trucking industry.[9] In the 1920s, wages across the US increased by 11 percent; in Minneapolis, they rose only 2 percent. The situation worsened with the coming of the Depression. By spring 1934, unemployed and dependants made up one-third of the population of Minneapolis and surrounding Hennepin County. Thousands of families were on a subsistence dole. Warehousemen earned $9 a week; truckers $12–18 a week for stints lasting between fifty-four and ninety hours.[10] Despite section 7a of the NIRA, Minneapolis employers, backed by the Citizens' Alliance, refused to deal with the city's AFL-led Teamsters' local. Early in 1934, the previously moribund local initiated a massive campaign to organize drivers and the inside workers – those employees who labored in warehouses and offices using transportation services. Through this effort, the local hoped to control the entire urban transportation industry, so that when the union struck, all of Minneapolis would be affected.

The 1934 struggle actually involved three separate strikes, each longer and bloodier than the previous one. The initial three-day confrontation in February gained bargaining rights for coalyard-workers. Building upon this victory, the local organized thousands of transportation workers, and by May was prepared to carry out a city-wide strike for union recognition. This strike, which lasted eleven days, was both violent and successful. Pickets halted almost all commercial trucks and common carriers, while major battles with police and a deputized citizens' army left two special deputies dead, and scores of participants injured. These confrontations brought federal mediators and the state's governor, Floyd Olson, into negotiations, and the strike quickly ended. The agreement between the local and employers, however, unraveled over an ambiguous passage concerning the rights of inside workers. When employers refused to recognize the local as representing these workers, Local 574 called another strike. During this longer, more militant five-week confrontation in July and August, union pickets again im-mobilized the city's transportation system. Tempers flared, and on July 20 – Bloody Friday – police fired into a crowd of pickets, injuring forty-seven, two of whom later died. Olson declared martial law, and the National Guard occupied Minneapolis. A strike stale-mate, which began in August, ended two weeks later with a settle-ment under which Local 574 gained the right to represent employees inside the major Minneapolis produce houses.

Several contemporary accounts described the strikes in re-volutionary terms. But, as Trotskyist strike leader Farrell Dobbs has pointed out, the struggle more closely resembled a traditional labor dispute than a proletarian uprising.[11] Local 574 was battling for traditional trade union goals: recognition, higher wages and seniority rights. Although some contemporaries (and their successors among New Left historians) idealized the revolutionary potential of the struggle, in fact militant postures vanished once union goals had been achieved.[12] This was also true of the auxiliary's actions that threatened traditional gender roles: once the immediate crisis ended, traditional ways reasserted themselves, and women's militancy became a distant memory.

The rationale for bringing women into the struggle itself illustrates the conventional nature of this dispute. The Trotskyists who led the strike, like most trade union men, were worried about the 'nagging wife syndrome' – that is, women pleading for their husbands to return to work in the face of dwindling financial resources.[13] To eliminate this problem, Carl Skoglund, prior to the May strike, proposed that the union mobilize workers' wives by forming an auxiliary.[14] The membership endorsed Skoglund's idea unenthusiastically, since most of them saw union activity as their occasional 'night out.'[15] Ignoring this objection, the Trotskyists quickly organized the women's group. They enlisted the wives of two Trotskyist leaders – Clara Dunne, a member of the Trotskyist Communist League of America, and Marvel Scholl (Dobbs), then a political neophyte.[16] Dunne and Scholl appeared at union meetings and urged members to recruit their wives, mothers, sisters or sweethearts into the auxiliary. At first, the men scoffed and jokingly demanded to know what work women could perform. Hoping to reassure them that auxiliary activities would not undermine women's traditional responsibilities, Scholl and Dunne listed a variety of tasks, none of which required women's participation on the front lines. Although most union members remained relatively unconvinced, some took the message home.[17]

By the beginning of May, about twenty-five women had responded. Once the strike began, the wives of men in other unions volunteered their services, but only relatives of Local 574 members could join the auxiliary. Actual membership probably never exceeded fifty women, most of them middle-aged. In fact, auxiliary members, on the average, were older than male pickets because they were primarily wives of long-time union members, who, through their marriages, had come to understand trade union principles.[18] Many of the union's new recruits, on the other hand, were young and novices in trade unionism. A woman who occasionally helped at strike headquarters recalls that, at the time, she, the 20-year-old wife of a local Teamster, knew nothing about trade unions. Although she did visit headquarters to discover what was going on, she was unable to give much time to the union's cause.[19] She may have been representative of other young women who remained at home because of children or because they had little understanding or sympathy with the local's goals.

Auxiliary leaders, particularly Scholl, under Trotskyist tutelage, shaped the inexperienced and disorganized women's group into a disciplined core of dedicated union supporters. Initially, women's militancy expressed itself in long hours spent at assigned tasks. Women, dressed in house-dresses, and girls, in overalls, worked shifts ranging from four to eight hours.[20] They frequently collapsed as a result of laboring beyond their designated times or forgetting 'to visit the commissary for something to eat.'[21] The auxiliary did not provide child-care – there was 'no place, no money, no nothing,' least of all a sustaining ideology. Women with small children split shifts with other family members – 'wives . . . daughters, and grandmothers . . . would divide the day . . . between them.'[22] Other mothers depended upon homebound relatives or friends for help.

Most auxiliary members easily accommodated themselves to their new, public roles. In the commissary, about twenty-five women were supervised by male volunteers from the sympathetic cooks' and waiters' union. Inexperienced in mass cooking, the women were soon preparing coffee, slicing bread and meat, and putting together sandwiches for thousands of people. Spam was the staple – to the point that Scholl recently confided how her stomach 'turns over' whenever she sees it on grocery shelves today.[23]

Other chores proved less formidable. In the office, women collected initiation fees and dues, issued union buttons, and sent new recruits to whoever was in charge of pickets. First aid required dressing minor cuts and bruises, using the medication auxiliary members solicited from their local druggists. They also canvassed 'mom and pop' grocers and butchers who depended upon working-class patronage for contributions; despite the success of such appeals, however, they ended up purchasing most of their supplies.

While reflecting conventional ideas about women's proper place, auxiliary activities also nurtured the seeds of women's autonomy. Indeed, as the auxiliary's responsibilities expanded, 'unfeminine' behavior emerged, and women's militancy threatened to spill over the boundaries of women's separate sphere. Auxiliary activity, then, had an ambiguous legacy. On the one hand, women militantly confronted male authorities; on the other, they willingly accepted limits on their behavior.

Women's roles moved beyond traditional expectations soon after the first bloody battle. Scholl recently described how she helped a doctor sew a striker's scalp into place with nothing 'more antiseptic than iodine,' and how, to avoid police, she drove three or four carfuls of injured pickets requiring hospitalization through the backstreets of Minneapolis.²⁴ That same evening, several auxiliary members, eager for action, joined male pickets to stop truck deliveries in Tribune Alley. Arriving at an ambush arranged by an *agent provocateur*, almost everyone was severely beaten by police and hired thugs. Skoglund later recollected that when they brought the women back to headquarters, 'all of them were mutilated and covered with blood, two or three with broken legs; several stayed unconscious for hours.'²⁵

Rather than convincing the Trotskyists that the auxiliary deserved a place on the picket line, the incident strengthened the men's resolve to bar women from picketing. Possibly, they intended to protect auxiliary members from police brutality. But their concept of how the auxiliary should function also influenced their decision. The Trotskyists envisioned the women's organization as a disciplined support group which would perform certain gender-related tasks within a stable, male-defined environment. This remained the plan, even though it was recognized that 'helpless' women facing hordes of armed authorities could be a powerful propagandizing tool. For example, a leaflet issued after the Tribune Alley ambush had pictured battered and bandaged women to dramatize 'what police and gunmen of the Citizens' Alliance do to workers when they ask for a living wage.'²⁶ Perhaps seeking similar opportunities, the union tried to recruit non-auxiliary women as pickets, but met with only minimal success.²⁷

Even as they sought to restrict the auxiliary, the Trotskyists acted ambivalently. Perceiving propagandizing possibilities, they sometimes used auxiliary members in volatile situations. On May 21, when the union expected violence, they ordered the auxiliary to stay away from the Central Market, but to march on City Hall. The women were instructed to demand that the mayor fire the police chief, withdraw the special deputies, and stop police interference with pickets.

Scholl led the march in her car, with Local 574's banner on top. Supporters waved placards telling the mayor to 'Take your hired thugs away,' and, as onlookers joined in, the crowd swelled. The women, encountering armed police, insisted upon seeing the mayor, and a small delegation, led by Scholl and Dunne, was allowed inside.²⁸ When the mayor refused to meet with them, the women reluctantly gave his assistant their demands.

When they rejoined the group gathered outside, they found two women urging the crowd to join the men in battle and accusing Scholl and Dunne of cowardice for their refusal to do so. Some might view these women as feminists seeking women's equal participation in the struggle, or as stooges, intent upon disrupting the march. Scholl offers a somewhat different interpretation. Identifying one woman as a New York Trotskyist sent to aid her Minneapolis comrades, she maintains that the incident involved some 'learned' New Yorkers who, thinking they were 'far superior' to the Minneapolis trade unionists, tried to take over.[29] Whatever their intentions, these two women were unsuccessful. Scholl and Dunne quickly silenced them, and the crowd dispersed. Media coverage was minimal, probably less than the Trotskyists expected, given the propagandizing potential of women demanding an end to police brutality at the moment that their husbands were being beaten.

When the May strike ended, shortly after the women's march, auxiliary numbers dwindled. By July, this process was reversed when Scholl and Dunne began recruiting again, following union orders to prepare for a longer, more violent struggle. Appeals in *The Organizer* and word-of-mouth messages emphasizing women's freedom 'from washing dishes and attending kids sixteen hours a day' brought in enough new members to formalize the structure of the auxiliary.[30] For the first time, elections were held, dues established, meeting dates set, and committees formed.

During this period, the women's activities continued to be extensions of domestic work, and, as before, innovation and expanded roles occasioned feminist undertones. As experienced caretakers, women assumed new responsibilities in caring for the union's needy. To obtain relief for workers not rehired, auxiliary members argued on behalf of individual applicants before the city's Board of Aldermen. Rarely successful in these endeavors, they had more luck in finding houses for evicted families. 'Dressing up in borrowed clothes and acting the part of women with good incomes,' auxiliary members rented homes in each tenant's name, and, with union funds, placed deposits on rent and utilities.[31] To aid the heavily indebted local, auxiliary members solicited money from other unions, clubs, auxiliaries and private individuals. One Saturday night, at an auxiliary-sponsored dance, free beer (via 'the back door of a brewery') and hotdogs (similar obtained) provided sustenance, as two orchestras enlivened the festivities – one playing while the other rested. With part of the $700 profit, auxiliary members purchased groceries for families on relief, a practice they continued throughout the ensuing strike.[32] Determined to cope with any medical emergency, the women also canvassed local pharmacies for 'antiseptics for the treatment of minor abrasions, colds and other slight ailments,' and collected cots, sterilizers, and instruments 'for minor surgery.'[33] Supervised by an auxiliary member, women and men sold *The Organizer* on street corners, in bars, restaurants, beauty parlors – or wherever they found a promising clientele. By July 16, when the union struck, auxiliary committees were in top form.

The strike, of course, brought new challenges. In the commissary, cooking took place on an unanticipated scale. Pickets in May had stopped all trucks coming into Minneapolis and had thereby antagonized or neutralized local farmers, but Teamsters and farmers had since then worked out a compromise. In exchange for a newly established and union-recognized produce market, farmers donated daily leftovers to the workers' kitchen. Members of the Farmers' Holiday Association also dispatched trucks to nearby states for contributions. Hot meals – meat, potatoes, vegetables, soups and stew – became daily commissary fare; on family day, Sunday, chicken was served. On an average, 5,000 meals were dished up each day; some days, 15,000, within a twenty-four-hour period.[34]

Tactically, the workers' kitchen was an inspiration. It not only fed its army well, but, just as importantly, it encouraged community solidarity – providing the only arena where the strikers from many different businesses, and their families, could stay in touch with each other and with strike events. Even if a woman didn't assist the auxiliary, coming to headquarters for a free meal exposed her to union activities – and perhaps undermined a tendency toward the 'nagging wife syndrome.'

Although stereotypical, commissary work also furthered women's autonomy. Imagine, as Meridel Le Sueur observed, the 'foreman . . . an efficient stout woman, bawling out . . . like any mother . . . a striker who had thrown the dregs of [his] coffee out the open window . . . "You aren't dry behind the ears yet," she says. "Don't you know we have to keep order here?" . . . Everyone listened . . . as if they were all ashamed. No one else will throw dregs or crumbs out the window.'[35]

Or picture women watching their husbands perform 'women's work.' For each meal, the strike committee assigned men to 'help' cook, wash dishes, clear tables, lift and wash pots and scrub floors. In her diary, organized from notes kept during the strike, Scholl recorded how you could always look at a woman and know if her husband was on duty: 'Her eyes would twinkle and she would probably think, "Now he knows what it's like." '[36] Presumably, men gave up this activity once the strike ended; for a brief period, though, women (and men) must have glimpsed 'another way.' Of course, men doing women's work may have reinforced conventional roles, if the other way became equated solely with crises, rather than everyday life.

In distributing *The Organizer*, women moved beyond traditional roles and into the public sphere. They faced the hostility of local citizens, such as the 'swell lady on Nicollet' Street who, when offered an *Organizer*, 'barked . . . "Where do you think you are, Russia?" ' and the harassment of local officials.[37] On August 4, the newspaper reported how a soldier approached a saleslady in a beer parlor, grabbed her papers, threw them to the ground, poured beer over them, spat, and then cursed and struck her. Although the paper threatened 'special steps' to prevent similar offences, it never specified how it would protect its distributors.[38]

Feelings of fear and intimidation also pushed women into non-conventional behavior. In a recent interview and in her diary, Scholl listed numerous intimidating episodes of harassment, arrests, beatings and shootings, as well as kidnapping threats against her children and rumors of possible assassinations. She recalled a vacant apartment across the street from her home with men positioned at the window at all times; a hole dug by the city on the corner of her street which was left unfilled and guarded by a group of men; and an evening when she returned home late to encounter a man hidden behind the woodpile, who, upon discovering Scholl, not her husband, fled.[39] Another auxiliary member relates that, in response to phone callers threatening to 'gun her family down,' her children 'didn't go out to play, [not] even on the front porch.' Accompanied to school by their grandmother, these children were warned 'not to talk to anyone and not to take anything from anybody.'[40] Both auxiliary members remember how they were 'scared to death' during the strikes. But, as Scholl explains;

> somehow or other, when you're in a situation like that, you don't have the same kind of fear you would have in what you could call normal life, and someone walked into your house or stood up in the dark . . . You're scared, you shake, and all . . . that stuff, but it's not the same.

Women (and men) needed to repress their fears since 'they had a job to do and . . . were determined to do it the best they could.'[41]

Perhaps the most fearful episode during the five-week strike was Bloody Friday. In her diary, Scholl described headquarters that day:

> Everything was different. Perhaps the fact that men were gradually being weeded out . . . helped create this atmosphere. Yet, I honestly believe there wasn't a woman . . . who had any idea just what was behind the feeling of dread. After the noon hour, headquarters was strangely empty . . . It was so quiet that it was almost eerie. Sensitivity was high, nerves tense, a quarrel broke out between two of the women. They had never especially loved one another and now . . . nerves cracked. Settling the battle . . . took a little time and gave the peacemakers a chance to work off some of our own steam. And then all too suddenly, the emptiness gave way to overcrowding, the stillness, to the awful siren of the ambulance, and the spotless white of the hospital to appalling red; blood red . . . When the first man was carried in, foaming at the mouth, gray as cement, unconscious, someone screamed . . . In less time than it can be told, forty-seven men . . . lay on improvised cots, their bodies riddled with bullet wounds . . . Action – water, alcohol, cotton, men and women bathing horrid blue welts from which blood oozed. Cutting away clothing. Lighting cigarettes for the men who lay there, gripping their hands, biting their lips, to keep from screaming. And then the scream of ambulances. Clear the way! Stand back! Let the cars into the garage. One by one they back in, and when they come out they are loaded with their cargo of suffering humanity . . . Full to the brim, they back out . . . until forty-seven men were on their way to beds of pain and some to oblivion.[42]

After Bloody Friday, auxiliary members spent hours caring for the wounded and cleaning headquarters. And, in the wake of this dramatic event, Minneapolis residents, including many middle-class women, volunteered to help the strikers.

When middle-class women appeared at headquarters, auxiliary leaders faced an unforeseen dilemma. Although these new volunteers could assist in several auxiliary tasks, class antagonism forced Scholl and Dunne to separate them from the bulk of working-class recruits. Middle-class women, 'so overcome with their own kindness,' unknowingly patronized their working-class peers.[43] To avoid confrontations, therefore, 'petit bourgeois' women were assigned to search for housing, to distribute The Organizer, to raise money, and to serve on the newly organized hospital committee, which provided hospitalized strikers with the 'creature comforts' they desired. Auxiliary leaders also acceded to the wishes of Mrs Carle, the stout commissary 'foreman' of Meridel Le Sueur's account, who, fearing middle-class women would question her orders, had refused to accept them on her crew.[44]

Carle's hesitation suggests that a second factor nurtured class antagonism – the relative autonomy of middle-class women. Because these women had little or no self-interest in advancing the union's cause, and probably volunteered out of emotional reactions to Bloody Friday or out of a desire to aid the 'oppressed,' they might have been less willing than working-class women to accept the authority of working-class men, and very reluctant to take orders from working-class women. Class differences, rather than their shared gender, shaped the relations between auxiliary members and their 'white gloved' allies.[45]

Of any single incident, Bloody Friday mobilized the largest number of new volunteers. It also had the most potential to radicalize auxiliary members, and indeed it was after this event that Scholl declared her intention to join the Communist League of America. Shocked by the day's events, and 'unclear what the League [was] all about, [she] knew whatever it [was], if it [was] against what happened,' she wanted 'to take part.'[46] Yet her response was exceptional: no auxiliary members followed Scholl's example.

Throughout Scholl's life, several factors nurtured her radicalization. These included a radical heritage in her family of origin, kept alive by her stepfather, a Debsian socialist. Scholl's relationship with this man was contradictory, but her rebellion against his authoritarianism and, possibly, an identification with his sense of injustice, may have fostered her life-long dislike of unjust authority. Also important were her non-status-seeking approach to life, her unhappiness as a housewife, and her self-education.

Perhaps most critical, though, was her marriage to Farrell Dobbs. It was through Dobbs, who became a Trotskyist after the February strike, that Scholl came to understand the union's struggle, and began to develop a revolutionary perspective. His radical affiliation also implicitly permitted her deviance, for 'she desire[d and was able] to go where [he] went, wherever that was to be.'[47] Other auxiliary members had ethnic backgrounds similar to Scholl's, most being Scandinavian or German, and were probably exposed to Minnesota's widespread radical heritage. But none, other than Dunne, was married to a Trotskyist.[48] Presumably, therefore, they lacked the access to a political education which Scholl's personal circumstances afforded her. More importantly, without their husbands' example or approval, these women, who accepted traditional ideas of spousal authority, were most unlikely to become revolutionaries, even if they wanted to. Ironically, among the few women married to Trotskyists in Local 574, only two – Clara Dunne and Scholl – embraced the Communist League. The others either remained neutral or were openly hostile, but none joined the auxiliary.

In examining the lack of radicalism among auxiliary members, the question arises as to why Clara Dunne, the auxiliary's president, was unable to politicize the other women. In practice, Dunne didn't lead the organization. Suffering from personal problems, which worsened as the strikes progressed, she sometimes failed even to appear at headquarters.[49] If anything, she may have been a negative model for a working-class woman's introduction to radical politics.

And so, except for Scholl, the auxiliary failed to produce class-conscious radicals. Nevertheless, the Trotskyists had originally perceived its radicalizing potential. From the early 1930s on, radical organizations, especially the Communist Party, acknowledged that the mobilization of working-class housewives might advance the class struggle. Communists initiated consumers' groups, councils for the unemployed, and auxiliaries, and, in the process, sought to educate participants politically.[50] The Trotskyists also followed this strategy, and, with the auxiliary, discerned an ideal opportunity to educate and recruit among this homebound population. Intending to continue the auxiliary once the strikes had ended, the Trotskyists also planned for a structured educational program on trade unionism.[51] The program never materialized during the strikes, probably because the small size and limited resources of the Trotskyist group prevented them from offering an educational program and waging a successful union strugle simultaneously.

But the absence of an educational program and their eventual decision to dissolve the auxiliary also reflect the fact that the Trotskyists accepted traditional ideas about gender, and evaluated women's abilities accordingly. This was particularly apparent in their reactions to the growth of a faction within the union and auxiliary, and in their attempts to control the auxiliary.

During the interval between the May and July strikes, some former members of the union's executive board and their supporters coalesced into a faction seeking to overthrow the Trotskyists. Relatively quiet until July, faction sympathizers among the women then initiated quarrels, resulting in hair-pulling matches, and spread rumors, using red-scare tactics to arouse fear. Aware of the trouble, Scholl knew nothing about its source and, throughout the strike, believed the fights resulted from women's inability to work together.[52] The Trotskyists decided not to tell Scholl and Dunne about the faction since they feared that auxiliary leaders lacked the experience to keep the women's organization functioning and deal with the ramifications of what was happening.[53]

More overtly, the Trotskyists' methods of controlling the auxiliary testified to their belief in women's subordination and to their desire to create a disciplined support group. Scholl became a direct link between the union and auxiliary by attending strike committee meetings, where she reported on the women's needs and received instructions.[54] Also, when an auxiliary activity appeared inefficient, the Trotskyists placed men in control. For example, responding to pickets' complaints in mid-July about 'food not get[ting] out fast enough,' the strike committee appointed five men to take 'full charge' of the commissary and to establish guidelines.[55] In addition, male committees seemed to parallel auxiliary committees, so that, if necessary, 'watchdogs' could oversee the women's actions.[56] Thus, while traditional gender ideology designated separate spheres, and thereby insured women's relative autonomy, it also perpetuated male authority, and a continual restraint upon that autonomy.

That the Trotskyists held conventional ideas about women should not be surprising. To imagine that, because they were revolutionary socialists, they might view women differently from the general public, would be to misread the hegemonic quality of traditional gender ideology during the 1930s, and the ways in which this ideology neatly fits into the ideas and practices of radical movements. According to radical theoreticians, the liberation of gender would follow the liberation of class. In practice, this meant that, in Minneapolis, men ran the strike and, if necessary, the auxiliary. It also meant that Trotskyists, like other radicals, concentrated more on organizing working-class men, especially in heavy industry, than on organizing either women wage-earners, viewed as temporary workers, or working-class housewives. Because of their isolation, relative lack of class consciousness, and obedience to spousal authority, this last group proved particularly resistant to radicalization. Given the Trotskyists' limited resources and ideological predilections, they might well have regarded the gains from organizing housewives as not worth the effort.

This attitude was evident in the decision to dissolve the auxiliary. By the end of the strike, the faction among the women had grown so vicious that the Trotskyists feared the auxiliary might become an effective base for the opposition. They therefore declared the women's organization had no future function.[57] Whether they actually believed this is doubtful, especially given their original inclination to continue the organization. Perhaps they feared the women's behavior was beyond control. Most likely, given the difficulty of radicalizing working-class housewives, they decided the risks outweighed the advantages. So, instead of educating auxiliary leaders on the faction's existence, and allowing the women to resolve the dispute themselves, or instructing them on how to do so, the Trotskyists moved to disband the auxiliary. The women 'just went home, feeling numb, knowing they [had done] a good job . . . but now suddenly kicked back into the kitchen. And, [for Scholl], it wasn't a good feeling, not a good feeling at all. Suddenly this whole new world that [she] had found outside [her] home was pulled out from under [her] feet.'[58]

For most women, these events spelled a return to conventional roles. Recently, an auxiliary member confided that, for a while after the strikes, she was 'completely lost.' But then, she went on, 'you know, you fall back into the routine of raising your family.'[59] No one revived the organization and, while some members saw each other at union gatherings, for most the traditional way of life probably reasserted itself.

Why didn't the women fight to continue the auxiliary? At the end of the strike, many of them, suffering from exhaustion and disrupted home lives, may have welcomed a respite from the daily turmoil. Furthermore, it is difficult to envision auxiliary members, who rarely questioned orders during the strikes, now challenging male authority. To do so required an autonomy or counter-ideology they did not possess. Even though they 'innovated' and 'deviated,' they rarely 'defied.'

Women's internalization of conventional gender ideology and the lack of an alternative ideology only partially explain their inability to challenge union orders. Also crucial were men's actions to discourage female autonomy. As has been shown, the Trotskyists actively curbed women's behavior and defused women's militancy. So, too, did the union rank and file. Most men only grudgingly accepted women's presence at headquarters. Occasionally, a picket demanded to know why a woman wasn't home where she belonged, or who was caring for her children while she was working. Although women responded with cutting retorts, these exchanges rarely moved them beyond traditional ideas of female subservience.[60]

One controversy which arose during the July strike is especially revealing about rank-and-file reactions to the auxiliary, when its presence constrained male behavior. Almost every evening, around 11 o'clock, prostitutes arrived at strike headquarters; sexual activities never took place inside the building, but they did occur in the parking lot outside. To conceal this from the auxiliary, the strike committee imposed an 11 p.m. curfew on women volunteers.[61] Paradoxically, however, men who condoned male patronage of prostitutes, and worried about the auxiliary's restraining influence, questioned the sexual actions of their newly liberated wives.

After the National Guard occupied Minneapolis, soldiers arrested male pickets and held them in a military stockade. An auxiliary committee visited the prisoners, supplying what they needed as far as military regulations would allow, listening to their complaints, and dealing with family matters such as the need for rent money or food. But, at a strike committee meeting, the union's president reported that the prisoners did 'not feel free to talk to the women, and [he, therefore] recommended that two men be put on the Committee to take care of Stockade matters.' As another strike leader explained, 'the men in the stockade [felt] that their wives in the kitchen, etc. [were] running around and [did] not feel like confiding such matters to the Auxiliary committee.'[62] While both divorces and marriages among strike participants took place, there was no evidence of married women 'running around.'[63]

In the 1930s, as the history of the auxiliary suggests, working-class housewives could not move beyond their conventional roles unless men permitted them to do so. Family structure, and the traditional gender ideology which enforced that structure, bound these women to their homes and limited their access to public institutions and ideas. At the same time, male unions could use that same structure and ideology to organize women into auxiliaries and, when necessary, to restrain 'unfeminine' actions. Men were critical to the auxiliaries, both as initiators and, by and large, as definers of female behavior. A woman might acknowledge, as Scholl recently did, that auxiliary work was 'where I was a person,' and auxiliary activities might push her into challenging male authority or testing the boundaries of women's separate sphere.[64] Nevertheless, men's traditional views on gender, and their active enforcement of those views, combined with women's own conventionalism to constrain any self-conscious feminism. Auxiliary activities did heighten women's sense of class inequities. While men might share that perspective, transforming it into a radical commitment still required the permission and, probably, initiation of men, particularly male relations.

The Depression itself only minimally affected the mobilization and actions of Local 574's auxiliary. Granted, economic deprivation nurtured the Minneapolis rebellion, and the passage of section 7a of the NIRA created 'a favorable psychology for the growth of labor organizations.'[65] Also, the Depression placed increasing psychological and monetary burdens on working-class housewives — burdens which might have motivated women's mobilization and inspired their militancy. But neither the form nor recruitment appeals were new — indeed, the union explicitly acknowledged the auxiliary of the Progressive Miners of Illinois as its model.[66] As such, Local 574's auxiliary might have been mobilized during any Teamster crisis prior to the time when substantial numbers of women entering the workforce limited the pool of potential auxiliary recruits.

On the other hand, the short life of Local 574's auxiliary did restrict its liberating potential. During the few hectic months of its existence, women had little time to reflect on the skills they were using, the ideas they were developing, or the actions they had taken. If the organization had been born long before the strikes, or had women with previous experience in the public sphere among its members, auxiliary members might have been more inclined to oppose union orders or resist a return to traditional ways. They might also have been more receptive to radical political views.

To explore this dynamic between the length of time of an auxiliary's existence, the presence of women active in the public sphere, and the transformation of women's consciousness of gender or class, it is useful to compare the history of Local 574's auxiliary with other cases — both crisis-borne and long-lived auxiliaries.[67] While unions have frequently used traditional gender ideology to mobilize working-class housewives, it has been suggested that women may have joined these organizations momentarily to liberate themselves from conventional domesticity.[68] But, since auxiliary organizers consistently used familial arguments, and since domestic concerns among these women generally overshadowed any recognition of individual needs, surely the most effective appeal was based upon women's roles within the family.

The limited literature on other auxiliaries implies that, although conventional ideology influenced their organizational form, some acted more independently than Local 574's. Because the interactions between auxiliaries and union authorities — and even among auxiliary members themselves — are relatively unanalyzed, the impetus for independence remains obscure. Some strike situations nurtured autonomous actions, as in the 1957 Mine, Mill and Smelters' strike, made famous in the documentary film *Salt of the Earth*. Here, women replaced men on the picket line, as their husbands, prohibited from picketing, assumed home and child-care responsibilities.[69] In other cases, politically active women inspired independent actions, such as Genora Johnson's founding of the Women's Emergency Brigade during the 1937 Flint auto strike.[70] Possibly, a combination of factors fostered the development and expression of women's autonomy, particularly within long-lived auxiliaries. We might even speculate that a female consciousness, reminiscent of the 'sisterhood' in nineteenth-century middle-class organizations, existed in long-lived auxiliaries, and that these organizations harbored a working-class 'women's culture,' conducive to nurturing women's independence. If so, auxiliary members, under certain circumstances, might have responded to feminist or radical appeals. Yet such responses were conditioned by the unchanging organizational form of the auxiliaries, rooted as they were in conservative gender ideology.

Notes

1 My thanks to people who read and commented on earlier versions of this chapter: the Berkeley Women and Work Study Group, Kim Chernin, Michael Rogin and Winifred Wandersee. I especially want to thank David Brody and Ruth Milkman, both of whom read more drafts than they probably wanted to. And while Marvel Scholl, who died in 1984, disagreed with my interpretation, I am forever grateful for the time she spent sharing her life with me. Without her help, this article would never have been written.

2 *The Organizer*, 2 July, 1934, p.3.

3 Elizabeth Jameson, 'Imperfect Unions: Class and Gender in Cripple Creek, 1894–1904,' in Milton Cantor and Bruce Laurie, eds, *Class, Sex, and the Woman Worker*, Westport, Greenwood Press, 1977, p.188.

4 Priscilla Long, *Mother Jones, Woman Organizer, And her Relations with Miners' Wives, Working Women, and the Suffrage Movement*, Cambridge, Red Sun Press, 1976, p.22.

5 *The Organizer*, 2 July, 1934, p.3.

6 Several historical studies, particularly on the nineteenth century, have examined how middling- or middle-class women, responding to domestic concerns, mobilized in the public sphere, and how that mobilization led to various manifestations of feminism. However, little work has been done on similar experiences among working-class housewives. For an analysis on how a female, but not feminist, consciousness arose among working-class women in Barcelona, out of the 'defense of . . . rights due them, according to the [sexual] division of labor,' see Temma Kaplan, 'Female Consciousness and Collective Action: The Case of Barcelona, 1910–1918,' *Signs*, vol. 7, no. 3, spring

1982, p.551. For studies on middle-class women, see Barbara Leslie Epstein, *The Politics of Domesticity: Women, Evangelism, and Temperance in Nineteenth-Century America*, Middletown, Wesleyan University Press, 1981; Ruth Bordin, *Woman and Temperance: The Quest for Power and Liberty, 1873–1900*, Philadelphia, Temple University Press, 1981; Carroll Smith-Rosenberg, 'Beauty and the Beast and the Militant Woman: A Case Study in Sex Roles and Social Stress in Jacksonian America,' *American Quarterly*, vol. 23, no. 4, October 1971, pp.562–84; Mary P. Ryan, 'The Power of Women's Networks: A Case Study of Female Moral Reform in Antebellum America,' *Feminist Studies*, vol. 5, no. 1, spring 1979, pp.66–85. Recent historical works have also analyzed organizations of women wage-earners. However, because these organizations more closely resembled those of working men than those of working-class housewives, these studies offer few insights into auxiliaries.

7   Although neither Bill Brown, the local's president, nor George Frosig, the vice-president, were Trotskyists, both men supported the Trotskyists. During the strikes, members of the local branch of the Trotskyist Communist League of America 'played an important assisting role,' as did a number of comrades sent to Minneapolis by the national office. Local 574 also had a number of secondary leaders; some were Trotskyists, others eventually joined the Communist League (Farrell Dobbs, *Teamster Rebellion*, New York, Monad Press, 1972, pp.54, 60, 104, 105, 117).

8   Particularly useful for understanding the 1934 strikes are: Dobbs, *Teamster Rebellion*; Charles Rumford Walker, *American City: A Rank-and-File History*, New York, Farrar & Rinehart, 1937; James P. Cannon, *The History of American Trotskyism*, New York, Pathfinder Press, 1972; Irving Bernstein, *Turbulent Years: A History of the American Worker 1933–1941*, Boston, Houghton Mifflin, 1971, pp.229–52; George H. Mayer, *The Political Career of Floyd B. Olson*, Minneapolis, University of Minnesota Press, 1951, pp.184–222; Walter Galenson, *The CIO Challenge to the AFL: A History of the American Labor Movement 1935–1941*, Cambridge, Harvard University Press, 1960, pp.478–86; Thomas E. Blantz, CSC, 'Father Haas and the Minneapolis Truckers' Strike of 1934,' *Minnesota History*, vol. 42, no. 1, spring 1970, pp.5–15.

9   Herbert Solow, 'War in Minneapolis,' *The Nation*, vol. 139, no. 3,605, 8 August, 1934, p.161.

10 Walker, *American City*, pp.59, 85.

11 Dobbs, *Teamster Rebellion*.

12 For a contemporary account that romanticized the conflict as a 'civil war' or 'class warfare,' see Walker, *American City*, pp.107, 113. The *Minneapolis Journal*, a pro-employer newspaper, was especially vitriolic in reporting on what it saw as a communist-led class struggle. See *Minneapolis Journal*, May–August 1934. For a New Left interpretation,

see Jeremy Brecher, *Strike: The True History of Mass Insurgence in America from 1877 to the Present*, San Francisco, Straight Arrow Books, 1972, pp.161–6, 251.

13 'Socialist Women and Labor Struggles, 1934–1954 – A Report by Participants,' *International Socialist Review*, vol. 3, no. 3, March 1975, p.21; Marvel Scholl, interviewed in her home, Berkeley, California, 11 March, 1980.

14 'Minutes of 5th Volunteer Organizing Committee Meeting of General Drivers held Monday, April 2nd, Hall #5, Labor headquarters,' 1934, personal files of Farrell Dobbs, Berkeley, California; Dobbs, *Teamster Rebellion*, p.68.

15 Dobbs, *Teamster Rebellion*, p.69.

16 Much of this analysis depends upon material from Scholl's diary (personal files of Marvel Scholl, Berkeley, California) and from recent interviews with her by the author. Problems arise, of course, in relying heavily upon one informant for the history of an organization. The problems of bias and hindsight are exacerbated by Scholl's marriage to Farrell Dobbs, and by her own revolutionary conversion during the strikes. There is also the potential problem of constructing an interpretation from the 'top down' – from the leader's perspective – rather than from the 'lived experience' of most auxiliary women. Wherever possible, Scholl's recollections were checked for internal consistency with existing documents, and through interviews with other auxiliary participants and union members. In 1934, Scholl was known as Mrs Dobbs. However, she requested that her name appear here as Marvel Scholl, her given name. She has used Scholl since the late 1930s, when she began writing for *The Northwest Organizer*, *The Organizer*'s successor.

17 Marvel Scholl, interviewed in her home, Berkeley, California, 11 March, 1980.

18 Farrell Dobbs and Marvel Scholl, interviewed in their home, Berkeley, California, 9 April, 1982.

19 Mrs Leona Sunde (wife of Earl Sunde), interviewed in her home, Minneapolis, Minnesota, 18 April, 1982.

20 Marvel Scholl, interviewed in her home, Berkeley, California, 23 April, 1981; Meridel Le Sueur, 'What Happens in a Strike,' *The American Mercury*, vol. 33, no. 131, November 1934, p.332.

21 Marvel Scholl, 'Ladies' Auxiliary,' unpublished paper, personal files of Marvel Scholl, Berkeley, California.

22 Marvel Scholl, interviewed in her home, Berkeley, California, 13 March, 1980; 'Socialist Women and Labor Struggles,' p.21.

23 Marvel Scholl, interviewed in her home, Berkeley, California, 11 March, 1980.

24 *Ibid.*

25 Skoglund, quoted in Walker, *American City*, pp.107–8; Dobbs, *Teamster Rebellion*, p.79; Minneapolis Farmer Labor Leader, 30 May, 1934, p.6; *St Paul Dispatch*, 21 May, 1934, p.2; *Minneapolis Labor*

Review, 1 June, 1934, p.2.

26 General Drivers' and Helpers' Union, Local 574, 'Working Men and Women of Minneapolis Support this Strike,' May 1934, Minneapolis History Collection, Minneapolis Public Library, Minneapolis, Minnesota.

27 *St Paul Pioneer Press*, 21 May, 1934, pp.1, 2.

28 Accounts of this event vary considerably, with estimates of the crowd ranging from 50 to 700 people. Marvel Scholl, interviewed in her home, Berkeley, California, 13 March, 1980. See also *The Militant,* 26 May, 1934, p.1; *St Paul Dispatch*, 21 May, 1934, p.2; *Minneapolis Tribune*, 22 May, 1934, p.2; *Minneapolis Star*, 22 May, 1934, p.6; Dobbs, *Teamster Rebellion*, p.86.

29 Marvel Scholl, interviewed in her home, Berkeley, California, 11 December, 1981.

30 Marvel Scholl, interviewed in her home, Berkeley, California, 24 March, 1980; 27 March, 1980; *The Organizer*, 9 July, 1934, p.2; Scholl, 'Ladies' Auxiliary.'

31 Scholl, 'Ladies' Auxiliary.'

32 Marvel Scholl, interviewed in her home, Berkeley, California, 18 March, 1980; Scholl, 'Ladies' Auxiliary.'

33 Scholl, Diary; *New York Times*, 5 August, 1934, section 1, p.20.

34 Dobbs, *Teamster Rebellion*, p.108; 'Mass Strike in Minneapolis, 1934,' *Red Buffalo*, nos 2 and 3, n.d., p.74; Scholl, Diary; *The Organizer*, 26 July, 1934.

35 Le Sueur, 'What Happens in a Strike,' p.331.

36 Scholl, Diary.

37 *The Organizer*, 20 July, 1934, p.2.

38 *The Organizer*, 4 August, 1934, p.2.

39 Scholl, Diary; Marvel Scholl, interviewed in her home, Berkeley, California, 27 March, 1980.

40 Mrs Rose Hork, interviewed in her home, Minneapolis, Minnesota, 1 May, 1982.

41 Marvel Scholl, interviewed in her home, Berkeley, California, 27 March, 1980.

42 Scholl, Diary.

43 Marvel Scholl, interviewed in her home, Berkeley, California, 30 April, 1981.

44 *Ibid.*

45 I am indebted to Elaine Black Yoneda, an early member of the San Francisco-based ILGWU Ladies' Auxiliary, for the term 'white gloved.' Although the term referred to middle-class allies, auxiliary members also used it to describe themselves when they dressed to look middle class (Discussion on Women's Auxiliaries, Labor History Workshop, Berkeley, California, 5 December, 1982).

46 Marvel Scholl, 'How I Came to Join the Party,' unpublished paper, personal files of Marvel Scholl, Berkeley, California.

47 *Ibid.*; Marvel Scholl, interviewed in her home, Berkeley, California, 1980–2.
48 Marvel Scholl, telephone conversation from her home, Berkeley, California, 8 April, 1982.
49 Marvel Scholl, interviewed in her home, Berkeley, California, 10 December, 1981.
50 See Elsa Jane Dixler, 'The Woman Question: Women and the American Communist Party, 1929–1941,' PhD dissertation, Yale University, 1974.
51 Marvel Scholl, interviewed in her home, Berkeley, California, 13 March, 1980, 10 December, 1981; *The Organizer*, 25 June, 1934, p.2.
52 Marvel Scholl, interviewed in her home, Berkeley, California, 15 April, 1980.
53 Farrell Dobbs, interviewed in his home, Berkeley, California, 15 April, 1980.
54 Marvel Scholl, interviewed in her home, Berkeley, California, 30 April, 1981.
55 'Strike Committee Meeting: Minutes of 23 July, 1934,' personal files of Farrell Dobbs, Berkeley, California.
56 Scholl contended that men only served on the commissary committee, but in her diary she referred to Chuck Cabana as the head of the hospital committee. In addition, later in the strike, men were appointed to the stockade committee, a group begun by the women to visit incarcerated pickets. If men did not serve on the auxiliary's committees, they must have had parallel committees. Marvel Scholl, interviewed in her home, Berkeley, California, 11 December, 1981; Scholl, Diary; 'Strike Committee Meeting: Minutes of 13 August, 1934, and 16 August, 1934,' personal files of Farrell Dobbs, Berkeley, California.
57 Dobbs, *Teamster Rebellion*, p.184; Scholl, 'Ladies' Auxiliary'; Marvel Scholl, interviewed in her home, Berkeley, California, 15 April, 1980.
58 Marvel Scholl, interviewed in her home, Berkeley, California, 15 April, 1980.
59 Mrs Rose Hork, interviewed in her home, Minneapolis, Minnesota, 1 May, 1982.
60 Marvel Scholl, interviewed in her home, Berkeley, California, 30 April, 1981.
61 Marvel Scholl, interviewed in her home, Berkeley, California, 11 December, 1981.
62 'Strike Committee Meeting: Minutes of 13 August, 1934,' personal files of Farrell Dobbs, Berkeley, California.
63 Marvel Scholl, interviewed in her home, Berkeley, California, 23 April, 1981.
64 Marvel Scholl, interviewed in her home, Berkeley, California, 18 March, 1980.
65 Maurice Goldbloom, John Herling, Joel Seidman and Elizabeth Yard, *Strikes Under the New Deal*, New York, League for Industrial Democracy, n.d., p.5.

66 *The Organizer*, 18 August, 1934, p.2; Cannon, *The History of American Trotskyism*, p.149.
67 Some auxiliaries have lasted for years. For example, the ILGWU Ladies' Auxiliary, which was initially mobilized during the 1934 San Francisco strike, still meets sporadically today (1983).
68 Sue Cobble, Discussion on Women's Auxiliaries, Labor History Workshop, Berkeley, California, 5 December, 1982.
69 The text of the film, along with commentary by Wilson and Rosenfeld, has been published in book form. See Michael Wilson and Deborah Silverton Rosenfeld, *Salt of the Earth*, Old Westbury, The Feminist Press, 1978, pp.117–46.
70 Sherna Gluck, 'The Changing Nature of Women's Participation in the American Labor Movement, 1900–1940s: Case Studies from Oral History, paper presented at Southwest Labor Studies Conference, Arizona State University, 5 March, 1977.

10

'We're no Kitty Foyles': Organizing office workers for the Congress of Industrial Organizations, 1937–50

Sharon Hartman Strom

The massive organizing drives of the 1930s concentrated primarily on the nation's mass production industries – steel, auto, rubber, electrical manufacturing – in which women were, at best, a minority of the workforce. By the 1930s, most women workers were already concentrated in 'pink collar' sales, service and clerical occupations, where they remain to this day. While unionizing these workers was never a high priority for the labor movement, some important efforts to do so were undertaken under the auspices of the fledgling Congress of Industrial Organizations. In this chapter, Sharon Hartman Strom recounts the previously unexplored history of the most important clerical workers' union within the CIO, the United Office and Professional Workers of America (UOPWA), which existed from 1937 to 1950. Setting her account against the backdrop of the rationalization and proletarianization of clerical work, Strom documents the progress of UOPWA organizing in the 1930s and 1940s in a wide range of workplaces, from publishing houses and direct-mail shops to the offices of small manufacturing firms. She contrasts the willingness of women office-workers to join unions with the limitations of the male-dominated CIO in relation to clerical unionism, in an analysis which does much to explain why most clerical workers, especially in the private sector, have remained outside the labor movement throughout the twentieth century.

In 1941, Local 16 of the UOPWA held its annual Stenographers'

Ball, attended by over 5,000 women and men. The winner of the beauty contest for the 'Queen of Stenographia' burst through a huge steno book on the stage and was crowned by movie actor Victor Mature. Ginger Rogers, recent star of the movie version of Christopher Morley's popular novel, Kitty Foyle, also attended the ball and personified the theme of the evening, the Kitty Foyle Frolic.[1]

A group of Boston clerical workers protested this glamorous portrayal of the secretary in the union newspaper. 'Foyle seemed to be mainly concerned about her romantic entanglements and not at all about her job,' they pointed out. 'As a matter of fact, it's never clear just what Kitty's job is. She has something to do with perfumes in a swank cosmetician's salon, calls her lady boss by her first name, opens branch stores and ends up at the age of twenty-eight in a fashionable women's hotel. If that's the typical white collar worker we'll eat Christopher Morley.'[2]

Kitty Foyle was but a fictional version of the picture of the woman clerical worker prevalent both in social commentary and in the labor movement itself in the 1930s and 1940s. The general presumption was that women office-workers were temporary workers, expecting to be rescued from a life of wage-earning by marriage (possibly to the boss), and interested only in clothes, movies and romance. Under these conditions, unionization was considered unlikely, if not impossible, to foster.

The indignant women who claimed 'We're no Kitty Foyles' were closer to the truth about the typical woman white-collar worker in this period, however. The secretary was as likely as most other working women to live at home with her parents, to 'bring her lunch to work in a paper bag,'[3] and to work in a dead-end job which would never be a career. Despite her uniform of hat, suit, nylon stockings and high heels, she was nearly as likely as her sister factory-worker to operate a machine on an office assembly line. And, given the opportunity, she might well join a labor union to go out on strike.

Background to unionism: Feminization and rationalization of office work

By the 1930s, the feminization of clerical work was largely complete, and the various functions of the office were already highly rationalized and mechanized. In contrast, the nineteenth-century office was typically a small male preserve, where the chief clerk, bookkeeper, copyists and messenger boys performed four functions: the supervision of the office work process, the keeping of financial records, the production of documents, and the transmission of information. In the 1880s, women were hired in increasing numbers as the production of documents and transmission of information was mechanized. By 1900, the widespread use of dictaphones, stencil duplicating machines, addressographs, envelope feeders, typewriters, pneumatic tubes and telephone equipment allowed employers to produce and transmit as many documents and bits of information as they pleased. Nearly all the workers who used these machines were women.[4]

In the second decade of the twentieth century, a similar mechanical revolution transformed bookkeeping. With the introduction of calculating machines and new accounting procedures, vast new clerical departments were created to meet managers' demands for expanded compilation of figures.[5] Substantial numbers of women began to work in bookkeeping departments after 1910, and the use of female bookkeeping machine operators in banks became general practice during World War I. By the 1920s, the typical bookkeeper had lost his ledger to an army of machine operators, most of whom were women. Women were 5.7 percent of all bookkeepers, cashiers and accountants in 1880; by 1910 they constituted 38.5 percent of the total. The ranks of women classified as stenographers, typists and machine operators, many of whom were doing some sort of book-keeping, continued to grow, and the total number of females working in offices tripled between 1910 and 1920. Women made up nearly half of the nation's office-workers by the end of World War I.[6]

While the employment of clerical workers increased steadily over the course of the twentieth century, even more rapidly than employment of industrial workers, the number of women seeking clerical employment increased at an even greater rate.[7] The rising age of compulsory schooling for teenagers and the ending of most child labor in the 1920s created a huge supply of potential clerks. Economist Paul Douglas argued flatly in 1930 that the high schools 'primarily served to recruit juveniles for clerical work.'[8] Discrimination against women in other kinds of education and training programs, the refusal of many middle-class parents to invest in college education for daughters, and the desire of many working-class parents to get their daughters out of factories and into offices left most women with no alternative to a commercial education.[9] As the office was mechanized and feminized, clerical wages fell steadily compared to those in manufacturing. By 1930, women clerks earned far less than skilled male workers in industry and substantially less than the average male wage-earner, although they were likely to earn a few more dollars a week than women in factory or sales jobs.[10]

The Depression created a golden opportunity for management further to debase the conditions and wages of office-workers. Clerical unemployment began to rise precipitously in 1932. Strictures against married women were more rigidly applied, although there was widespread evasion of these rules by women workers, including outright deception of employers. Women over thirty-five, who had always been likely to be excluded from office work, had particular trouble finding jobs. The slashing of wages was nearly universal, as was the cancelation of paid vacations and the institution of compulsory overtime without pay. A seven- or eight-hour day and paid vacations had long been two of the chief attractions of clerical work compared with jobs in manufacturing.[11]

These measures slowed the rate of increase in the employment of office-workers until the late 1930s. The crisis of women looking for clerical work, which was already serious before the Depression began, became more acute by 1933 for a number of reasons. Many middle-class women and men recently trained in the professions were unable to find jobs as teachers, librarians or editors and turned to clerical employment instead. Due to the lack of manufacturing jobs for teenagers, many working-class parents sent their children through high school, where they invariably took commercial courses. And many middle-class families, who might have sent daughters to college in better times, desperately needed their children's wages to help pay the mortgage and buy the groceries. Observers noted that the educational level of clerical workers in America was higher in the mid-1930s than it had been ten years before, although most employers did not think anything but a high school education was necessary for the jobs they offered. The ongoing proletarianization of office work was thus masked in the 1930s by the number of middle-class men and women who took office jobs because better jobs were not available.[12]

Clerical workers routinely complained about speed-up, production quotas, piecework rates and bonus plans during the 1930s. These measures were easiest to institute in large, highly mechanized firms like those in the direct-mail industry, where workers produced commercial letters for businesses which did not have in-house addressograph and duplicating machinery. Bonuses and piecework rates were typically paid to dictating and billing machine operators in New York City. There was also renewed managerial interest in the elimination of private secretaries, long considered a luxury many junior executives could do without.[13]

Mechanization was another way of cutting costs. One businessman threatened that office machinery 'could dispense with one quarter of the total number of clerks in the country . . . Instead of a five-day week, they can take a continuous vacation.'[14] Business schools instituted courses on office machines and were encouraged by both businessmen and office-machine manufacturers to train women students in their use. Between 1929 and 1935, American businesses invested about $500 million in office machines; by 1937, the *Wall Street Journal* reported a 'cheering profit outlook' for companies like Remington Rand, IBM, Burroughs and Addressograph Multigraph. As World War II approached and business began to expand again, these manufacturers could not keep up with new orders.[15]

Depression commentators who were sympathetic to office-workers saw office machines as the nemesis of the bookkeeper and the secretary. The office, they said, was becoming more and more reminiscent of a factory assembly line, with women operating the machinery, and men supervising the women. Indeed, by 1930 about half of all office-workers were in offices of more than fifty workers, and there were six women using an office machine for every man.[16] But there were limits to the specialization of labor in this period. Only with the postwar application of advanced tabulating machines, computerized information banks and word processing, was it possible to achieve a degree of control comparable to the factory assembly line.[17] In the 1930s, many clerical workers still performed a variety of tasks in a small office using two or three different machines in the course of a day. And even in larger offices, groups of seven or eight workers were still subject to the direct, personal control of supervisors or bookkeepers, not machinery.[18]

The intimacy of office life and the character of the division of labor in the office created special problems for anyone who sought to unionize clerical workers. The male boss still enjoyed a paternalistic relationship with his secretary, who could be, as *Fortune* magazine emphasized, 'someone to balance his checkbook, get him seats in the fourth row, take his daughter to the dentist, listen to his side of the story, give him a courageous look when things were blackest, and generally know all, understand all.'[19] Boss and secretary alike might view union membership as personal disloyalty. And both men and women had additional reasons to remain ambivalent toward organizing. By giving men more professional titles and paying them higher wages, businesses were able to coopt them as supervisors of women clericals – the 'factory-workers' on the office floor. When men feared that women and the machines they used were a threat to their jobs and wages, they tended to turn to professional associations rather than to industrial unions. And those women who were private secretaries or head bookkeepers mirrored this complex relationship between management and men. Kay Bell, who had been reared by a widowed working mother, had risen to a $45-a-week job as a private secretary at the Columbia Broadcasting System by 1935. Earning three times the wages of the average woman clerical worker, she had been able to establish bank accounts, life insurance policies and go out to lunch. She enjoyed bridge, horsebackriding and aquaplaning. She did not belong to a union.[20] There were, it seemed, enough Kitty Foyles to give the stereotype some reality.

The CIO and office-worker unionization

In the years before World War I, most unionized office-workers were male. AFL unions for postal clerks, telegraphers and railroad clerks monopolized these jobs for white, native-born men, for whom they sought higher wages and better working conditions. However, the workers in one recently feminized occupation organized a very successful union in the 1910s – the telephone operators' department of the International Brotherhood of Electrical Workers (IBEW). Responding to the mechanization, rationalization, and scientific management of the telephone business, women operators staged a series of militant strikes against telephone companies and, during World War I, against the federal government itself. By 1921, there were 25,000 women in the United States and Canada who belonged to IBEW. But union membership declined drastically in the 1920s as the huge Bell system gained a near monopoly over telephone business, fostered company unions and used aggressive union-busting tactics. Male IBEW linemen, telephone installers, cable splicers and switchboard men insisted that women be assigned to a separate unit to avoid their being swamped by 'petticoat rule'; women operators were thus left out on a limb with limited financial resources. By 1924, membership had fallen to 1,200 workers.[21]

Bookkeepers', stenographers' and accountants' unions were also organized before World War I in cities like Chicago, Kansas City and New York, but they too suffered severe declines in the 1920s; by the end of the decade, there were only a few dozen left throughout the country — mostly made up of secretaries of labor unions.[22] In Boston, the Bookkeepers', Stenographers' and Accountants' Union (BSAU) used its union label to maintain a monopoly on office work for trade unions and spent almost no time organizing clerical workers.[23]

By the mid-1930s, these long-dormant locals began to feel militant pressure from clerical workers with industrial union sympathies. The dramatic struggles of working people in the textiles and manufacturing industries in New York, Philadelphia and Boston, inspired militants — many of them leftists — to wrestle for control of the old AFL locals. In 1937, they carried a sizeable group of dissidents with them into the CIO. That year, the CIO granted national charters to three white-collar unions: the United Office and Professional Workers of America (UOPWA), the United Federal Workers (UFW), and the State, County and Municipal Workers of America (SCMWA). Despite the competition they faced from already established AFL locals, all three grew substantially over the next few years, until their disappearance following expulsion from the CIO in 1950 for refusing to eliminate communist members.[24]

The CIO was far more receptive to women than the AFL had been, but male industrial workers still tended to view women as temporary workers and potential wives and mothers, not as equals in their unions. In industries like textiles, garment-making, electrical manufacturing and meat-packing, women were so numerous that they had a major impact, as rank-and-file members, on CIO strikes and organizing efforts in the 1930s. But they were underrepresented at conventions, and almost entirely excluded from national offices and the policy-making decisions of most CIO unions. They were the 'Sweethearts of the CIO,' more often portrayed in union literature as bathing beauties than as strikers, more in need of recipes and sewing patterns than of strike pay.[25]

The predominant industrial unionist's view of clerical workers lumped them together with management, and office-workers in general were viewed as potential spies for management. This reflected the general invisibility of women workers within the labor movement, as well as an automatic assumption that 'girls' who worked in offices would be easily manipulated by supervisors or bosses. Male unionists evidently saw nothing wrong with signing contracts through the 1930s and 1940s which exchanged gains for blue-collar members for agreements eliminating office-workers' bargaining rights. CIO organizing thus resulted in no raises or even pay cuts for many office-workers, whose wages were already desperately low.[26]

Nor did the CIO really encourage its office-worker unions to organize effectively. The UFW and the SCMWA were given authority to organize government employees, but their leverage was limited, since virtually all of these workers were prohibited from striking. This situation produced particular strategies for public workers, such as lobbying for higher pay with legislatures, negotiating upgraded job classifications, or staging slowdowns or other job actions on the office floor. The UOPWA, in contrast, could imitate the tactics of industrial unionism by using the strike. But the CIO drastically limited UOPWA's jurisdiction when it allowed existing industrial unions in steel, auto, electrical manuacturing and rubber to claim any organized office-workers for themselves. UOPWA successfully organized office-workers in steel and rubber in 1938 and 1939, but was then forced to give them up to the United Steel Workers (USW) and United Rubber Workers (URW). With the exception of some progressive locals of the United Auto Workers (UAW) and the United Electrical Workers (UE), few CIO unions included clerical workers in their contracts, and therefore these industrial union monopolies were tantamount to a 'no-union' policy for clerical workers employed by manufacturing firms.[27] Noting that office-workers in industry frequently contacted the UOPWA because 'the plant unions did nothing to organize them,' one UOPWA editorial complained about raids by industrial worker unions:

> there are hundreds of thousands of white collar workers over whom the big industrial unions like Steel and Auto claim jurisdiction, who are not organized and who could absorb all the expenditure of time, effort and money if these big industrial unions were to seriously attempt to organize rather than raid UOPWA and criticize our organizational work.[28]

The situation was further exacerbated by a series of National Labor Relations Board (NLRB) rulings that clerical and manufacturing employees should not be part of the same bargaining units. As office-workers comprised 14.2 percent of all workers in manufacturing by 1938 and would increase their proportion over the next decade, these policies were found to undermine the solidarity of workers and to alienate clerical workers. The UAW was the first major CIO union to attempt to organize clericals, but did not do so until 1941 – and then only half-heartedly.[29]

The CIO did give the UOPWA organizing jurisdiction over industries dominated by office-workers, but banks and insurance companies had no tradition of industrial unionism and were precisely the workplaces where the sexual division of labor made worker solidarity highly unlikely. So the UOPWA concentrated on those offices in small manufacturing firms which could be organized without attracting the ire of other CIO unions, and on paperwork factories – direct-mail shops, credit clearing houses, publishing firms and advertising agencies.

The potential clientele of UOPWA also included professional workers who worked in offices, and the union did attract social workers, editors in publishing, advertising people; during World War II, architects, engineers and technicians were also enlisted. The thinking behind combining professional and clerical workers in the same union ran along several lines. It seemed logical to group together all so-called 'white-collar' workers, or all workers who did not work in manufacturing. Moreover, the left, which dominated the CIO clerical unions, had traditionally lumped all white-collar workers together as 'middle class.' Despite the fact that leftist economists and labor organizers were more aware than anyone else of the 'proletarianization' of women in office work, they were apparently unable to develop any notion of organizing them separately. This probably had a lot to do with the prevalent view, both among leftists and CIO unionists, that women workers were usually dominated by their male supervisors, and that men, as heads of families and permanent members of the workforce, were more important to organize than women.

The UOPWA was thus plagued with an inherent contradiction from the start. Including professionals meant that many offices could be organized as a whole and that skilled workers, who generally had more leverage with management, might be induced to write contracts which included ordinary clerical workers and even win them some benefits. Certainly, excluding professionals would have eliminated the services of a large body of politically sophisticated and committed left-wing unionists, some of whom were women. On the other hand, the sexual division of labor in the office meant that male professionals might seize the union organizing process as a means of preserving a monopoly over their occupations and the sexual hierarchy of labor in the office.[30] It is probably no accident that the unionized social workers, most of whom were women, were the most likely of the UOPWA locals to include clericals in their contracts and to welcome them as union members. As one organizer recalls, 'The social service employees ... were much more progressive. They were women, and they dealt with people in trouble, and they had a much more progressive outlook.'[31] A 1948 strike by agencies of the Jewish Federation of Los Angeles included directors, social workers, clerical staff, maintenance workers, nursery school mothers and a children's picket line.[32]

Professions dominated by men were less likely to include women workers in contracts, and the UOPWA routinely allowed technicians, book and publishing editors and insurance agents to set up locals which excluded clerical workers and assigned them to special locals, effectively dividing locals along craft and sexual lines. The bulk of the UOPWA's paid organizers were assigned to male locals, often supported by dues from women's locals; the latter were told to use volunteers for their own efforts. Aware that this more closely resembled AFL unionism than the supposed 'organize the unorganized' policy of the CIO, one woman unionist recalled:

The force of any desire to set up their independent entities overpowered any broad philosophical concept of becoming one big union . . . We feared the idea of a return to craft unionism. But there was a difference. White collar work, unlike a production industry like steel or auto, had such a great variety of skills and employers that to try to get everybody who was in the union to agree on the demands of one category just seemed like an insurmountable task. And it was a hindrance to the efficiency and the speed with which a group of workers . . . were able . . . to develop strategy.[33]

Nowhere were these internal contradictions of the UOPWA more apparent than in its attempts to organize the insurance industry. Evidently male insurance agents employed by the largest companies were the first to seek union help. They had suffered a loss in status and income as a result of the Depression. There were virtually no women insurance agents, although thousands worked for the companies as clericals. Organizing the insurance companies seemed to make sense, both in political and union terms. 'The insurance companies are the reservoir of finance capital,' wrote UOPWA president Lewis Merrill, 'and they use the funds of these companies for the purpose of controlling and dominating all commerce and industry.'[34] The union poured a lot of money and organizing effort into the unionization of the insurance business, but the agents insisted on their own locals, which basically functioned as craft unions. They refused to write contracts which included women workers. A Boston woman who was trying to organize secretaries at the time recalled the elitism of the insurance agents with some bitterness:

> The insurance agents were almost totally male; they were older than the office workers; they were much more 'set in their ways'; and I would say they had very strong male chauvinist attitudes. For instance, they never brought the office workers into the insurance workers' union. I don't ever remember seeing an office worker in an insurance office in their unions. If they joined they came into the general local of the office workers. The logical place for them to be would have been the insurance agents. They were dealing with the same employers, the same industries. But that didn't happen.[35]

The snobbery of the insurance agents was so embarrassing that Merrill felt compelled to bring it up at an eastern regional conference in 1939. Clerical workers, he said,

> can be your friends and proudest and firmest allies in the situation. They are natural members of our union. We understand them. We have a program for them. We have a natural home for them. Don't treat them as if they don't belong, because if you can't win them, we are storing up trouble for ourselves . . . Let us face the issue frankly. They are snobbish arguments. 'They are young,' 'What do they know,' 'They are females,' 'They are little ones,' 'How can they enter the work of a union,' 'They only earn this and that,' etc. . . .
>
> The facts are that they are exploited by the same companies as yourselves . . . I assure you that when we organize these clerical workers, and we can — we have thousands of clerical workers organized in the International Union elsewhere, why not here? — those sitting in the swivel chairs in the head offices will certainly feel that it is a hot seat.[36]

The UOPWA had successfully organized insurance agents at most of the major insurance corporations by the end of World War II. But the insurance companies capitalized on the conservatism of the agents by launching a red-baiting campaign in 1948 and instituting company unions which later affiliated with the AFL. These unions explicitly excluded clerical workers.[37]

The extent to which the UOPWA was organized along sex-divided lines was masked by the presence of men in office-worker locals who were bookkeepers and accountants and by the women members who thought of themselves as professionals, leftist intellectuals, or something other than 'just secretaries.' Most social workers were women, and there were thousands of women bookkeepers and data clerks. Some were editors or advertising writers. Many of the women who were active in the UOPWA in its infancy came from working-class families where reading and intellectual improvement were a part of growing up. As one woman organizer said of her childhood home, 'we had books, music, and a very strong desire to better ourselves through the Labor Movement.'[38] Many young leftist women, particularly in the larger cities where the UOPWA was strongest, had put themselves through city colleges or night school to become teachers, librarians, economists and social workers, but could find nothing other than office work. They tended to set themselves apart from what they perceived as the more flippant, 'ordinary' secretary. One woman who was president of a UOPWA local in New England had earned a college degree in teaching but went to work in a credit clearing house. She felt more comfortable with social workers than with secretaries, and prided herself on her political commitment: 'I once had an offer from a young man,' she recalled, 'to be with him or go to a meeting and I said, "Well, if I have a choice I'll take the meeting." '[39]

Labor union secretaries, the backbone of many of the early UOPWA locals, tended to view organizing in manufacturing as the heart of the CIO labor struggle. Often these women had boyfriends or husbands who were organizers in the dramatic industrial strikes of the 1930s. Most of them were uninterested in feminism and believed women's rights would come along with socialist revolution. Many of these men and women agreed with the left's position that white-collar workers were the most likely supporters of fascist ideology, and potential enemies of the industrial labor movement. The real grievances of office-workers got short shrift in this kind of analysis.[40] Even an independent leftist like Florence Luscomb, the first president of Boston UOPWA Local 3 and an active feminist, adhered to this view. She wrote in 1937:

> Next month I am to be elected president of my trade union . . . so my activities for the next year will be largely CIOish. With the struggle sharpening between fascism and the working democracies I don't know of any more crucial field of endeavor than the militant trade union movement. And if the members of the middle class here are the potential fascists they were in Germany, certainly the white collar unions have a contribution to make.[41]

Leftists patronized female clerical workers by claiming they were difficult to organize, likely to side with their bosses, and uneducated in the larger issues of industrial democracy and union solidarity. Leftists seemed unaware of the ways in which these undocumented pronouncements colored their own methods of organizing or became self-fulfilling prophecies in the field.[42] The UOPWA newspaper was dominated by male union struggles and rarely discussed the particular issues faced by clerical workers. It did include a regular column entitled 'Susie the Secretary,' which followed a mythical but naive Susie to the CIO convention in Philadelphia in 1937:

> I thought I'd go for the ride and would be bored by the meeting, because I've always thought speeches were awfully dull . . . But was I mistaken! . . . Why, it makes you feel so strong and hopeful to know that other people feel the way you do and it encourages you to want to really do something instead of just putting up with a measly little job . . . I don't know either if there are any other girls in my department who have sense enough to stick together. They seem to be just out for themselves and not to care about how anyone else gets along. I used to be pretty dumb too, thinking that unions were just for common laborers and mechanics, so perhaps I can show them that organization is the thing.[43]

In November, Susie announced that she was 'beginning to feel that I have a real place in the union now . . . I'm on the Social and Entertainment Committee. Doesn't that sound gay – and important too?'[44] The New York Joint Council of the UOPWA ran a series of women's forums in 1939–40 which included talks on civil service exams, office machines, dress and makeup, 'The Most for your Money' (with a speaker from the Consumers' League), 'Marriage and its Problems' and, finally, 'Women in Society Today.'[45]

Of course, in some ways these stereotyped views of women's interests reflected the real needs and values of rank-and-file women and men of the UOPWA. Women did need budgeting information because of their tiny wages, and knowing how to dress and wear makeup was required of most women workers on the job. The membership of the UOPWA, like most of the office workforce in the country, was young, interested in social events, and largely destined to become wives and husbands. The 'Queen of Stenographia' balls drew thousands of office-workers in New York and other cities and became important fund-raisers for strike funds and union salaries. An appeal by Local 16 in 1939 to clericals to attend the 'stenos' ball,' where they could 'refuse to take dictation from anyone except those two masters of swing, Lucky Millinder and Enoch Light,' was bound to be enticing.[46]

We need to remember, however, that women – and men – who

assumed these traditional roles could still be militant unionists. Sometimes, the combination of traditionalism and militancy made for effective strike drama, as in the Efficient Letter campaign of 1937:

> Efficient Letter pickets plan a picket line wedding. All the girls were busy getting white dresses and flowers while the boys were preparing to wear new signs. The wedding procession in honor of Miss Low Wages and General Bad W. Conditions was to be headed by a page boy, explaining that real weddings could not take place because of low wages, insecurity, no vacations, and similar causes.[47]

Moreover, despite their tendency to accept traditional sex roles and to reject any discussion of feminism as a 'bourgeois reform,' leftists who dominated the CIO office-worker unions were committed to a far more progressive position on both race and sex than their counterparts in other white-collar unions. One of the great achievements of the UFW was a consistent attack on the barring of blacks from civil service examinations and on Jim Crow practices in federal offices. The UOPWA organized black insurance workers and fought to integrate the direct-mail industry. 'Equal Pay for Equal Work' was a slogan all of these unions endorsed. In 1942, the UFW worked to eliminate a nearly $200 difference in yearly salary between stenographers and workers in typing pools. Two years later, Eleanor Nelson became the first woman ever to head a CIO national union when she was elected president of the UFW.[48]

Women and men office-workers did respond, sometimes dramatically, to the opportunity to join unions during the 1930s and 1940s. In New York, Philadelphia and Chicago, where there were large numbers of office employees and where the Communist Party had attracted so many young people, groups of office-workers in manufacturing firms, credit clearing houses and the direct-mail and publishing industries joined BSAU locals (which would soon after affiliate with the UOPWA) when the Wagner Act of 1935 made collective bargaining legitimate. These locals, which had previously been dominated by male accountants, bookkeepers and women secretaries of labor unions, rapidly attracted large numbers of women clerical workers. There were changes in local leadership as well. By 1937, Local 16 still had a male president, but the vice-president, recording secretary and treasurer were all women, as were three of the five paid organizers and more than half of the members.[49]

One of the first in the wave of successful strikes by office-workers in the 1930s took place at Macaulay Publishing, New York, in 1934.[50] In 1936, small office staffs of women struck firms manufacturing auto parts and slide fasteners. At the New York Margon Corporation that year, seven women who joined a quickly settled machinists' strike at their factory were fired. After a protracted strike by the office-workers, during which the machinists crossed the BSAU picket line and the company sent in goon squads, Margon moved the plant to New Jersey to avoid dealing with the union. At the Simmons Company in Cleveland, by contrast, 300 machinists joined the locked-out office staff of twenty and refused to negotiate a separate contract.[51] Later in 1936, several hundred office-workers, mainly women, joined a ten-day strike initiated by warehousemen of a Gimbels department store in Philadelphia. As sitdowns in the manufacturing industries began to make news, women who worked in the office of Frost Cleaners and Dyers, in Detroit, sat down to secure the reinstatement of two fired workers. In Philadelphia in 1937, successful sit-ins by workers at Vitagraph and Universal film-exchange offices won wage increases.[52]

Thirty-three office-workers at the Maidenform Brassiere Company in Bayonne maintained a successful picket line; 1,000 factory-workers refused to cross it. Nineteen office-workers with a sense of humor at another brassiere company went on strike in 1940, demanding an 'uplift in wages because the company kept them flat-busted.' After a five-week strike, which included picketing of Woolworth and Grants, both Maidenform retailers, the women won a union contract.[53]

The larger corporations proved more difficult to crack. The UOPWA lost an important strike in 1941 at L. Sonneborn Sons, a national oil and paint firm, despite a lengthy and well-organized strike. In the same year, the UOPWA reported that textile concern Lowenstein and Sons had capped a four-year effort to win collective bargaining rights for 450 office employees with 'intimidation, firings, and that good old stand-by, red-baiting.' The union lost the NLRB election in August by twenty-four votes.[54]

Paperwork 'factories' were easier to penetrate. The first national president of the UOPWA, Lewis Merrill, was fired in 1930 for trying

to start a union at the New York Credit Clearing House (CCH), and
became a paid union organizer for BSAU. In 1936, 225 office employees at CCH won a contract under the leadership of union
steward Lena de Pasquale. Four years later, CCH office-workers
organized friends, relatives and union supporters in a 'telephone
picketing' campaign which swamped CCH's seventy-seven trunk
lines and helped to win a strike. In 1938, the managers of Romeike
Press Clipping Bureau resorted to a lock-out to end contract negotiations and 'fled to New Jersey in the dead of the night.' Union
organizers managed both to force the firm back to New York and to
win a union contract.[55]

Some of the UOPWA's most effective organizing took place at
firms which published directories and catalogs or produced commercial letters and direct mail. These document-producing firms
were often operated on an assembly-line basis. They tended to be
completely mechanized and to have eliminated skilled workers.[56] On
the other hand, many of the small direct-mail shops still used typists,
mimeograph operators and hand stuffers to process orders in firms
resembling old-fashioned sweatshops. Workers were paid by the
piece, and speed-up was a common complaint. Workers were often
laid off for days and then called in to work as long as sixteen hours a
shift. The UOPWA reported in 1942 that direct-mail houses in New
York paid wages substantially below the minimum wage. Men constituted 'an unduly high proportion of higher-paid people,' and
women usually received far less than the minimum income established in several states for a single woman living alone or with her
family. Most direct-mail workers were women, many of them over
twenty-five and married.[57]

Direct-mail workers first tried to organize at Globe Mail Service in
September 1936, when 103 employees went out on strike. The
average salary at Globe was $10 a week. Pay was docked for lateness
or for minor infractions, and overtime was compulsory. Workers
were out on strike for eight months before the NLRB found the
company guilty of refusing to bargain collectively. Ordered to
recognize the union, Globe then changed its name to avoid compliance. The New York UOPWA won its first contract in direct mail
at the renamed Press Mail Service in March 1937, winning a weekly
wage of $18 minimum for mailing-equipment workers and $21
minimum for regular office staff.[58]

In October 1937, eighty-five employees of the Efficient Letter Company went out on strike. Their wages were as low as $6 a week; some of the 'temporaries' had worked as long as eighteen years. Thugs were hired to break up the picket line, and seven unionists were arrested. The UOPWA protested in court, the cases were dismissed, and more pickets were sent to join the strikers. The UOPWA secured the help of the League of Women's Shoppers to expose 'the whole letter shop racket in which women work for 25¢. and 30¢. an hour,' and organized picket lines in front of New York firms which refused to boycott the company. These included the offices of General Motors, General Electric, Gulf Oil, the Lily Tulip Cup Corporation, Bellevue Hospital and the New York *Journal*. By December, pickets were being arrested for harassing scabs, while the case awaited a hearing before the New York Labor Relations Board. Just before New Year's Day, the board ruled in favor of the strikers and ordered the Efficient Letter Company to negotiate with Local 16; by the spring, the workers had a union contract.[59]

In 1938, workers at Sampson and Murdock, a large printer of city directories in Boston, approached UOPWA Local 3 and asked unionists to present the firm with a contract. G. D. Marcy, the 92-year-old president of the company, announced that he would liquidate the firm rather than deal with the CIO. When a stockholder suggested selling the company, Marcy replied that he was more interested in smashing the union. He revealed that the Northern Publishers' Association 'was vitally interested and considered this a test case.' Members of the association vowed to 'aid the firm in its anti-union moves,' and promised to 'use a blacklist to prevent employees from getting employment with other directory publishers.' Despite appeals to the NLRB, Sampson and Murdock went out of business and fired all of its workers. One organizer felt this episode demoralized the Boston UOPWA for many years to come:

> They were organized. They were solid, and they were organized by our union . . . They were on the verge of setting up a committee to have a contract . . . The company folded up shop and left town. That was the closest we ever came to a contract in Boston. The workers were solidly together and they were *all* fired. It was *that* ruthless.[60]

Detroit, a much stronger union town, was the target of a more successful campaign to organize 1,500 directory and direct-mail workers at R. L. Polk. A successful contract was negoiated for what was then the largest single group of clerical workers to come into the union. Victories at smaller branches of Polk in Cleveland and New York soon followed, and in the fall of 1942 the UOPWA in Detroit convinced Polk to break a longstanding color bar by hiring 250 Afro–Americans.[61]

In August 1941, the UOPWA launched a national campaign to organize the direct-mail industry, chiefly aimed at the more than 20,000 workers in 300 New York letter shops. After a dispute with the independently unionized lithographers over jurisdiction, the New York campaign proceeded smoothly, with letter-shop workers coming into the CIO at a rate of more than 100 a week. Union members from organized shops handed out leaflets and talked with workers in unorganized ones. In November, the union negotiated a master agreement covering 4,000 letter-shop workers, winning new minimum wage rates, paid vacations and union shops. The victory was not complete, for there were still thousands of workers not covered by the agreement – especially among the temporaries, many of whom were women. Piecework rates were retained, and overtime could still be made compulsory. One recalcitrant shop, McKenzie Service, launched a 'two-week reign of terror' to avoid unionization, with 'mass arrests of union members, armed goons roaming the shop, and a lockout after the breaking off of negotiations.' But McKenzie finally signed the contract on December 31.[62]

The 1941 letter-shop campaigns coincided with a general quickening in the pace of clerical worker organization on the eve of World War II. In that same year, in Birmingham, Alabama, the office employees of Sloss-Shefield Iron and Steel voted to come into the UOPWA under the novice hand of Ida S. Jones. In Chicago, meanwhile, Afro–American office-workers and tenants picketed together against Mid-City Management, a real estate firm which exploited both its workers and its customers. The UOPWA won its first victory at a bank in New York, and office-workers at companies in Oakland, San Pedro, Chicago and Newark came into the union.[63]

World War II brought an immediate halt to open strikes because of the no-strike pledge. But even during the 1930s, despite the strike victories, office employees lost ground in wages and salaries relative to larger and better-established industrial unions in manufacturing.

Average wages in manufacturing increased by 28.9 percent between 1941 and 1943, while wages for non-manufacturing workers declined by 2.9 percent. The government estimated that the cost of living went up 33 percent during the war, and the AFL and CIO said the increase in the cost of living was closer to 50 percent.[64] Employers were continually replacing men with women at lower rates of pay during the war, and this was also when mechanization of the office really took hold, as C. Wright Mills has noted.[65]

The UOPWA had a difficult time fighting these developments because its dominant policy, like that of the other left-led unions, was to maintain production and win the war. Until 1940, the office-workers' union did not seem to be much affected by the Communist Party's position on foreign policy. After the period of the 'phony war,' however, the Communist Party's concern for the fate of the Soviet Union and weekly reminders of the need for a second front did tend to take up space previously devoted to the activities of workers. Even then, the office-worker papers were never mere propaganda sheets. The tenor of union life changed dramatically because of the no-strike pledge, but this was the case in all CIO unions, not just the leftist ones. Jessica Mitford, who joined the UFW during the war, recalled how vitiating the policy was:

> But what did we actually do in the union, aside from attending endless meetings at which we enunciated and reaffirmed our policy of all-out support for the war effort and passed resolutions demanding the opening of a second front? Even at the time I was hard put to it to explain our raison d'être to outsiders. One of . . . [my husband's] relations asked what the advantages were in belonging to a union in circumstances where wages and conditions were not issues, and the strike weapon was expressly prohibited by law.[66]

The UOPWA urged men to go to war and women to entertain them in canteens or to take war jobs. 'Sweethearts' of the CIO replaced women pickets as clericals in UOPWA locals across the country were asked to chip in and help 'win the war.' In 1943, the Boston local reported that it had recruited 400 office-worker hostesses for the union's canteen on Tremont Street, and every issue of the UOPWA newspaper showed smiling young women waiting to serve 'the boys' punch and swing around the dance floor.[67] Some of the leftist women who had been key leaders in their locals took jobs in war plants or entered the professions, taking up the opportunities the war created for women.

After the war ended, the UOPWA staged a number of successful organizing drives among office-workers. The union grew by half between 1946 and 1948. Boston showed signs of new life, with victories at the Credit Bureau and the Association of Jewish Philanthropies. At the Arthur Murray Studios in New York, 350 dancing instructors joined the UOPWA, and a number of banks were organized.[68] But this flurry of activity proved shortlived. The tolerance that had existed for communists in the 1930s in industrial unions now vanished. The Taft-Hartley Act of 1947 required union officers to sign affidavits stating they were not members of the Communist Party. When, like several other leftist unions, the UOPWA refused to cooperate, raids by other AFL and CIO unions greatly weakened it. By 1948, a small group of dissident insurance agents had won control of the national; they renamed the union newspaper *Career*. In 1950, the UOPWA was expelled from the CIO and, after briefly merging with several other progressive unions, it passed out of existence entirely. Employers eagerly seized upon red-baiting tactics to kill CIO office-worker unionization.[69] Former UOPWA activists found themselves fair game for the House Un-American Activities Committee (HUAC) and state investigatory commissions on communism.[70]

Clerical workers in the postwar period thus found themselves either entirely without unions or back in the jurisdiction of male craft unions which had no intention of seriously representing them at the bargaining table. The AFL established the Office and Professional Employees' International Union (OPEU) in 1945, but it was largely a union for the benefit of male office-workers and professionals. When Jean Maddox went to work as a secretary in California at a firm with a contract with OPEU in 1952, she found that 'none of the rank and file members seemed to know what the Executive Board was doing, grievances weren't being handled and union meetings were rarely held for want of a quorum of 25 members.' The UAW did not actively attempt to organize clerical workers until 1961.[71] And by the time office-worker organization revived in the 1970s, the history of the industrial union era had been all but forgotten.

Conclusion

The CIO era presents an ambiguous legacy for the vast numbers of women in clerical jobs today. The continued mechanization and feminization of office work in the 1930s and 1940s were probably inevitable consequences of the growth of American capitalism. It is difficult to say whether the exigencies of the Depression provoked more efficient organization of office work. It is clear, however, that with the coming of World War II, the rapid need for mobilization, systematization and government regulation of industry expedited the institution of cost accounting, mechanized office work and job classification in all but the most marginal firms.

Women clerical workers faced these developments with almost no protection from exploitation. In the 1930s, hundreds of thousands of working-class and middle-class young women had entered the already overcrowded occupation. This trend was to continue unabated after the war, as education levels climbed without any progress toward removing sexual discrimination in the professions, business or education. With the removal of most strictures against married women, moreover, office employment was flooded with a whole new group of workers seeking to keep pace with rising standards of living and inflation.

The AFL had responded to the changing nature of office work, when it responded at all, by shunting office-workers into ill-financed locals – or, in even more quixotic fashion, arguing for an apprenticeship system which would exclude the new-style high school clerks and machine operators. Of course, this was completely ineffective, given the continued deskilling and proletarianization of office work. Industrial unionism of the kind adopted in CIO struggles in auto, rubber and textiles, would have been a far better device for bringing women and men into office-worker unions in the 1930s. It had the potential for dissolving the hierarchy of labor in the office and factory, a hierarchy constructed along sexual and class lines. Sometimes this potential was realized; more often, though, office-worker unions continued to be institutions which mirrored the sexual division of labor at work. Male unionists shaped policy in such a way as to win benefits mainly for themselves and to prevent women from climbing out of the lower levels of clerical work. Indeed, the seeming 'solidarity' of professional and office-workers in the 1930s was more rhetorical than real.

That women clericals were able to organize themselves as effectively as they did in the 1930s and 1940s was remarkable, under the circumstances. And it is tempting to ask what might have happened after 1950 if the office-worker unions had not been driven from the CIO. Office-worker organization was at a new high, the first inroads in banks had been made, and there was a whole new generation of younger workers who had been introduced to unions during the war. The indifference of the CIO and its collusion in the red-baiting of these unions was both tragic and ultimately self-destructive. Workers who would form the most rapidly expanding part of the labor market in the future were virtually abandoned. The vast majority of women workers were once again cut adrift from the labor movement, which continued to ignore both their exploitation and their potential for militancy.

Notes

1 'Kitty Foyles Frolic at Steno Ball,' *Office and Professional News*, vol 7, February 1941, p.2. Hereafter cited as *OPNews*.
2 'We're No Kitty Foyles,' in *ibid.*, p.7.
3 *Ibid.*
4 See report of the International Labour Office, 'The Use of Machinery and its Influence on Conditions of Work for Staff,' *International Labour Review*, vol. 36, October 1937, pp.486–516; and M. W. Davies, *Woman's Place is at the Typewriter: Office Work and Office Workers, 1870–1930*, Philadelphia, Temple University Press, 1982.
5 H. Braverman, *Labor and Monopoly Capital: The Degradation of Work in the Twentieth Century*, London and New York, Monthly Review Press, 1974, p.305; A. D. Chandler, Jr, *The Visible Hand: The Managerial Revolution in American Business*, Cambridge, Mass., and London, Harvard University Press, 1977, especially pp.455–61; C. W. Mills, *White Collar: The American Middle Classes*, New York, Oxford University Press, 1951, pp.191–3; and D. Nelson, *Managers and Workers: Origins of the New Factory System in the United States, 1880–1920*, Madison, University of Wisconsin Press, 1975, pp.34–78.
6 E. Erickson, 'The Employment of Women in Offices,' US Women's Bureau Bulletin no. 120, Washington, DC, 1934, p.16. Erickson is the best general source on the evolution of women's jobs in offices between 1910 and 1930, but see also G. Coyle, 'Women in the Clerical Occupations,' *Annals of the American Academy of Political and Social*

Science, vol. 143, May 1929, pp.180–7, and J. M. Hooks, 'Women's Occupations Through Seven Decades,' US Women's Bureau Bulletin no. 218, Washington, DC, 1947, pp.74–7.

7 International Labour Office, 'Use of Machinery,' p.513; J. Köcka, *White Collar Workers in America, 1890–1940: A Socio-Political History in International Perspective*, London and Beverley Hills, Sage Publications, 1980, p.94. For an analysis of similar developments in England, see F. D. Klingender, *The Condition of Clerical Labour in Britain*, London, Martin Lawrence, 1935, p.25.

8 P. H. Douglas, *Real Wages in the United States, 1890–1926*, Cambridge, Mass., Harvard University Press, 1930, p.366. As David Lockwood notes, 'universal public education meant that every literate person became a potential clerk' (*The Blackcoated Worker: A Study in Class Consciousness*, London, George Allen & Unwin, 1958, p.37). As early as 1928, there were between three and five clericals seeking jobs for every one available in New York State, a greater disparity than in any other occupation (Coyle, 'Women in the Clerical Occupations,' p.187).

9 See S. H. Strom, 'Old Barriers and New Opportunities: Working Women in Rhode Island, 1900–1940,' *Rhode Island History*, vol. 39, May 1980, pp.43–55.

10 Douglas, *Real Wages*, pp.363–6; L. Corey, *The Crisis of the Middle Class*, New York, Covici, Friede, 1935, p.250. Also see A. G. Maher, 'Bookkeepers, Stenographers and Office Clerks in Ohio, 1914 to 1929,' US Women's Bureau Bulletin no. 95, Washington, DC, 1932. For an excellent summary of women's wages in different occupations in this period, see S. P. Benson, ' "A Great Theater": Saleswomen, Customers, and Managers in American Department Stores, 1890–1940,' PhD dissertation, Boston University, 1982, pp.284–97. One problem with comparing median manufacturing wages and clerical wages for women is that there was a wider range of salaries for women clerical workers than for industrial workers, so that the starting salaries for the lowest-paid clerical workers were considerably lower than the median and fell even more drastically during the Depression. A 1937 survey found starting salaries for file clerks as low as $8 a week; transcribers, $12; and bookkeepers, $12.50. See 'Business Survey Shows Low Office Salaries,' *Ledger*, vol. 3, January 1937, p.6.

11 See Erickson, 'Employment of Women in Offices'; 'Women Who Work in Offices,' US Women's Bureau Bulletin no. 132, Washington, DC, 1935; H. Byrne, 'Women Unemployed Seeking Relief in 1933,' US Women's Bureau Bulletin no. 139, Washington, DC, 1936; 'Office Work and Office Workers in 1940,' US Women's Bureau Bulletin nos 188–1, 2, 3, 4, 5. Coyle ('Women in the Clerical Occupations,' p.183) argues that some married women circumvented employers' preferences for single women by retaining their maiden names in the 1920s. For a good overview of these trends during the Depression see L. Scharf, *To Work and to Wed: Female Employment, Feminism, and the Great Depression*,

Westport and London, Greenwood Press, 1980, pp.98–108, 119–20.

12 Scharf, *To Work and to Wed*, pp.86–109; W. D. Wandersee, *Women's Work and Family Values, 1920–1940*, Cambridge, Mass., and London, Harvard University Press, 1981, pp.84–102; 'Women in Business II,' *Fortune*, vol. 51, August 1935, pp.51 and 53.

13 Erickson, 'Employment of Women in Offices,' pp.11 and 32; Coyle, 'Women in the Clerical Occupations,' pp.184–5; Scharf, *To Work and to Wed*, p.99; V. Solomon, 'Modern Times Becomes Workers' Modern Menace,' *OPNews*, vol. 6, May–June 1940, p.7; O. Pell, *The Office Worker – Labor's Side of the Ledger*, New York, League for Industrial Democracy Pamphlet, 1937; M. J. Stuart, 'Robots in the Office,' *New Republic*, May 25, 1938, pp.70–2.

14 Quoted in L. Gordon, *White Collar Workers Organize*, New York, UOPWA Pamphlet, n.d. (*c.*1938), p.7.

15 Scharf, *To Work and to Wed*, p.99; Stuart, 'Robots,' p.70; 'Labor Saving Equipment,' *Ledger*, vol. 3, March 1937, p.4; 'Business Machine Sales Soar – Office Jobs Don't,' *OPNews*, vol. 7, March 1941, p.7; Mills, *White Collar*, p.193.

16 Mills, *White Collar*, p.198; M. E. Pidgeon, 'Women in the Economy of the United States,' US Women's Bureau Bulletin no. 155, Washington, DC, 1937, p.75.

17 For the consequences of this kind of equipment on office work see I. R. Hoos, *Automation in the Office*, Washington, DC, Public Affairs Press, 1961; E. N. Glenn and R. L. Feldberg, 'Degraded and Deskilled: The Proletarianization of Clerical Work,' *Social Problems*, vol. 25, October 1977, pp.52–64; and Braverman, *Labor and Monopoly Capital*, pp.319–56.

18 Lockwood, *Blackcoated Worker*, p.78.

19 'Women in Business II,' p.55. For a good analysis of the role of the private secretary, see Davies, *Woman's Place*, pp.129–62.

20 *Ibid.*, p.52.

21 The best account of sexual conflict in the railroad and telephone unions is M. W. Greenwald, *Women, War and Work: The Impact of World War I on Women Workers in the United States*, Westport and London, Greenwood Press, 1980, pp.185–232.

22 R. L. Feldberg, ' "Union Fever": Organizing among Clerical Workers, 1900–1930,' *Radical America*, vol. 14, May–June 1980, pp.53–67. Also see Köcka, *White Collar Workers*, pp.228–9; and J. E. Finley, *White Collar Union: The Story of the OPEIU and its People*, New York, Octagon, 1975, pp.4–6.

23 As related by F. H. Luscomb in E. Cantarow, S. G. O'Malley and S. H. Strom, *Moving the Mountain: Women Working for Social Change*, Old Westbury, Feminist Press, 1979, p.40.

24 F. Peterson listed 1943 membership figures for the CIO office-worker unions as: UOPWA, 43,000; UFW, 33,000; and SCMWA, 38,000 (*Handbook of Labor Unions*, Washington, DC, American Council on

Public Affairs, 1944). For helpful summaries of these unions see G. M. Fink, ed., *Labor Unions*, Westport, Conn., and London, Greenwood Press, 1977, pp.257–60, 304–7. Köcka (*White Collar Workers*, pp.355–6) lists somewhat smaller numbers, but does not explain why he differs from Peterson, who received membership information directly from the unions. In 1946, the more successful SCMWA (not to be confused with AFSCME, an AFL rival union) merged with the UFW to become the United Public Workers (UPW). Both the UPW and the UOPWA expired shortly after being expelled from the CIO in 1950.

25 For a fuller treatment of the CIO's views on women, see S. H. Strom, 'Challenging "Woman's Place"': Feminism, the Left, and Industrial Unionism in the 1930s,' *Feminist Studies*, vol. 9, summer 1983, pp.359–87.

26 Köcka, *White Collar Workers*, p.226; Pidgeon, 'Women in the Economy,' pp.76–7; 'Wage Cuts in Steel Offices Hit by Union,' *Ledger*, vol. 4, February 1938, pp.1 and 8; C. D. Snyder, *White Collar Workers and the UAW*, Urbana, University of Illinois Press, 1973, p.31.

27 'Begins Organizing of Akron Rubber Company Offices,' *Ledger*, vol. 4, May 1938, p.8; 'Organizing in Akron,' in *ibid.*, November 1938, p.1; 'Union Grows in Rubber Company,' *OPNews*, vol. 6, March–April 1940, p.1; 'Organizing the Unorganized White Collar Workers,' *Career*, vol. 2, October 15, 1949, p.4. Also see E. M. Kassalow, 'White Collar Unionism in the United States,' in A. F. Sturmthal, ed., *White Collar Trade Unions: Contemporary Developments in Industrialized Societies*, Urbana, University of Illinois Press, 1966, pp.344–6.

28 'Organizing the Unorganized White Collar Workers.'

29 Köcka, *White Collar Workers*, pp.23, 223–8; Snyder, *White Collar Workers and the UAW*, p.45.

30 For example, the Federation of Westinghouse Independent Salaried Unions protested against the employment of married women in their offices before World War II (Köcka, *White Collar Workers*, p.231).

31 Interview with A. Prosten by S. H. Strom, February 5, 1977. On the progressivism of social workers in general, see N. Glazer, *The Social Basis of American Communism*, New York, Harcourt, Brace & World, 1961, p.142.

32 Interview with Matilda Chernin and Maury Rosen by S. H. Strom, May 27, 1983.

33 Prosten interview. In 1938, the Newspaper Guild signed a contract which granted increases to editorial, building maintenance and mechanical workers but did not mention 'members of the bookkeeping and clerical departments' ('Newspaper Guild Gains Three New Victories,' *CIO News*, vol. 1, February 26, 1938, p.1).

34 For a helpful but anti-communist account of the CIO insurance drive, see Harvey J. Clermont, *Organizing the Insurance Worker: A History of Labor Unions of Insurance Employees*, Washington, DC, Catholic University of America Press, 1966; 'President Merrill Outlines Tasks

Facing Unions,' *Ledger*, vol. 5, January 1939, p.1.
35 Prosten interview.
36 'Merrill Addresses Eastern Regional Conference,' *OPNews*, vol. 5, February 1939, p.3.
37 Clermont, *Organizing the Insurance Worker*, p.176.
38 F. W. Fox, 'Telling it the Way it was with Harry and Frances,' unpublished typescript in the possession of the author, p.1.
39 Interview with C. Levy Mills by S. H. Strom and S. Halpern, November, 15, 1975.
40 For a more detailed analysis of the left's position on both feminism and the importance of organizing office-workers to ward off fascism, see Strom, 'Challenging "Woman's Place," ' pp.367–8 and 374–5.
41 Letter, *c.*1937, F. H. Luscomb Papers, Schlesinger Library, Radcliffe College.
42 Mary Heaton Vorse, for instance, charged that 'office girls by the score . . . signed the cards furnished them by the Citizens' Committee' during the General Motors strike in Anderson, Indiana, in 1936 (*Labor's New Millions*, New York, Modern Age Books, 1938, p.138). The problem with this kind of statement, of course, is that it does not say how many industrial workers signed such cards, whether any office-workers did not sign them, or whether this example was repeated or contradicted elsewhere.
43 'Susie Steno Discovers the Union,' *Ledger*, vol. 3, June 1937, p.6.
44 'Susie Socializes,' in *ibid.*, November 1937, p.5.
45 'Forums, Classes, Arts and Sports,' Program of the New York Joint Council, UOPWA, 1939–40.
46 'New York Awaits Stenos' Ball,' *Ledger*, vol. 5, January 1939, p.3. The 1938 ball netted more than $2,000 for New York Local 16 (P. K. Hawley, 'Local 16 Reports,' November 21, 1938).
47 L. Gordon, 'Strike Highlights,' *Ledger*, vol. 3, November 1937, p.3.
48 'Stenos Want In-service Training,' *Federal Record*, vol. 4, September 25, 1942, p.4. Nelson was the daughter of a Republican congressman from Maine, a graduate of Wellesley and, along with her vice-president, Dorothy Bailey, a graduate of industrial relations from the University of Minnesota. They had worked for the US Department of Labor before becoming union organizers for the UFW. When elected to the presidency of UFW in 1944, Nelson was married to a second mate in the merchant marine, had a small child, and used her own name.
49 'Union Election Results,' *Ledger*, vol. 3, November 3, 1937, p.3; Gordon, *White Collar Workers Organize*, p.19.
50 Gordon, *White Collar Workers Organize*, pp.20–1.
51 *Ledger* (vol. 2) reports: M. Nathan, 'The Margon Strike' and 'Unity Pledged at Joint Rally,' March 1936, p.5; M. Nathan, 'The Margon Strike Continues,' April 1936, p.9; 'Cleveland Office Workers and Machinists in Joint Strike,' November 1936, p.9.
52 *Ledger* reports: 'Store Clerks Win Philadelphia Strike,' vol. 2, December

1936, p.1; '17 Win in Sit-down,' vol. 3, January 1937, p.1; 'Sit-in Brings Film Raises,' vol. 3, January 1937, p.1.

53 Brassiere Company Workers Win Union Recognition,' *Ledger*, vol. 3, July 1937, p.1; 'Bra Strikers Ask "Uplift" in Wages,' *OPNews*, vol. 6, November–December 1940, p.1.

54 *OPNews* (vol. 7) reports: 'Sonneborn Strikers Win Coast-to-Coast Support,' February 1941, p.1; 'Strike Spirit Rises as Sonneborn Accounts Fall,' March 1941, p.8; 'Local 16 Maps Changes in Sonneborn Strike,' May 1941, p.8; 'Lowenstein Sees Red as NLRB Poll Draws Near,' July 1941, p.1; 'Local 16 Contests NLRB Election at Lowenstein,' August 1941, p.3.

55 Gordon, *White Collar Workers Organize*, pp.3–4; 'Union Recognized in Credit Firm which Fired Merrill More than Six Years Ago,' *Ledger*, vol. 3, September 3, 1937, p.1; 'CCH Pact Renewed,' *Ledger*, vol. 4, November 1938; 'Local 16 Pickets CCH by Telephone,' *OPNews*, vol. 6, February 1940; Hawley, 'Local 16 Reports,' p.15.

56 'Brief Submitted by Local 16, UOPWA, CIO in Arbitration Proceedings with the Mail Advertising Service Association, Inc. for the Establishment of Hourly and Piece Work Minimum Wage Sacles,' UOPWA papers, September 1942, pp.8–9. Also see International Labour Office, 'Use of Machinery,' p.495.

57 International Labor Office, 'Use of Machinery,' pp.9–11, 55–7, 61–2.

58 *Ledger* reports: 'Labour Board Hears Globe Mail Strikers,' vol. 2, December 1936, pp.1–2; 'Globe Mail Decision Expected from Washington,' vol. 3, January 1937, p.1; 'Contract Won in Mail Firm,' vol. 3, March 1937, p.1.

59 *Ledger* reports: 'Solid Strike Forged against Efficient Letter Sweatshop,' vol. 3, November 1937, pp.1 and 3; 'Labor Board Hears Efficient Letter Company Case, Strike Strong,' vol. 3, December 1937, p.1; 'Board Edict Aids Strikers,' vol. 4, January 1938, p.1; 'Efficient Company Strike Win,' vol. 4, February 1938, p.2.

60 'Unionism "Fate Worse than Death" to Boston Firm, Tries to Liquidate,' *CIO News*, vol. 1, May 7, 1938, p.7; Prosten interview.

61 *OPNews* reports: 'UOPWA Signs Pact for 1500 at Polk,' vol. 7, June 1941, pp.1 and 2; 'Local 26 Signs Second Big Direct Mail House,' vol. 7, July 1941, p.1; 'Polk Workers Win Pact in New York, Poll in Cleveland,' vol. 7, August 1941, p.1; 'Detroit Socks Jim Crow,' vol. 8, October 1942, p.1.

62 *OPNews* (vol. 7) reports: 'UOPWA Opens Big Drive in Direct Mail Field,' August 1941, pp.1–2; 'Victory in Key Election Spurs Letter Shop Drive,' September 1941, p.1; 'Union Opens Direct Mail Contract Talks for over 1500 Lettershop Workers,' October 1941, p.1; 'DMOC Wins Master Pact,' November 1941, p.7; 'Strike Climaxes Reign of Terror at McKenzie,' December 1941, p.2; 'McKenzie Bows to Union after Two-Month Strike,' vol. 8, January 1942, p.1.

63 *OPNews* reports: 'Two New Contracts,' vol. 6, March–April 1940, p.2;

234 *Sharon Hartman Strom*

'Southern Steel Office Staff Scores Labor Board Victory,' 'Strikers, Tenants Win Hearing in Chicago Council,' 'Conmar Parley Begins after Election Victory,' vol. 7, August 1941, pp.3 and 8.

64 These figures are cited in two UOPWA pamphlets by L. Merrill: *A Salary Policy to Win the War*, September 1943, p.5; and *You Can Get It: How White Collar Workers Can Win Higher Pay*, n.d. (c.1946), p.5.

65 Mills, *White Collar*, p.193; 'Business Machine Sales Soar – Office Jobs Don't; Chandler (*The Visible Hand*, p.476) observes that World War II put a 'capstone' on economic developments between 1920 and 1940, and set the stage for 'impressive growth' in the postwar years. The mobilization of the wartime economy allowed smaller firms who were subcontractors to the larger corporations with government contracts to learn 'about the modern methods of forecasting, accounting, and inventory control.

66 J. Mitford, *A Fine Old Conflict*, New York, Knopf, 1977, p.54.

67 'Organizing an Office Workers' Canteen,' *UOPWA Organizers' Bulletin*, vol. 4, March 10, 1943.

68 For a summary of these strikes and new contracts see 'Officers' Report to the 7th Constitutional Convention of the UOPWA, CIO,' Brooklyn, New York, March 1, 1948, pp.9–11.

69 'Is National CIO Interfering in UOPWA?' *Career*, vol. 1, December 1948, p.14; 'More Taft-Hartley Affidavits Filed,' *Massachusetts CIO News*, vol. 5, June 1948, p.4. In 1949, for instance, Boston Union News Company employees were told the company would not negotiate with the UOPWA and 'began "inviting" workers to attend AFL meetings on company time where they were told they would be "saved from Moscow domination" and that everybody would get a $5 raise if the AFL won' (*Career*, vol. 2, January 1949, p.1).

70 Cantarow, O'Malley and Strom, *Moving the Mountain*, pp.42–3.

71 *Jean Maddox: The Fight for Rank and File Democracy*, Union WAGE Pamphlet, Berkeley, Cal., 1976, p.9; Snyder, *White Collar Workers and the UAW*, p.57.

11

Organizing the United Automobile Workers: Women workers at the Ternstedt General Motors parts plant

Ruth Meyerowitz

The United Automobile Workers' Union (UAW), like most of the industrial unions formed in the 1930s, had a predominantly male constituency. But there were also some factories in the UAW's jurisdiction – in the auto parts branch of the motor industry – where women were quite numerous. In this chapter, Ruth Meyerowitz analyzes the role of women in the UAW's organizing drive in one such factory, the Detroit Ternstedt General Motors parts plant, which played an important role in the union's broader General Motors (GM) drive. Drawing on archival material and extensive oral history interviews, Meyerowitz analyzes the social and political composition of Ternstedt's female union activists, and demonstrates their critical role in the organizing drive's success. Although these women were organized along with their male counterparts, in accordance with the logic of industrial unionism, the UAW gave little attention to the special needs of women workers. There was no systematic effort to encourage women's union leadership, and most of the women activists involved in the Ternstedt drive gradually disappeared from the scene. Their story is part of the contribution of the 1930s generation of rank-and-file women activists to building the Congress of Industrial Organizations, a contribution which has never been fully recognized.

In 1937, men and women at the Ternstedt General Motors parts plant in Detroit organized a unit of the UAW. Women made up half of the total labor force in this factory, which employed between 12,000 and 16,000 workers. Such a large female labor force was unusual in the automobile industry, and as a result of male prejudices, union drives at sites with so many women workers were rare. But because the Ternstedt women were employed in a strategically important factory, the UAW's desire to organize male auto-workers led union men to organize their female co-workers.

The union drive at Ternstedt was typical of many such drives in basic industries in the 1930s, despite the plant's unusually high proportion of females. The organizing occurred during the period of economic recovery, between 1935 and 1937, when conflicts between labor and management escalated throughout the nation. As employment increased in the auto industry in 1937, workers became more confident of finding work and were more willing to risk union activity. There was an upsurge of unionization throughout the auto industry at this time, culminating in the UAW's first major victories in 1937.

General Motors was the UAW's primary target in its drive to establish a national union of automobile-workers. The prototype of the huge, modern corporation, GM was by this time larger than Ford, and also seemed less intransigently anti-union. By September 1936, the UAW's national leadership had decided to concentrate on unionizing GM. The dramatic Flint sit-down strike against GM in December 1936 and January 1937 was only the first stage of the struggle to organize GM. The UAW's victory in Flint encouraged the unionization of other plants in the GM empire, including the Ternstedt parts plant in Detroit.[1]

Auto union organizers, like other CIO unionists in the 1930s, organized women along with men in mass production industries. When given a choice, however, they preferred to organize workers of their own sex, and the plants and industries they targeted for unionization were predominantly male. Women workers were generally left in the position of either unionizing themselves or remaining unorganized.

Although UAW men were reluctant to organize them, women – both as wives and as workers – made central contributions to the union's victories in the late 1930s. Without them, the UAW might have failed to win some of its key battles. What explains women's activism, in the face of union hostility or indifference? During the

1930s, unionists from union families or from the ranks of the Socialist, Communist and Proletarian Parties, provided the leadership which encouraged wives and women workers to organize. These organizers were predominantly women, though there were some men. Whether male or female, however, they were not feminists: they sought neither equal rights nor female emancipation. The absence of an independent feminist movement in this period also meant that women were ill-equipped to organize in their own interests. Within the labor movement, for both men and women, a politics of class prevailed over a politics of sex. Even the communists, who were most sensitive to the greater exploitation of women, and periodically raised 'women's issues' within the unions, did not do so consistently. Nor did they encourage women to aspire to union leadership; those who did win such posts were not actively maintained in office.

The history of the Ternstedt organizing drive illustrates both the strengths and the weaknesses of the UAW's relationship to women workers in the 1930s. It shows that plants in mass production industries with large numbers of female employees could be unionized, and that a few dedicated men and women could organize thousands of workers. In spite of resistance from the all-male executive board of UAW Local 174, a handful of organizers from the amalgamated local on Detroit's West Side, where the Ternstedt plant was located, unionized this factory. They employed what was then an unusual tactic – a slow-down, rather than the more dramatic and popular sit-down strike. Developed as a creative response to the no-strike clause in the national contract signed by the UAW and GM in early 1937, the slow-down was very well suited to organizing women workers. As a tactic of on-the-job resistance, it occurred during work-time and thus interfered minimally with women's family responsibilities.

Women played a leading role as rank-and-file organizers at Ternstedt, and the role of the organizer – both male and female – was critical. Although conditions in the plant were poor, they were better than at many other factories employing women at this time. Workers' grievances alone did not spontaneously generate a union. Rather, the successful drive at Ternstedt was the product of hard work by skilled organizers who, in 1937, secured union recognition, and then went on to consolidate the union's power over the next four years – despite renewed recession, layoffs, and intense managerial resistance to the UAW.

The Ternstedt drive reveals the limitations of the UAW leadership's attitudes toward women, as well as the obstacles women activists faced within the union following the initial campaign for recognition. In addition to serving as organizers, women became rank-and-file union leaders, stewards and sat on committees in the UAW of the 1930s. Several were elected as delegates to union conventions, and a few went on to win union office. But the absence of a feminist consciousness within the UAW in this period meant that efforts to sustain women labor leaders in official union positions were minimal. As a result, women dropped out of union activities far more frequently than their male counterparts. By the end of World War II, most of the generation of women activists who had first helped to organize the UAW had either left the plants or dropped out of union activity. Younger women in the plants therefore had few models of successful female labor leaders.

Women workers in the Ternstedt plant

In 1937, the Ternstedt General Motors parts plant was the largest GM parts factory in Detroit, and probably in the nation. Composed of five buildings, the plant was in the heart of Detroit's West Side. Ternstedt first hired women in large numbers during World War I and continued to employ them in accordance with the sex-stereotyped view that females could easily handle the small parts – mostly door handles and chromium trim – it manufactured. The company could also pay them less than men. Although auto work has generally been considered a male preserve, women actually worked in a range of jobs throughout the automobile industry well before the shift to war production swelled the ranks of the female labor force during World War II. The auto industry's 'female' jobs were primarily in the factories of the small parts suppliers, like Ternstedt, where wages were lower, as well as in sex-segregated jobs in the major auto plants.

A handful of the women at Ternstedt were in their fifties and sixties when the organizing began in the mid-1930s. These women had worked in factories from the age of ten or eleven – long before

Alva K. Ternstedt established the company in 1917 – bringing in falsified birth certificates to circumvent the compulsory schooling and child labor laws. When Stanley Nowak, the Ternstedt organizer on the staff of the UAW's West Side local, arrived in Detroit in 1924, he found women employed at Dodge, Packard and Ford, as well as at GM. But with between 6,000 and 8,000 women workers, Ternstedt alone employed approximately half of all the females in Detroit's auto industry's workforce in 1930. The figures were very high even in comparison with other types of female industrial employment in the 'Motor City.' For example, the cigar plants where many women worked were relatively tiny, employing only 200 or 300 women.[2]

The women workers at Ternstedt came from several distinct ethnic and cultural groups. The native-born had migrated to Detroit from depressed farm and mining regions in the 1920s, in response to the successful labor recruitment campaigns the city's manufacturers had conducted, which swelled auto industry employment by 30 percent in that decade.[3] Among the women were a large group of southerners, called 'hillbillies,' including both rural migrants and the wives and daughters of coal miners from the anthracite regions of Kentucky and southern Illinois. Those from mining families were familiar with unionism, and would prove to be the most likely to support the UAW. There were also women who had previously lived in Michigan's farming areas, as well as Eastern European immigrants, predominantly second-generation Poles. Like those with mining backgrounds, the Polish women were more likely to join the union than were those of other ethnic groups. Some German and Hungarian women also worked in Ternstedt. Most of the latter lived in Del Rey, a Hungarian neighborhood near the plant.

Until the Depression, most of these women saw themselves as temporary workers, and were not likely to press for higher wages, steady employment or job security. But these patterns changed in the 1930s, as male unemployment and underemployment forced more and more women to enter the workforce. By 1940, 35 percent of all working women were married. The old rule that a woman should quit her job as soon as she found a husband broke down. Yet wives faced widespread prejudice, since they were viewed by many as taking jobs from male heads of households. Although few working-class families contained two steadily employed breadwinners, the prejudice against hiring married women persisted. To get jobs, many married women pretended to be single. They were fired if their employers discovered the truth. Ternstedt, however, was one of the few workplaces in Detroit willing to employ married women.[4]

Only a minority of women were employed in basic industries in this period, and so in that respect Ternstedt's women workers were atypical.[5] Otherwise, though, their experience was generally representative of the female workforce as a whole. Most had less than an eighth-grade education, and many probably could not read. Becky Laing Kimsley, one of Ternstedt's rank-and-file organizers, thought that even among the second-generation ethnic workers, few of the women had gone past the second or third grade. They all worked out of economic need. Nearly all were part of a family economy. Many were the first generation of women in their families to work regularly outside the home for wages.

Because of Ternstedt's unusually liberal policy in regard to marital status, a majority of the factory's female employees were married. Others, widowed or divorced, were heads of households, while single women worked to help support parental families. Ternstedt worker Ann Dankowitz believed many of the single girls were totally under the domination of their families and turned all their earnings over to them, receiving only a small allowance in return. Others worked because of changing conceptions of an adequate standard of living. They took jobs to buy the material possessions they wanted. For working-class families to acquire such goods as automobiles, daughters and sometimes wives had to work. Nevertheless, Ternstedt's managers expressed the conventional view that women worked only for 'pin money.' When Becky Laing Kimsley complained about women's low wages in the 1937 negotiations, an assistant to plant manager Skinner proposed that those women who could not make ends meet on their own wages find a man to support them. But under Depression conditions, even if a woman followed this advice, she was likely to be forced periodically to seek work outside the home.[6]

On the job, women workers faced many of the same conditions which their male co-workers complained of – seasonal work and frequent layoffs; competition between ethnic groups; widespread abuses of authority; tyrannical foremen; favoritism; job insecurity; low wages and long hours; the shapeup and the arbitrary shifting of workers from one machine or job to another; work that was dangerous and unhealthy; complex piecework and incentive pay systems; and the infamous speed-up. In addition, most women experienced sexual harassment and abuse.[7]

At Ternstedt, each plant had its own structure and personality; yet the work in the five plants was similar. Plants 16, 18, Main and Fleetwood each housed a tool and die operation, punch presses, and assembly divisions. Employees in the Main Plant and Plant 18 were overwhelmingly female, while Fleetwood had a large concentration of women workers. On the second floor of Plant 18, for example, there was hardly a man to be found. More than half of this female majority were second-generation Poles and Hungarians in their late twenties.

A sexual division of labor pervaded the organization of work. Most of the men were skilled and semi-skilled; most of the women, semi-skilled or unskilled. The few skilled jobs at Ternstedt were in tool and die and in polishing, and both were exclusively male. Although women worked in every other area, they were clustered in the semi-skilled punch- and drill-press jobs, and in assembly where work was 'unskilled.' They also handled stock, worked as bench hands, on clip lines and on weatherstripping. In the graining and spraying departments in Plant 18, they handled stock and blew holes.[8]

However, the existence of separate job classifications for men's and women's work did not mean that women and men necessarily worked in separate sections of the factories. They often worked side by side, and they cooperated in the slow-downs and wildcat strikes which marked this period. This was especially true on assembly lines and in the polishing sections, where one group could not stop work without affecting all the others. Although a few Ternstedt women worked in traditionally 'male jobs,' rigid segregation of tasks along sex lines was usually maintained, and the jobs accorded to women were always assigned lower rates of pay.[9]

The union drive

When the West Side local first discussed the possibility of organizing Ternstedt, the UAW's drive against GM was at its height. Yet the union had not made any attempt to unionize Ternstedt, the largest plant on Detroit's West Side except for the Ford Motor Company. The UAW considered the plant impossible to organize, simply because half of its employees were female. In spite of many examples to contradict this presumption, the male executive board of West Side Local 174 believed that women were harder to organize and less militant than men.

There was general debate within the labor movement at this time about the possibility of organizing the 'backward stratum' of women workers. Some argued that women could actually set the workers' movement back if they were incorporated into unions in large numbers. They claimed that women were essentially conservative, due to their family responsibilities and social conditioning, and warned that women would retard men unless special appeals were made to them. On the other hand, other organizers suggested that, precisely because of their different roles in the family and the community, women could play a leading and unifying role in labor struggles. Dramatic instances of this occurred in the 'auxiliaries' and 'emergency brigades' created by wives and women workers during the organizing drives in auto. Women in Flint, for example, played a central role in winning the sit-down through organizing strike support as an extension of the kind of support they felt they owed to their men as wives, mothers and family members.[10]

Throughout the history of labor in the US, unions have generally agreed to organize women only after outbreaks of militancy and independent organizing by the women workers themselves. Ternstedt was unusual in this respect, for it was a male unionist who pressed the UAW to undertake the project of organizing the plant, despite its large concentration of women workers. Stanley Nowak, the union's Polish workers' organizer, believed the plant could be unionized, because of his previous successes in organizing women workers in Detroit's cigar factories. But when Nowak first suggested organizing Ternstedt to the executive board of the West Side local, he was met with many objections. Not only were half of the workers in the plant women, but, the board members pointed out, a majority were rural southerners, presumed to be anti-union. Nowak believed this last impression was incorrect. He thought that about half the women were southerners, but the other half were Poles.[11] And because most of the Poles were American-born, he thought, they would be relatively easy to organize. But not even Nowak recognized that among the 'southern women' in the plant were a number of migrants from mining areas, many of whom had had experiences with the United Mine Workers' union. Their background would lead these women to become the backbone of the Ternstedt drive.[12]

In spite of their reservations, the executive board agreed to assign Nowak the task of organizing the plant. The drive began while the Flint sit-down strike of 1936–7 was still under way. It went through several distinct stages.[13] Nowak's first step was to identify pro-union workers inside the plant, to create an organizing committee, and to identify and publicize the workers' grievances. He followed workers into local bars and restaurants and talked to them about problems in the shop. After learning what the issues were, he wrote about them in the next morning's leaflets. In his contacts with Ternstedt workers, the organizer observed that the men responded more than the women, although his approach to workers in bars and restaurants necessarily excluded most of the women, who went home after work to their daily round of family and child-care chores. While other drives included visits to workers in their homes, Nowak concluded these calls would take too much time. Home visits, however, might have proved an effective way of reaching female employees. As soon as three of the women organizers – Irene Young Marinovich, Becky Laing Kimsley and Martha Strong – enlisted, it became easier to approach women.

The organizers

Ternstedt's rank-and-file organizers tended to be men and women in their twenties and thirties. More militant than the older workers, who had experienced significant working-class defeats after World War I, they were survivors of the Depression and had managed to retain jobs and reasonably steady employment even in the depths of the years 1929–33. Most came from the upper strata of the working class. They tended to be white, native-born of Northern European descent, and more educated than their co-workers. Most of the women organizers were the wives and daughters of coal miners who had migrated north to Detroit after the union defeats in the mining regions of the country in the 1920s and the collapse of the coal industry in 1929. The women were either semi-skilled or unskilled workers, in contrast to the male organizers, who tended to be either skilled tradespeople working in tool and die, or former coal miners.

Irene Young Marinovich, Martha Strong, Becky Laing Kimsley, Irene Kotlarek, Margaret Lipscomb, Lena Saline and Mary Kaluszak were among the women who became rank-and-file organizers, union activists and stewards. They identified themselves to Nowak early in the drive, and were quickly assigned to official union tasks. They were all highly disciplined, committed organizers. All were elected stewards in their departments; all played leading roles in the slow-down. Most of them had learned about unions before taking jobs at Ternstedt. Irene Young Marinovich and Martha Strong experienced unions in the mining regions of the country in the 1920s, while Becky Laing Kimsley's father was an organizer. They brought their union sympathies and the skills acquired in the struggles of the 1920s and early 1930s to the organizing drive. In addition, Irene Young Marinovich was a member of the Communist Party, whose small presence at Ternstedt belies its tremendous influence in the organizing drive.

As the drive progressed, Nowak held public meetings. With women's growing attendance, the problem of reaching them lessened. As more women organizers were recruited, they built support for the union among workers of both sexes. Although several of the women activists left their factory jobs when their husbands or families could afford to keep them at home, the fact that they were temporary workers did not make them less militant while they were in the plants. At times, their sense of indignation about deteriorating conditions and less fear of the consequences of losing their jobs if their husbands were employed, or if they could return to parental families, made them the best organizers.[14] Nowak believes that, in general, women were more militant and more effective organizers than the men:

> One thing about women in a place like Ternstedt, once they are convinced, they are sometimes more courageous, in some respects, than men are. They have more nerve. They are more aggressive in approaching men and asking them to join the union. When a woman approached a man that was hesitant and urged him to join, it was less likely to turn into an argument that could get physical than if a male organizer did it.[15]

Irene Young Marinovich attributed the pro-union sentiment among the Poles to Nowak's work and to the character of Detroit's Polish community. Nowak had solid ties to this community with its strong leftist component centering on the Polish-language newspaper, *Glas Lodowy* (*People's Voice*), and several ethnic halls. Slovenian Hall and Dom Polski Hall, two of these cultural centers, became union meeting places during the drive. A number of Poles became stewards in the union's early days, and their example probably encouraged their compatriots. In addition, Nowak held special meetings for the Polish women workers. The Hungarian community, in contrast, proved more difficult to recruit. When Hungarian women joined the union, they paid their dues but rarely became active. No Hungarian organizer played a role similar to Nowak's; no union meetings seem to have been held in Hungarian, nor were there any special efforts to reach Hungarian women. Fewer Hungarians became rank-and-file organizers.[16].

Women workers had to overcome greater obstacles than their male counterparts to join the union or to become active. Their difficulties stemmed from the commonly held assumption that the women were temporary workers and, more important, from the union's own indifference to the special problems of women workers on and off the job. Few community facilities eased the burdens of housework and child-care, so women found it difficult to participate; married women and single parents encountered the greatest barriers. The pressures to accomplish all their work made the women feel they had no time to stop for meetings, although they supported and participated in the strikes. Kimsley recalls:

> You didn't hear women say, 'My husband or my father doesn't want me to go to the meetings.' The women had a lot of things to do at home and didn't have time to stop either before or after work for meetings. It was essentially a function of having two jobs. None of our women got that actively involved. It was the men who could attend the meetings.[17]

For the handful of women activists, the conflict between union and family demands was often painful. Both called on precious time which had to be squeezed out of the few hours remaining after the standard working week of fifty-four hours. A good husband 'allowed' his wife to participate actively in the union – as long as she carried out all her other responsibilities. An unusual husband 'encouraged' her union activities. In neither case did the husband expect, nor did his wife insist, that he help with housework or child-care. The only help a mother and wife could usually get with these tasks came from daughters, but these girls often deeply resented a mother's union activities for that reason.[18]

Union work in these years took time. A woman serving as a steward or sitting on a committee could expect to spend at least two nights a week in long meetings handling grievances. Moreover, there were additional union meetings to attend. Several of the activists would have participated more had their families not drained their time. Even though she was a committee member, Becky Laing Kimsley recalls that caring for her daughter as a single parent limited her participation in the union. When stewards' classes were established, she could not attend because she had no one to care for the girl. Although some of the men from her section attended, virtually no women did. Yet even activists who would have participated more extensively had they themselves had help with family and child-care responsibilities, failed to integrate an analysis of their own situation into their understanding of why women had lower rates of participation in the union. Instead, they repeated the traditional explanations. Kimsley considered women 'pretty much home-bodies' who were hard to drag out to meetings after work. Nor were there financial incentives for union work or rewards in the form of higher status among one's peers. Many of these positions required much work without pay or status, and it was therefore hard to recruit people to fill them.[19]

Under these conditions, it is not surprising that it was the single women who found it easiest to be active. Martha Strong's experience illustrates the way in which single women could choose to organize their lives around the union:

> I worked the midnight shift and lived alone in an apartment near my job, so I had more time. I could go to meetings during the day and still do my job. Well, not many people would have given that much time, but I was happy to do it because I believed we needed that union.[20]

Most women with families, however, found Strong's level of commitment impossible. Most of Ternstedt's female activists were unmarried, had no children, and were inspired either by a political commitment to a workers' society, or by a history of unionism in their families. Of the women rank-and-file activists, only Becky Laing Kimsley and Irene Young Marinovich had children at the time. Kimsley's activism was especially remarkable, as she was a single parent, and under considerable pressure from her child to stay at home 'like other mothers.'

Irene Young Marinovich believes that political affiliation was the most important factor in the self-selection of union activists, among both men and women. She estimates that at least 75 percent of the stewards and committee members in the early days of the union were members of a leftist political organization. The most active such groups in Ternstedt and in West Side Local 174 at this time were the Socialist, Communist and Proletarian Parties.[21]

In the early days of the Ternstedt drive, there were two small but important victories which did much to allay workers' fears that those allying with the union would be fired. After being elected steward, Martha Strong openly wore her union and steward buttons in the plant and began signing up members. When she was confronted by plant superintendent Jim Pirtle and asked why she had joined the union, she told him it was because of the speed-up, which had forced her to triple production over a five-year period, without any increase in pay. She fully expected to be fired, but Pirtle did not even threaten her with the loss of her job. This was a turning-point in the organizing drive, for it persuaded other workers in Plant 16 that they, too, could join the union and keep their jobs. People who had union application forms began signing them and paying dues. Women took application forms home to their husbands employed at Ford and began to bring in dues from them, as well.[22]

Although the struggle to keep Irene Marinovich employed was more difficult, that victory, too, galvanized the drive. Marinovich was elected steward for her plant at the first union meeting she attended. When she began to distribute union buttons and cards the next day at work, she was immediately fired for falsifying company records, since she had joined the plant under her maiden name. It was clear that the real cause of her being fired was her union activity, however. She reported the incident to the local; as a probationary employee, however, she did not expect the fledgling UAW to fight for her reinstatement. Nevertheless, the union did press the case, fearing that they would never succeed in organizing the plant if she was not rehired. Although the company transferred Marinovich immediately upon her reinstatement to another job in a different building, the result of the victory was that every worker on her floor signed a membership card. 'They got me back to work,' she recalls, 'and I was a probationary employee. So the women there thought, "If they could get her back to work, and she didn't have seniority, then there's a chance for us!" '[23]

The slow-down

The UAW's victory in Flint in February 1937 gave further impetus to the drive in Ternstdt, and created new challenges. As a subdivision of GM, Ternstedt was covered by the master agreement GM signed, recognizing the UAW for the first time. The agreement provided that management must recognize and negotiate with the union throughout the corporation. But many local plant managers, including Skinner at Ternstedt, refused to comply with the agreement and meet with union representatives. Meanwhile, the new agreement prohibited the UAW from striking.

As Ternstedt's management persisted in its refusal to recognize the UAW, the organizers sought new tactics to force it to come to the bargaining table. While the sit-down strikes which had proved so effective in Flint seemed the logical method, the no-strike clause in the new GM–UAW agreement ruled out similar action, since the union wanted to show its responsibility and good faith. In addition, the organizers faced the problem of persuading more workers at Ternstedt to join the UAW, in the face of management's intransigence. By March 1937, only one-third of the workers had signed union cards.

As the organizers discussed tactics, Nowak recalled having read about a slow-down in Vienna. American workers in the garment trades had used the slow-down, but it had not been used as a unionizing technique in auto. Nowak feared the workers would not have the discipline to stay at their machines and continue to produce at the lower rate. This method did cut production at the same time as meeting the formal requirements of the contract. The slow-down presented another difficulty for management: they would have to pay workers, but would not get production. For the workers, the financial sacrifice was less than in an ordinary strike. Although they could not earn piece-rate bonuses, they would receive their hourly wages. In March 1937, the UAW called a stewards' meeting at Ternstedt to plan this action.[24]

Although all the Ternstedt buildings were represented at this planning meeting, most of the stewards attending were from union strongholds in the Main Plant and Plant 18. Openly planning an illegal tactic in this way was an unusual action, for the plan could easily have been sabotaged had any of the stewards attending the meeting informed the company. But in contrast to the Ford Motor Company and other GM plants where there were stool-pigeons, Ternstedt had no leaks. Nowak thought the company spy system was weak at Ternstedt because Skinner had an unrealistic view of the loyalty of the workforce, and relied entirely on his supervisors for intelligence. This allowed the union to plan and execute the slow-down under optimal conditions.[25] Marinovich recalls: 'We met together with a few of the stewards and the committeemen and decided how we would do this and keep it from the company. It was one of the best-kept secrets ... The company was really taken by surprise.'[26]

Most workers had never heard of a slow-down and did not understand the legal significance of the contract. Although they favored forms of struggle with which they were familiar – either an outside strike or a sit-down – Nowak was able to persuade them to adopt this new technique. Marinovich and other leaders built support. They told trusted men and women that on a certain morning they would go to work, but cut production back by half. On the second day, they would cut back by another half – and so on, until they produced practically nothing. Marinovich warned them against taking breaks and sitting down. People were expected to be at their machines and at work all day so that the company could not fire them. Most important was to stay at their machines and cut production back to nothing.[27]

For ten days between April 1 and April 10, the workers cut production back to a fraction of their normal output. Several female stewards took the lead – Irene Kotlarek, Margaret Lipscomb, Lena Saline, Becky Laing Kimsley and Mary Kaluszak. From the initial planning group of 200 stewards and committee members, the action spread by word of mouth. Sustaining the slow-down and insuring its success required constant organization, hard work, persuasion and an ability to recognize and cope with the additional stress created by the new pace of work and the constant demands by foremen to increase production. 'The slow-down was one of the most magnificent things I have ever seen,' Marinovich recalls. 'All my life I will always remember how *hard* it was and how I couldn't believe before it really happened that the women would really participate like that.'[28]

The slow-down became an organizational strike to get people into the union. It was particularly effective given the ethnic and sex divisions among Ternstedt's employees, the fact that such a large portion of the workforce was female, their fear of unions, and the general reluctance among both male and female employees to challenge management. Marinovich speculates that Ternstedt's large group of female employees meant that it could not have been organized with traditional methods. Since it occurred during work-time, the slow-down interfered least with family responsibilities; it also gave employees a sense of their power:[29]

> Stanley was right when he said we could not have organized that plant if we hadn't had a slow-down. That showed the workers the strength that they had there. It gave them confidence that they had the ability to close down that damned plant because that's what we did. We didn't walk out because of the contract. But we slowed it down until they realized we had the power to do it – girls who never joined the union, who didn't intend to join the union, and a lot of men, too. It really caught fire. They weren't losing any wages, they were working, they came in every day.[30]

After recognition: women at Ternstedt

The slow-down won the UAW recognition from the company and brought management to the bargaining table. This, however, was only the first step toward a viable union. Within the plants, support was strong but uneven, and varied from department to department depending upon the consciousness of the workers and their informal leaders. Union leaders at this point had a dual goal – to win concessions from management which would improve wages and working conditions, and to create full support for the union among Ternstedt employees. Throughout the following year of tedious work, the union continued to gain members by building on the support it had won during the slow-down.

Although management had now recognized the union, it remained reluctant to negotiate with the UAW or to implement the concessions it had promised. Less than two months after the company had agreed to collective bargaining in response to the slow-down, management once again refused to meet or negotiate with the bargaining committee. Workers and unionists had to resort to new pressure tactics several times in 1937 in order to force the company to deal with the union. In June, afternoon shiftworkers initiated a spontaneous sit-down, which brought new concessions from management. The corporation agreed to abolish piecework and instituted a day rate. This not only eliminated rate disputes, but also significantly reduced the power of the foremen. Now, foremen had fewer opportunities to demand favors or to distribute jobs and overtime on the basis of their personal preferences.

Women at Ternstedt made some real gains as a result of unionization. Sex differentials remained, but working conditions improved. Sexual harassment and sexual abuse diminished as unionization weakened the power of the foremen to demand favors in exchange for employment. While these changes were significant, they resulted from changes primarily designed to ameliorate conditions for men. Few problems which specifically affected women workers were addressed, and improvements in the workplace affecting females only were rare.

There were many reasons for this. First, women had little power or influence in the UAW. From the local up to the international, power lay in male hands. Few women in the UAW achieved leadership positions, and even fewer retained them for any length of time. In comparison with their numbers in the union, they were underrepresented. Those women who did win leadership positions usually remained in the lower ranks as stewards and committee members while men occupied the more powerful union positions in vastly disproportionate numbers.[31]

The organizers of the UAW in the 1930s also lacked a feminist consciousness. In comparison with both earlier and later periods, the absence of special attention to women's concerns on the part of labor organizers is especially conspicuous during this time. While activists did sometimes raise issues of particular relevance to women workers, they lacked any systematic analysis of women's social position. Because they failed to understand the way the structures of society and of the union perpetuated male supremacy, they did not see the need for fundamental change. Instead, they identified a handful of issues affecting women and raised them in a manner uncharacteristic of their organizing on other union issues. They did not attempt to coordinate their efforts with other advocates, or to win support from women. Rather than building caucuses and undertaking some form of political preparation, they simply raised these issues at public forums – in meetings and conventions – hoping to find a sympathetic audience. Nor did Ternstedt's female activists appeal directly to women workers for their support on traditional union issues. Given the lack of preliminary work, it is not surprising they had less success than when they organized around concerns affecting both sexes.

Sexism also pervaded the structure and ideology of the UAW. Although some female organizers were more sensitive to the problems of women workers than their male colleagues, many were not. There was no independent mass feminist movement in the 1930s and 1940s. The consciousness of the organizers and the discussion of women's issues in both Ternstedt and the UAW generally reflected this absence. None of Ternstedt's female activists organized around the special problems of women workers, and none consistently incorporated an awareness of women's issues into union work.

At Ternstedt, women activists did not coordinate their efforts in raising women's issues. Although several of them felt women could be unionized more easily if the UAW addressed their particular concerns as women, both in regard to the family and to the work-place, they considered the class issues they had in common with their brothers more important. Both men and women throughout the UAW treated the issues which affected workers as a class more seriously than those which impacted primarily on women. These values left intact prevailing sex biases and male privileges. Beneath the surface, tensions between the sexes simmered and women's resentments over their relegation to a subordinate status remained unacknowledged, sabotaging any real unity between male and female laborers in this generation of unionists.

Women activists at Ternstedt were also isolated from each other. When they did meet, they rarely worked together and did not provide a support system for each other. Moreover, when women became active in the union, they followed a pattern common in all kinds of organizations – they held jobs primarily at the lower levels. Few were rewarded with paid staff jobs or elected to upper-level positions. In the UAW, women activists served primarily as organizers, stewards and committee members, and participated on grievance and bargaining committees. Women were occasionally elected delegates to the GM conferences, and to the state, CIO and international union conventions. Irene Young Marinovich was elected recording secretary of West Side Local 174 in 1938, while Martha Strong was elected one of Ternstedt's two representatives to the local's executive board. Both served on the executive boards of the Ternstedt unit and the West Side local in these years. However, no other women held top leadership posts in either of these units. In contrast, a number of the men who were active in the West Side local at the time – Walter Reuther, George Edwards and Stanley Nowak, for instance – went on to develop careers in the labor movement and in city and state politics.[32]

For those women who were socialists and communists, the decision to remain rank-and-file leaders may have been a deliberate choice, influenced in part by the party's desire to disperse its members throughout the union structure while keeping a strong base among the rank and file. Or perhaps it resulted from their unconscious adherence to conventional notions of a woman's place. However, it is clear that few men encouraged women activists to aspire to union office, to think about careers in the upper echelons of the union, or to run for leadership positions. Few women were urged to participate actively in union business beyond the initial struggle to organize the unions.

Under these circumstances, it is not surprising that only two women achieved top leadership positions within the West Side local. Thus, women's issues received inadequate attention, because men were reluctant either to raise or to endorse demands for the equitable treatment of women workers. Those who did support these issues were usually the same small handful who actively encouraged women to participate in the local.[33] Given the UAW's superficial and frequently discriminatory treatment of its female members, women workers had even fewer reasons to become active or to aspire to leadership.

Sexism took many other forms at Ternstedt. It affected the vast majority of women who were not activists even more directly. Male unionists were uncomfortable when it came to treating women in the plant and in the union as equal co-workers. Married women, in particular, continued to face discrimination and prejudice: often, their employment was contested by those workers and union leaders who believed that married women belonged at home. Other male unionists found it difficult to take female workers seriously and to prosecute their grievances. Even though the union publicized and opposed the most blatant practices designed to keep women subordinate in the plant and in the union, these efforts were insufficient to make equality for women workers a union priority in the 1930s, or to create equitable treatment in practice.[34]

Conclusion

The experience of women workers and unionists at the Ternstedt plant reveals a great deal about the female experience in the labor movement of the 1930s. Several factors facilitated the unionization of these women. The presence of a male organizer who believed that women could be organized – and who was willing to unionize them – was critical, as was the recruitment of female organizers who spoke directly to the women workers. The presence of women in local leadership positions, both in the organizing and in the union, also played an important role. While Ternstedt's women leaders were atypical in that they had acquired union sympathies prior to coming to work in the plant, they were able to convince other women workers of the value of unions. If women workers had not believed that the union could address their needs, they would not have joined it; and it was the women leaders who effectively won them over to a belief that the union could improve their wage, remedy health and safety concerns, and eliminate favoritism and sexual harassment.

Union victories in the course of the GM drive also encouraged women to join the UAW. The dramatic role of women in the Flint sit-down against GM not only showed that the UAW could win recognition from a giant anti-union corporation, but also that women could play important roles in union drives. At Ternstedt, the example of several union activists who kept their jobs despite company harassment persuaded others to risk joining the union. Without the contribution of women with radical political backgrounds, the Ternstedt unit might never have come into being. Most of the active organizers were native-born and from union families. Few were part of the ethnic communities from which the majority of the plant's female workers came. Most of the women leaders came from non-traditional families, and few were married. They were thus not subject to the intense pressures traditional families exerted in favor of conventional female roles and anti-unionism. A large proportion of Ternstedt's activists, both male and female, were politically radical. Their work in the union and their views of women reflected the larger radical movement of the time, and despite that movement's limited vision of equality between the sexes, Ternstedt women workers might never have been unionized at all had it not existed.

The Ternstedt experience illustrates the fact that women workers in the 1930s were neither less easily organized nor less militant than men. But the contribution they made to the building of the UAW was never fully recognized. Indeed, this entire generation of women activists gradually disappeared from the union – either because they retired from the plants once their husbands or families could manage without their earnings, or because of the lack of any systematic support for women union leaders. Despite the critical contribution of women to the building of the UAW, then, their legacy has remained invisible to subsequent generations of women autoworkers.

Notes

1 Sidney Fine, *Sit-down: The General Motors Strike of 1936–37*, Ann Arbor, University of Michigan Press, 1969, pp.121–48.
2 'Some Facts and Figures about Ternstedt,' *The Ternstedt Flash*, April 16, 1940; Margaret Nowak, 'The Making of an American: The Story of Stanley Nowak, Michigan's Pioneer Labor–New Deal Legislator,' unpublished manuscript, p.201, Stanley Nowak Collection, Wayne State University, Archives of Labor History and Urban Affairs (hereafter: WSU Archives); Ruth Meyerowitz, interview with Irene Young

Marinovich, Detroit, July–August 1975; Ruth Meyerowitz, interview with Stanley and Margaret Nowak, Detroit, August 1975; US Bureau of the Census, *15th Census of the US, 1930, Population*, Washington, DC, US Government Printing Office, 1933, vol. 3, part 1: *Reports By States*, Table 10, p.1, 164; US Bureau of the Census, *16th Census of the US, 1940, Characteristics of the Population*, Washington, DC, US Government Printing Office, 1943, vol. 2, part 3, *Reports By States*, p.916.

3 Edward Levinson, 'Technology and Employment in the Automobile Industry,' p.1, Edward Levinson Collection, WSU Archives, Box 1, Folder: 'Ford Wages and Finances.'

4 Meyerowitz interviews with Marinovich and Nowak; Ruth Meyerowitz, interview with Martha Strong, Detroit, July–August 1975; William Bryce, interview with Irene Young Marinovich, Detroit, July 1974; 'Sounding Off,' *The West Side Conveyor*, March 1, 1938; Lois Scharf, *To Work and to Wed: Female Employment, Feminism, and the Great Depression*, Westport, Connecticut, Greenwood Press, 1980, chapter 5.

5 Nearly half of the women gainfully employed in Detroit in 1930 were concentrated in three occupational groups: domestic and personal services; the wholesale and retail trades (exclusive of automobiles); and hotels, restaurants and boarding-houses (*Fifteenth Census*, vol. 3, p.1,164).

6 William Bryce, interview with Becky Laing Kimsley, Detroit, 1974; William Bryce, interview with Ann Dankowitz, Detroit, August 1975; Meyerowitz interviews with Strong and Marinovich.

7 Bryce interviews with Kimsley and Dankowitz; William Bryce, interview with Ann Vivian, Detroit, August 1975; Meyerowitz and Bryce interviews with Marinovich; Meyerowitz interview with Strong. Virtually all the women auto-workers interviewed commented on the problem of sexual harassment and the prevalence of exchanging sexual favors for jobs. Women who refused to participate in this exchange reported receiving poorer work assignments, less work, less tractable machines, and constant harassment from foremen. (The term 'shapeup' refers to the selection of a few people to work from a larger pool who have been called in and expect to work.)

8 Meyerowitz interviews with Marinovich and Strong; Bryce interviews with Marinovich and Kimsley. William Bryce, interview with Jack White, Detroit, August 1974.

9 Meyerowitz and Bryce interviews with Marinovich; Bryce interviews with Kimsley, Dankowitz, Vivian and White; Meyerowitz interview with Strong.

10 Patricia Yeghissian, 'The Emergence of the Red Berets,' *University of Michigan Occasional Papers in Women's Studies*, no. 10, winter 1980, pp.30–56; Mary Heaton Vorse, *Labor's New Millions*, New York, Modern Age Books, 1938.

11 This view of the plant's ethnic composition ignored the large number of

Hungarian women concentrated in Plants 16 and 18. Bryce interviews with Marinovich, Vivian, Kimsley and Dankowitz; Meyerowitz interviews with Nowak and Marinovich.

12 Former miners were central to other union drives in auto. See John G. Kruchko, *The Birth of a Union Local: The History of UAW Local 674, Norwood, Ohio, 1933–1940*, Ithaca, NY, Cornell ILR Press, 1972.

13 'West Side Local 174, UAW–CIO: A History, 1936–1952,' p.10, WSU Archives.

14 Meyerowitz interviews with Strong and Marinovich. This pattern of militance was common among women who were temporary workers. Other studies which discuss this include: Miriam Cohen, 'The Role of Women in the Organization of the Men's Garment Industry, Chicago, 1910,' in Dorothy McGuigan, ed., *New Research on Women at the University of Michigan*, Ann Arbor, Center for Continuing Education of Women, University of Michigan, 1974, p.81; Thomas Dublin, 'Women, Work and Protest in the Early Lowell Mills,' and Lise Vogel, 'Hearts to Feel and Tongues to Speak: New England Mill Women in the Early Nineteenth Century,' both in Milton Cantor and Bruce C. Laurie, eds, *Class, Sex, and the Woman Worker*, Westport, Connecticut, Greenwood Press, 1977.

15 Meyerowitz interview with Nowak.

16 Bryce interviews with Marinovich and Vivian; William Bryce, interview with Stanley Nowak, Detroit, April 1974.

17 Bryce interview with Kimsley.

18 Meyerowitz and Bryce interviews with Marinovich; Bryce interview with Kimsley.

19 Bryce interview with Kimsley.

20 Meyerowitz interview with Strong. For a similar finding regarding women in the United Electrical Workers, see Ronald Schatz, 'Union Pioneers: The Founders of Local Unions at General Electric and Westinghouse, 1933–1937,' *Journal of American History*, vol. 66, no. 3, December 1979, pp.559–602.

21 Meyerowitz and Bryce interviews with Marinovich; Bryce interview with Kimsley.

22 Meyerowitz interviews with Strong and Marinovich.

23 Meyerowitz interview with Marinovich.

24 Meyerowitz and Bryce interviews with Nowak and Marinovich.

25 In contrast, the Flint sit-down was planned by a handful of leaders with diversionary maneuvers designed to throw company spies off the track. See Fine, *Sit-down*, p.26. At the Detroit Parts Company, the leadership implemented a slow-down without discussing it with other workers. See Peter Friedlander, *The Emergence of a UAW Local, 1936–1939: A Study in Class and Culture*, University of Pittsburgh Press, 1975, pp.87–92.

26 Susan Hartmann, interview with Irene Young Marinovich, Detroit, 1974.

27 *Ibid.*; Meyerowitz and Bryce interviews with Nowak and Marinovich.

28 Elaine Crawford and Judith Longley, interview with Irene Young Marinovich, Detroit, 1975.
29 Bryce, Crawford and Longley, Meyerowitz and Hartmann interviews with Marinovich; Meyerowitz and Bryce interviews with Nowak; Bryce interview with Kimsley.
30 Hartmann interview with Marinovich.
31 See Ruth Meyerowitz, 'Women Unionists and World War II: New Opportunities for Leadership,' paper presented at the Organization of American Historians' meeting, San Francisco, April 1980; Jack Crellin, 'Anti-woman Bias Alleged,' *Detroit Times*, March 1, 1953.
32 Meyerowitz and Bryce interviews with Marinovich; Meyerowitz interview with Strong; Bryce interviews with White and Kimsley; Meyerowitz interview with Nowak; *West Side Conveyor*, August 13, 1938; 'Minutes of the Executive Board of West Side Local 174,' December 2, 1938, and February 10, 1939, in WSU Archives; Robert Conot, *American Odyssey*, New York, William Morrow, 1974, pp.437–8.
33 Meyerowitz interviews with Marinovich and Strong.
34 *West Side Conveyor*, March 1, 1938; Meyerowitz and Bryce interviews with Marinovich and Strong.

12

Women and the United Automobile Workers' Union in the 1950s

Nancy Gabin

During World War II, when women were drawn into industrial employment in massive numbers to fulfill wartime production demands, their involvement in the labor movement, and especially the young industrial unions formed in the years immediately preceding the war, also grew dramatically. Both during the war and in the period leading up to it, female union membership increased sharply, and many secondary leadership posts were assumed by women. Much attention has been given by feminist labor historians to the immediate postwar demobilization period, when the sexual division of labor in industry reverted to its pre-war form, and women's union membership also dropped sharply. The general presumption has been that women's wartime gains in the labor movement were liquidated in the late 1940s and in the 1950s, as the 'feminine mystique' took hold in the larger society. In this chapter, however, Nancy Gabin suggests that the situation was considerably more complex. Focusing, like Meyerowitz, on the case of the United Automobile Workers, one of the best-studied unions in the literature on the 1930s and 1940s, Gabin shows that while women did not overcome the longstanding obstacles to sexual equality either in industry or in the union during the 1950s, the gains made in the war years were not entirely lost. On the contrary, the institutionalization of women's concerns within the UAW's structure and official policies during the war years insured the survival of women's union activism into the postwar period, providing an important bridge to the late 1960s and 1970s, when the resurgence of feminism sparked a renewal of women's activism within the unions.

The 1950s are usually characterized as a decade of quiescence and consensus, a period in which conservative values and attitudes were vigorously and unanimously asserted. The popularity of the 'feminine mystique,' which prescribed marriage and motherhood as the source of female fulfillment, and the absence in these years of a feminist movement suggest a pervasive reaction against the changes in women's role brought about by World War II. The erosion after 1945 of the wartime gains made by women in the male-dominated basic industries and unions, and the expansion of the unorganized tertiary sector, where most of the women who entered the labor force after the war found jobs, are often taken as evidence of working women's presumed disaffection from unionism and their lack of interest in collective action in the 1950s.[1]

The history of women's activism in the UAW during the 1950s, however, suggests a different perspective on the decade. In a period regarded as the nadir of modern American feminism, women in the UAW exposed the dynamics of sexual inequality in the auto industry and in the union. Evidence of their activism is found in the persistent voice and influence of women within the union, the official commitment of the UAW to anti-discriminatory principles and policies, and the concerted effort of female unionists to eliminate unequal wage rates, sex-based occupational classifications, separate seniority lists and contractual restrictions on the employment of married women.

Women's activism in the UAW during the 1950s was a legacy of the preceding decade. By forcing issues of concern to women on to the union's agenda and establishing a presence for women within the UAW bureaucracy during World War II, female auto unionists mitigated the devastating impact of postwar reconversion. Although the proportion of women in the automotive labor force fell from a wartime high of 26 percent to 9 percent, just two percentage points greater than in the pre-war period, the gains made by women in the union during the war insured the survival of gender-conscious protest. Recent scholarship exploring the dynamics of gender relations in industrial unions has concentrated on the case of the UAW, the quintessential Congress of Industrial Organizations union. Although this work has added greatly to our knowledge about women, work and unionism, it has focused almost exclusively on the 1940s. The efforts of women in the UAW to combat sexually discriminatory employment practices in the 1950s reveal their continuity with those of the preceding decade and suggest the enduring importance of the trade union as an arena for female activism.[2]

The wartime background

The massive influx of women into auto plants during World War II irrevocably changed the role and status of women in the UAW. Largely ignored by the male-dominated and male-oriented union during its period of organization in the late 1930s, women took advantage of wartime conditions to increase their voice and influence in the union. At the urging of women activists, the UAW publicly supported the institution of federally funded child-care facilities, devised a model maternity clause for inclusion in contracts, and implemented a novel and widely acclaimed union counseling program for women new to the industry. To further meet the needs of women, who by 1945 represented 28 percent of the union's membership of one million, the UAW established the Women's Bureau as an office of the War Policy Division in the spring of 1944.[3]

The placing of the bureau in the War Policy Division, however, indicated the short-term and limited character of the UAW's commitment to women auto-workers. Although the policies enacted by the UAW during the war secured for it a reputation as one of the few unions to treat women workers fairly, they were essentially palliatives, treating the symptoms rather than the causes of sexual inequality in the industry. The sexual division of labor, which defined women's and men's work as separate and unequal, historically had confined women to a small number of poorly paid jobs in auto plants. The successful integration of women into 'men's' jobs during World War II had the potential permanently to widen women's access to employment and to contravene their marginal status in the industry. The codification of the sexual division of labor in sex-based job classifications, wage rates and seniority agreements, however, was preserved and extended during the war, women holding 'male' jobs only for the duration. Although 85 percent of female UAW members surveyed in the summer of 1944 said they wanted to keep their better-paid jobs in the auto industry after the war, neither employers nor male unionists would permit wartime exigencies to alter permanently the sexual composition of the auto labor force.[4]

In the absence of any fundamental change in the structure and organization of work, the postwar expulsion of wartime women workers was a foregone conclusion. Women in a number of locals, especially those in the Detroit area, individually and collectively protested management's discriminatory practices and urged the UAW to defend the hard-won principle of seniority and safeguard women's right to exercise seniority in transfers, layoffs and recalls. Male unionists, however, concerned about veterans' seniority and job rights and the prospect of a return to the high unemployment levels of the 1930s, seldom recognized management's treatment of women as unfair or discriminatory. Despite its verbal commitment to protect the rights and interests of women workers, the UAW's international leadership had no interest in coordinating and sustaining a challenge to the sexual division of labor. Deprived of much-needed support and influence in their confrontations with management, most women were denied access to postwar jobs in the auto industry.[5]

Although the results of the reconversion protest actions were meager, they did give women unionists a new awareness of the arbitrary and discriminatory character of the sexual division of labor. Lillian Hatcher, assistant director of the UAW Women's Bureau since its inception, remembers that 'we began to look a little differently at the whole question of equal job rights for women . . . when the . . . layoffs and recalls came and there were all sorts of innuendos about not calling back women because allegedly there weren't any jobs open that they could perform.' Women leaders realized that 'to say that she wanted to be classified forever as a female worker was hurting the working woman . . . because there were many jobs that were tagged male occupations that women could perform as well as any other person.'[6]

Female activists were determined that the UAW should not ignore the lessons of reconversion. To enhance 'the strength and solidarity of our Union as a whole,' the Council of Women Delegates informed the 1946 convention, the UAW should give 'increased attention and aid . . . to the status of women workers.' The sexual division of labor received their special censure. The classification of jobs as male or female not only permitted unequal wage rates regardless of equal or comparable job content, but also limited women's access to employment. Separate male and female seniority lists compounded these problems. Because they differentiated workers on the basis of ascribed characteristics rather than skill, ability or job assignment, these practices, codified in contracts, both perpetuated women's marginal and unequal status in the industry and compromised the UAW's commitment to industrial unionism. Reminding male unionists that 'the basic security for each and every Union worker is to be found in a Union contract' and that 'full membership rights are pledged to every worker regardless of . . . sex or marital status,' women urged the UAW to fulfill the democratic promise of industrial unionism and defend women against discriminatory employment practices.[7]

Framed in the language of industrial unionism, this feminist perspective on the position of women in the auto industry received the endorsement of the UAW leadership. In June 1946, the International Executive Board (IEB) granted the Women's Bureau, which had been in limbo since the dissolution of the War Policy Division, permanent status by incorporating it into the newly established Fair Practices and Anti-Discrimination Department. This action symbolized the IEB's recognition of the legitimacy of the demands made by women during the years of war and reconversion, and provided them with a permanent platform for extending their gains and helping to sustain gender-conscious activism.

In the late 1940s, the Women's Bureau, in conjunction with female leaders who had survived the reconversion layoffs, formulated a postwar agenda and developed strategies for mobilizing rank-and-file women. The bureau conducted conferences and workshops to educate women and men about the causes and consequences of sexual discrimination, advised local unions in contract negotiations, and assisted individual women workers in filing grievances and appeals. Reviving a strategy that had proved successful during the war and reconversion periods, the bureau also encouraged women to organize local union women's committees to advocate the interests of women in the plants. The formation of regional women's committees in the late 1940s and the establishment of the National Advisory Council to the Women's Bureau in 1950 not only gave women greater visibility within the UAW, but also institutionalized a communication and support network for women unionists. By the end of the decade, the Women's Bureau and female activists had acquired the experience and the confidence to inaugurate a campaign to extend equal rights and opportunities to women in the auto industry. Reflecting on the history of women in the UAW, Lillian Hatcher recalls the early 1950s as a time 'when we were really down to [the] serious business of eliminating discrimination as it might have been directed in contracts.'[8]

Women's issues in the 1950s

A principal goal of women auto unionists in the postwar period was the elimination of discrimination against married women. The scarcity of jobs during the Great Depression had made the position of married women in the plants especially tenuous, and discriminatory practices were written into many early collective bargaining agreements.[9] The demand for labor during World War II eased restrictions on the employment of married women. Although the entrance of large numbers of married women into the workforce during the war had begun to undermine the ideology of the 'family wage,' a number of employers and local unions entered into verbal and written agreements after 1945 that recodified discriminatory policies. Some contracts forbade the hiring of married women and required the resignation of single female employees who married. Other agreements provided that if a married woman could show cause for employment – for example, if her husband was incapacitated or in the service – she might be allowed to work, but only under certain onerous constraints. The contract between Local 72 and the Nash-Kelvinator Company in Racine, Wisconsin, allowed married women thus hired to accumulate seniority only in the department in which they worked rather than in accordance with the contract's provision for plant-wide seniority. They were, moreover, the first to be laid off regardless of any seniority they might have accumulated. Local 391 had a particularly insulting way of insuring a married woman's gratitude; she had to pay the local one dollar per week for permission to work.[10]

In contrast to the experience of the 1930s, female auto unionists after World War II decried discrimination against married women as a violation of the rights of all women to determine their own lives. Acutely aware of their vulnerable position in the plants, married women in the 1930s had countered criticism of their employment not by appealing to the union to protect their right to equal treatment, but by emphasizing the injustice of an economic system that compelled wives and mothers to seek employment outside the home.[11] In the postwar era, too, women did not claim that employment in auto plants was a fulfilling alternative to domesticity. 'The number of women working for the sheer joy of working,' explained Ceceyle Carrigan, a Local 887 officer, 'is at best infinitesimal.' Women argued, however, that men impugned the democratic principles of industrial unionism by advocating discrimination against married women. Defending the right of women to equal protection under union contracts, regardless of marital status, women unionists in the 1950s maintained that a woman's decision to work was simply beyond the purview of the UAW. 'Who is to say a woman should work or should not?' asked Mildred Szur at the 1955 convention. 'Where is our democracy in this country if a woman cannot be a free individual and make up her own mind? I think that when you start telling women you can or cannot work,' Szur concluded, 'you are infringing upon their civil rights, which I, as a woman, resent.'[12]

In the postwar period, the UAW changed its policy regarding the employment of married women. Although this was in part a response to women's protests, it reflected the greater presence of married women in the labor force after the war as well. In the 1930s, union leaders had adopted an ambivalent policy, deferring to local autonomy and the family-wage ideology rather than taking a principled stand on the issue.[13] After World War II, the international leadership made discrimination against married women a violation of the UAW's fair practices policy and condemned attempts to make married women the scapegoat for the problem of unemployment in the industry. Abandoning the earlier concessions to local autonomy, the IEB now ordered local unions to comply with international policy and abolish practices that discriminated against married women. For example, in reviewing a case involving the discharge of four married women from the Nash-Kelvinator plant in Grand Rapids, Michigan, the IEB Appeals Committee noted with annoyance that the local union officers 'seem to have their own definition of the word "discrimination." One of the local union witnesses went so far as to state that the International Union might continue to follow its policy with no complaint from Local 206 so long as the Local Union was permitted to follow its policy.' Reminding the local officers that the IEB had taken 'drastic action' and revoked the charter of Local 1014 in Dallas, Texas, for colluding with the Braniff aircraft company to discriminate against blacks, the committee directed Local 206 to negotiate the reinstatement of the four women with compensation for time lost and to 'cease and desist from this practice in the future.'[14]

The elimination of wage inequities proved to be a more difficult task than the abolition of discrimination against married women. The UAW's official support for the principle of equal pay for equal work offered women auto-workers some relief from wage discrimination. In 1949, women employed as crane operators, drill grinders, engine testers and platers at the West Allis, Winconsin, plant of Allis Chalmers, an agricultural implement manufacturer, took advantage of a clause in the company's contract with Local 248 providing for equal pay for equal work and filed a grievance demanding wages equal to those paid men in the same jobs. The company admitted having violated the contract but refused to compensate the women for the wages they had lost over the years. In a celebrated decision, the union–management umpire ruled against the company, awarding 207 women $112 each in back pay. The UAW's equal pay policy, however, reflected a limited commitment to gender equity. To its credit, the UAW officially forbade the inclusion in contracts of the most blatant forms of discrimination, such as unequal hiring-in rates and dual wage scales without reference to job assignment. But the widespread use of separate 'male' and 'female' job classifications, which enabled employers to pay women less than men for equal and comparable work, did not receive the UAW's censure.[15]

The experience of women employed by the Auto-Lite Corporation plant in Vincennes, Indiana, demonstrated the limits of the UAW's equal pay policy. Local 675's agreement with Auto-Lite provided for separate 'male' and 'female' job classifications and sex-differentiated wage scales, and so inequities could be retained despite the policy. For instance, the day and evening shifts of the punch-press operation were classified as 'female' and accorded the rate of $1.05 per hour; the 'graveyard' shift of the same operation was classified as 'male' and accorded the rate of $1.25 per hour. In July 1951, an international representative informed the local that its agreement complied with neither the UAW's equal pay policy nor the national contract with the Electric Auo-Lite Corporation, which stipulated that women employed in jobs 'normally performed by men' were to receive equal pay. The predominantly male local leadership and membership ignored the representative's appeal. Eight women punch-press operators, however, 'having been sold the idea of equal pay for equal work,' filed a grievance demanding that they receive the $1.25 hourly rate paid to male punch-press operators.[16]

The company cited the local agreement's provision for separate wage scales and rejected the women's complaint. Asserting that it was acting in the interest of consistency and contractual conformity, the company offered to pay male rates on the punch-press job only if the local union agreed to put men on all the shifts. If the local union refused, the job was to remain in the 'female' classification and receive the lower rate. The company clearly preferred to pay higher wages for the one job rather than concede the point and risk having later to pay higher wages to female employees in other similarly equal jobs. The local, however, not only saw an opportunity to provide more work for men, but also feared that advocating women's right to equal pay in the one instance would set a precedent for women to be hired for other 'male' jobs. Instead of defending the female members, the local membership accepted the company's proposal and the women on the two shifts were laid off.

Requesting assistance from the Women's Bureau, the laid-off women protested the local's action. 'We have been holding our present jobs since the factory started, paying dues as required for the protection of our jobs,' they complained. 'We feel this is a discrimination against the women.' The Women's Bureau stated in its report on the matter that, in light of both the national agreement and the international's 'firm equal pay policy,' Local 675 'should have had the grievance processed to a successful conclusion and with the local membership support.' Local 675, however, refused to follow the bureau's recommendation to negotiate with the company for the reinstatement of the women to the day and evening shifts with pay equal to that of men on the night shift. 'We have been treated wrong by our local,' the women told Caroline Davis, director of the Women's Bureau, in November 1951, but said in desperation that they would accept the lower rate of pay if only they could get their jobs back.[17]

Lacking the power to enforce policy, the Women's Bureau referred the women's case to the IEB for adjudication. The Appeals Committee acknowledged that the women lost their jobs 'solely because of the fact that they made a demand for equal pay for equal work in accordance with the well-established policy of the Union,' and ruled that they be reinstated in their former jobs with the higher male rate of pay. The committee, however, also recommended that the punch-press operation remain classified as a 'male' job and that 'future additions or replacements shall be made on the basis of a classified male job.' Presenting the committee's report to the IEB, Leonard Woodcock explained: 'That's necessary because in the Auto-Lite master agreement you have male jobs and all jobs are classified as one or the other.' No member of the IEB questioned the relevance of separate classifications for the same job or seemed concerned that the practice discriminated against women by denying them both equal pay and equal access to employment. Concerned only to preserve the highest rate possible, the IEB took the path of least resistance and rendered its decision a Pyrrhic victory for women auto-workers.[18]

The attitude of the IEB notwithstanding, the UAW's women leaders were fully aware of the threat that sex-based occupational classifications posed to the goal of achieving sexual equality in the auto industry. In the 1950s, the Women's Bureau repeatedly emphasized that unless the UAW pressed employers to determine wage rates solely on the basis of job content rather than on the sex of the operator, its equal pay policy was meaningless. But, alert to the way in which the labeling of jobs as male or female endowed the sexual division of labor with an aura of legitimacy, the bureau also urged the UAW to eliminate occupational classifications based on sex from contracts altogether. Having conducted a campaign to obtain equal pay for female employees in six General Motors parts and accessories plants, the Women's Bureau reported regretfully that the UAW's 1955 negotiations with GM had yielded only a 50 percent reduction in wage differentials ranging from ten to twenty-six cents an hour. Caroline Davis hailed the union's success in eliminating all references to sex in job titles from the contract, however, recognizing the potential for achieving not only wage parity but greater employment opportunities for women as well. Arbitrarily defining women's place in the industry, sex-based job classifications were discriminatory not only because they denied women equal pay for equal work, but also because they limited women's prospects for employment in auto plants, prevented them from using seniority rights in layoffs and recalls, and excluded them from training and promotional opportunities.[19]

Contractual discrimination was not the only problem that women confronted in the postwar era. Entering the political arena outside the UAW, women auto unionists turned to the federal government for assistance in combating hiring-gate discrimination, a practice over which the UAW had little control. Women in the UAW also began to question the benefits of state laws designed to protect the health and safety of women workers. Often out-dated and un-realistic, restrictions on hours and on weight-lifting often operated to prevent women from being hired, recalled to work or promoted to better jobs.

The employers' lack of interest in integrating women more fully into the auto labor force prevented female job seekers from obtaining employment in auto plants. Recalling the great demand for women workers during World War II, the *Detroit Free Press* remarked in 1953 that 'Rosie feels something like Typhoid Mary when she applies for a factory job.' The Women's Bureau received reports that auto-manufacturers refused to hire women, claiming that 'female' jobs were already filled. According to Octavia Hawkins, a Local 453 officer, National Malleable Steel Products in Chicago did not hire any women between 1950 and 1953 but did add new male employees to its workforce in these years. In 1955, Agnes Loveland of Local 174 reported that although Ternstedt, a division of GM in Detroit, hired a substantial number of men in 1950, it had not hired any women since 1944. Offering a different perspective on the problem, Anna Pastuszka complained that Detroit auto plants were refusing to hire women over the age of thirty-five. Confirming this, the Women's Bureau reported to the 1955 convention that employers 'who once refused to hire persons because of sex . . . have now further increased this harried number by adding age restrictions.'[20]

Women in the UAW first sought the government's assistance in challenging hiring-gate discrimination at the end of World War II. During the effort to establish on a permanent basis the Fair

Employment Practices Committee, which monitored the hiring of blacks by companies with federal defense contracts, women auto unionists considered lobbying for the inclusion of sex as a category in the proposed legislation. However, in order to ease passage of the bill, they decided not to do so. The failure of the FEPC bill prompted the UAW to devise a model fair practices clause for inclusion in contracts. Issued in the late 1940s, the clause enjoined employers from discriminating on the basis of race, national origin, creed, sex or marital status 'in the hiring of employees or in their training, lay off, discipline, [or] discharge.' The clause, however, had little effect on actual hiring practices. Employers refused to concede their prerogative in hiring, asserting that the union's relationship was with job holders and not job seekers.[21]

US involvement in the Korean war revived demands for a federal fair employment practices policy. In response to pressures for a new wartime FEPC, Harry Truman created the Committee on Government Contract Compliance in December 1951. The UAW leadership supported the effort by women auto unionists to have sex included in the compliance code's section 18, a clause directing government contractors not to discriminate against job applicants or employees on the basis of race, creed, color or national origin. Despite evidence that government contractors were refusing to hire women for defense jobs, the effort to include sex in the new compliance code failed in the face of employer opposition and lack of commitment on the part of Labor Department officials.[22]

During the 1950s, civil rights activists campaigned for fair employment practices committees at the state level, and women in the UAW again pressed for the inclusion of sex in anti-discrimination guidelines. Fearing that it would either jeopardize passage of the legislation or distract attention from racial discrimination, Will Maslow, director of the American Jewish Congress's Commission on Law and Social Action, told the secretary of the Michigan Co-ordinating Council for FEPC in 1955 to 'resist any efforts [by women auto unionists] to include sex as a prohibiting ground.' 'Perhaps I am a purist,' Maslow explained, 'but I believe that discrimination because of sex, age or physical disability are entirely different problems from discrimination because of race or religion or national origin.' President Kennedy's 1961 executive order prohibiting discrimination in hiring by employers with government contracts also led to tension between women leaders in the UAW and civil rights advocates. Asserting that the elimination of racial discrimination should receive priority, Kennedy's Commission on the Status of Women refused to comment on the absence of sex as a category in the order. Caroline Davis, a member of the commission, was angered by its failure to recognize the equally pernicious problem of sexual discrimination in the labor market. She filed a minority report stating that 'the UAW is in favor of including the word "sex" in the existing Executive Order #10925 as the most expeditious method of removing the scourge of discrimination from the woman worker.'[23]

The increasingly negative attitude of women auto unionists toward protective legislation for women workers also branded them as mavericks in the 1950s. They had first recognized the disadvantages of these laws after World War II, when states reimposed restrictions on the employment of women that had been suspended for the duration of the war. Employers, citing protective laws, now dismissed wartime female employees and replaced them with men with lesser seniority. In the 1950s, protective legislation denied women hiring and promotional opportunities. Charging that the limits for weight-lifting by women were unnecessarily low, Ceceyle Carrigan reported that North American Aviation in Los Angeles was 'using state laws to keep us in lower classifications. Many of us have ten or more years' seniority and are still in the lowest classifications.' Midland Steel in Detroit denied the transfer of several female employees to a higher-classified and better-paying grinding job, stating that the work was appropriate only for men. The company referred the women to a letter from John Reid, Michigan's Commissioner of Labor, which stated that because the grinding wheels lacked suction hoods on the blowers, the use of women on the job would violate sections of the state's 1909 law protecting the health of female wage-earners. Despite the obvious double standard, neither Reid nor Midland Steel deemed the work equally as unhealthy for male employees.[24]

Employers also used protective legislation as a smokescreen for discriminatory practices. The president of Local 1055 reported that the number of women in his plant 'grew less every day' because the company had combined lighter jobs held by women with heavier jobs held by men and denied women access to the new jobs, claiming – erroneously – that state laws forbade their employment on such work. With 'all the women squeezed out into the street,' the local president 'won the battle' by 'forcing the state inspector to come back in and then working him over for awhile and telling him . . . that I would appeal the case if he didn't render a fair decision.' Women employed as punch-press operators in the power-brake division of Midland Steel met with a similar fate. Automation had progressively reduced the number of jobs available to women; in 1956, the company transferred the entire operation to its new plant in Owosso, Michigan. Already having had 'a problem finding jobs which the women are capable of performing,' Local 410 negotiated an agreement with the company whereby the 'displaced' women would quit, surrender their seniority rights and receive severance pay. Anxious to retain their employment, two women requested transfers to crane operation, a male-classified job but one which women had performed ably during the Korean war. John Perry, a management spokesman, affirmed the company's willingness 'to promote and upgrade employees to jobs where possible and where they possess the required ability,' but reported that 'restrictions that govern female employees' prevented Midland Steel from employing women as crane operators. Unable to specify the terms of the 'restrictions,' Perry claimed that 'it is not advisable for women to operate cranes because of the climbing, jarring and shaking involved in this work.' Midland, moreover, had hired women as crane operators during the war 'only because no men were available for employment at that time.' 'We were not satisfied with their work then or now,' Perry protested lamely, 'but it was one of those conditions we had to live with.'25

The labor movement's support for protective labor legislation placed women auto unionists in an awkward position in the postwar era. According to Lillian Hatcher, they realized as early as the late 1940s that protective laws 'negated opportunity for women to move up into better paying jobs and to receive equal pay for equal work.' Conflict over the Equal Rights Amendment, however, had long before polarized the women's movement, and the UAW's friends and allies steadfastly refused to consider that protective laws might discriminate against women. While publicly denouncing the ERA as 'a pernicious and anti-social piece of legislation which will perpetuate exploitation and discrimination,' the UAW's women leaders sought to raise the issue of protective legislation for debate in the 1950s.

During the conferences conducted in 1955 by the National Manpower Council to investigate ways to use more effectively the nation's womanpower, women auto unionists were among those who contended that 'the existence of differential legislation provides employers with a justification for hiring men for work which women have in fact done or could undertake.' Opposition to ERA became an increasingly untenable position for women auto unionists by the 1960s. In 1970, the Women's Department (formerly the Women's Bureau) drafted a resolution calling for ratification of the ERA. In approving the resolution, the UAW became the first labor union to endorse the amendment.[26]

Conclusion

Despite the importance of their goals and actions during the 1950s, women did not attain equal status as workers or as unionists during this first postwar decade. Patterns of job segregation changed little, and women remained clustered in a few, predominantly female occupations. Not only did the rates for 'women's jobs' form the bottom of the industry's wage structure, but rates for women and men in the same job categories also remained unequal. Although male and female job classifications were eliminated from many contracts, the principle of separate seniority for women and men persisted to define the sexual division of labor. Most notably, the UAW's contract with General Motors, the largest single employer of women in the industry and the biggest of the 'Big Three' auto-manufacturers, retained dual seniority rosters for male and female employees.[27]

The hostility of male auto-workers to the idea of sexual equality was a principal reason for the limited progress made by women in the 1950s. The comment made by one male delegate at the 1955 convention was characteristic. 'The sacrament of matrimony bears out the fact that the man has the responsibility of providing for his family,' he asserted. 'Let's not leave this convention with the understanding that a woman has the right to compete with a man for a job.' Stating the problem clearly and explicitly, a report prepared by the Women's Bureau on the status of women foundry-workers commented that 'no one but a blind fool would believe that in the UAW–CIO prejudice against women working, against equal pay, against women holding the same or comparable jobs as men, against women's participation on an equal basis with men in the local union has been eliminated.'[28]

The failure of the UAW leadership to define the status of the union's anti-discrimination policies indicated its own ambivalence toward the intents and purposes of women unionists. The IEB did not provide the Women's Bureau with any power to enforce union policy, even after it granted the unit departmental status and doubled the size of its staff in 1955. The Women's Department 'wanted to be effective,' Florence Peterson, an international representative, recalls, 'but the cards were stacked against it.' Endowed with only 'the power of moral persuasion,' the department could do little to prevent discrimination at the local level. 'If I had been Caroline Davis,' Peterson remarks acerbically, 'I think I would have wanted to go out and shoot myself.'[29]

As its decision in the Local 675 case demonstrated, the IEB was itself inconsistent not only in enforcing union policy, but also in promoting and protecting the interests of the female membership. Dorothy Haener, an international representative from 1952 until her retirement in 1982, remembers how 'depressing' it was to learn that the staff at Solidarity House, the UAW's national headquarters in Detroit, were just as 'bitterly opposed to the concept of women moving upward or having a job' as the men in the rank and file. Excluded from direct participation in contract negotiations, female staff members were unable themselves to advocate the needs of women auto-workers at the bargaining table. 'I learned about sex discrimination at Solidarity House,' says Peterson. 'Any woman who has worked for the union has to fight to avoid being tied to the desk because, at least in those years, that was the appropriate place [for women].'[30]

Although certainly important, the hostility of male unionists to the principle of sexual equality does not in itself explain the persistence of discrimination against women in the auto industry in the 1950s. Many of the women's demands were casualties on 'the industrial battleground' of labor–management relations after World War II. The UAW accomplished a great deal for its members in the postwar era, but it sacrificed a measure of control over shopfloor issues for high wage and benefit packages. Cost-of-living increases, the annual

wage improvement factor, pension plans, and supplemental unemployment benefits were won at the bargaining table in exchange for
agreeing not to contest management's prerogative in determining the
structure and organization of work in auto plants. According to
David Brody, 'when it took up the problem of unstable employment
in the auto industry, the UAW had two choices: either to deal with
the causes, or to protect its members from the consequences. By
choosing the latter, the UAW actually conceded away its interest in
the former.' The elimination of job classifications and seniority
rosters based on sex, practices that made women especially vulnerable in layoffs, were explicit challenges to managerial prerogatives
— challenges the UAW was incapable of making in the 1950s.[31]

The inability of women activists to mobilize their constituency
also helps to account for the slow pace of change in the 1950s.
Although its intentions were good, the Women's Bureau misjudged
some of the consequences of its program to increase female participation in union activities. The purpose of the program was both to
improve the image of women in the union and to expand the number
of women in local leadership positions. Local union women's committees, however, often assumed responsibility for fund-raising and
social services, activities that not only distracted attention from
shopfloor issues but confirmed many men's notions about women's
proper place. Involvement in union political action committees,
encouraged by the bureau, also consumed valuable time and energy.
These methods of developing female activism tended to deflect
criticism of union responsibility for discriminatory practices in the
plants, and to promote trade union loyalty at the expense of gender
consciousness.

Although they were unable to mobilize a broad-based feminist
movement within the UAW, the strategies adopted by women
leaders were not without results. The very existence of the Women's
Bureau and the UAW's official anti-discriminatory policies, moreover, were resources for women in the plants. When, for example,
women in Local 206 became aware of international policy forbid-
ding discrimination against married women, they filed a grievance to
protest their discharge out of line with seniority and took it to the
Women's Bureau after the local supported management's rejection
of their complaint.[32] By successfully pressing the UAW to commit
itself, if only verbally, to anti-discriminatory principles, women

leaders helped to alleviate the oppressive effects of dominant social ideology about women.

The activism of women in the UAW during the 1950s was the result of what Alice Kessler-Harris, in characterizing the history of women in the postwar period, calls 'the radical consequences of incremental change.'[33] The successful effort of women activists during World War II to integrate issues of concern to women into the union's agenda and to establish a presence for women in the union leadership provided both the inspiration and the resources for mobilization in the postwar era. Although frustrated by the indifference, and at times the active hostility, of union men, women activists remained committed to the UAW. They continued to challenge the union to fulfill its promise to protect the rights of all its members to equal treatment, carrying on the philosophy of engagement and gender-conscious protest they had developed in the 1940s. Challenging assumptions not only about women in blue-collar occupations, but also about the origins of the rebirth of feminism in the 1960s, the history of women in the UAW during the 1950s illuminate a convergence of gender and trade union consciousness.

Notes

1 The standard treatment of women in the 1950s is William Chafe, *The American Woman*, London, Oxford University Press, 1972, pp. 199–225. Alice Kessler-Harris reassesses the 1950s in the light of the efforts of policy-makers to challenge sexual discrimination in the labor market in *Out to Work*, New York, Oxford University Press, 1982, pp.300–11.

2 Figures for female employment in automobile and automotive equipment production are derived from US Bureau of Labor Statistics, *Handbook of Labor Statistics, 1947*, Washington, DC, Government Printing Office, 1948, p.18, and US Bureau of Labor Statistics, *Labor Statistics, Employment and Earnings, United States, 1909–1975, Bulletin No. 1312-10*, Washington, DC, Government Printing Office, 1976, p.299.

   Studies of women and the UAW in the 1940s include, Nancy Gabin, ' "They Have Placed a Penalty on Womanhood": The Protest Actions of Women Auto Workers in Detroit-area UAW Locals, 1945–1947,' *Feminist Studies*, vol. 8, no. 2, summer 1982, pp.373–98; Nancy Gabin, 'Women Workers and the UAW in the Post-World War II Period: 1945–54,' *Labor History*, vol. 21, winter 1979–80, pp.5–30; Lyn Goldfarb, *Separated and Unequal: Discrimination Against Women Workers After World War II*, Union for Radical Political Economics

Pamphlet, Washington, DC, 1976; Ruth Meyerowitz, 'Women Unionists and World War II: New Opportunities for Leadership,' paper presented at the Organization of American Historians' Conference, San Francisco, California, April 1980; and Ruth Milkman, 'The Reproduction of Job Segregation by Sex: A Study of the Sexual Division of Labor in the Auto and Electrical Manufacturing Industries in the 1940s,' unpublished PhD dissertation, Berkeley, University of California, 1981.

3   The number of women employed in auto plants jumped from 28,300 in October 1941 to a wartime high of 203,300 in November 1943. US Bureau of Labor Statistics, *Handbook of Labor Statistics*, 1947, p.18; Gladys Dickason, 'Women in Labor Unions,' *Annals of the American Academy of Political and Social Science*, vol. 251, May 1947, p.72.

4   *UAW Research Report*, vol. 4, August 1944, pp.1–2; Ruth Milkman, 'Redefining "Women's Work": The Sexual Division of Labor in the Auto Industry During World War II,' *Feminist Studies*, vol. 8, no. 2, summer 1982, pp.337–72.

5   Gabin, ' "They Have Placed a Penalty on Womanhood." '

6   Transcript of interview with Lillian Hatcher, 'The Twentieth-century Trade Union Woman: Vehicle for Social Change,' Oral History Project, Institute of Labor and Industrial Relations, Ann Arbor, University of Michigan, p.83.

7   *Proceedings of the Tenth Convention of the UAW–CIO, March 23–31, 1946, Detroit*, UAW, 1946, pp.328–9.

8   Interview with Hatcher, p.32. The National Advisory Council consisted of women representatives from each of the union's regions. I examine the activities of the Women's Bureau during the postwar period in chapter 5 of my dissertation-in-progress, 'Women Auto Workers and the United Automobile Workers' Union, 1935–1955.'

9   Gabin, 'Women Auto Workers and the UAW,' chapter 2. For discussions of discrimination against married women in the 1930s see Kessler-Harris, *Out to Work*, pp.250–72, and Lois Scharf, *To Work and to Wed*, Westport, Greenwood Press, 1980, chapter 3.

10 George Addes to Local 391, n.d. (1948), UAW War Policy Division–Women's Bureau Collection, Box 5, Folder 12, Walter P. Reuther Library, Archives of Labor and Urban Affairs, Wayne State University, Detroit, Michigan (hereafter: ALUA).

11 Gabin, 'Women Auto Workers and the UAW,' chapter 2.

12 *Proceedings of the Fifteenth Constitutional Convention of the UAW–CIO, March 27–April 1, 1955, Detroit*, UAW, 1955 (hereafter: *1955 Convention Proceedings*), pp.53 and 56.

13 Gabin, 'Women Auto Workers and the UAW,' chapter 2. In the early 1950s, the UAW asserted that it had eliminated discrimination against married women from its collective bargaining agreements. Although this statement ignored the persistence of discriminatory verbal agreements, the increase in the relative number of married women in auto plants

between 1940 and 1960 is evidence of a substantial decrease in the extent of discrimination. Between 1940 and 1950, the proportion of married women in the female automotive labor force rose from 55 percent to 67 percent. In 1960, 74 percent of all women auto-workers were married (US Bureau of the Census, *United States Census of Population, 1940*, vol. 3, part 1, Washington, DC, Government Printing Office, 1943, p.115; US Bureau of the Census, *United States Census of Population, 1950*, vol. 4, part 1, chapter B, Washington, DC, Government Printing Office, 1956, pp.96 and 98; and US Bureau of the Census, *United States Census of Population, 1960*, vol. 2, part 7, chapter A, Washington, DC, Government Printing Office, 1963, p.180).

14 Appeal Hearing Report, May 20, 1952, Emil Mazey Collection, Box 40, Local 206-2 Folder, ALUA.

15 *Ammunition*, vol. 8, no. 1, January 1950, p.11.

16 Agreement, Auto-Lite Battery Corporation and UAW–CIO Local 675, March 7, 1951; National Agreement, Electric Auto-Lite Company and UAW–CIO, 1951; Fair Practices Appeal, February 12, 1951; and Women's Bureau Appeal Hearing Report, October 15, 1951. All in Emil Mazey Collection, Box 39, Folder 1, ALUA.

17 William Groeber to William McMahon, August 10, 1951; Fair Practices Appeal, September 12, 1951; Women's Bureau Appeal Hearing Report, October 15, 1951; and Dorothy Williams to Davis, November 1, 1951. All in Emil Mazey Collection, Box 39, Folder 1, ALUA.

18 IEB Appeal Committee Report, September 9, 1952, Emil Mazey Collection, Box 39, Folder 1, ALUA; Minutes of the September 15–18, 1952, IEB Meeting, pp.326–7, UAW–IEB Collection (unprocessed), Box 6, ALUA.

19 Women's Bureau Report, *1957 UAW President Report*, Detroit, UAW, 1957, p.172D.

20 *Detroit Free Press*, August 30, 1953; *Proceedings of the Fourteenth Constitutional Convention of the UAW–CIO, March 22–27, 1953*, pp.62–4; *1955 Convention Proceedings*, p.53; and Women's Bureau Report, *1955 UAW President Report*, Detroit, UAW, 1955 (hereafter: *1955 Women's Bureau Report*), p.93D.

21 Mildred Jeffrey to Frieda Miller, November 4, 1946, Box 867, Autoworkers' Folder, Women's Bureau Papers, Record Group 86, National Archives, Washington, DC (hereafter: RG 86/NA).

22 *1955 Women's Bureau Report*, p.93D; Summary of Actions Taken by the Women's Advisory Committee on Defense Manpower, n.d. (1953), Box 965, Equal Pay Folder, RG 86/NA.

23 Marvin Meltzer to Maslow, February 2, 1955, Maslow to Meltzer, February 8, 1955, and Emanuel Muravchik to Meltzer, February 21, 1955, in Jewish Labor Committee Collection, Box 8, Folder 13, ALUA; UAW, *UAW Women's Department 25th Anniversary, 1955–1980*, Detroit, UAW, 1980; interview with Dorothy Haener, 'The Twentieth-century Trade Union Woman,' Oral History Project, pp.60–4.

24 Gabin, 'Women Auto Workers and the UAW,' chapter 4; *1955 Convention Proceedings*, p.53; Reid to Julian Kuhn, October 26, 1956, UAW Local 410 Collection, Box 12, 1956 Folder, ALUA.

25 *1955 Convention Proceedings*, p.53; Zigmunt Mizejewski to Emil Mazey, May 3, 1956, and Grievance #1741, May 9, 1955, UAW Local 410 Collection, Box 17, Kay Darvin *et al.* Folder, ALUA.

26 Hatcher interview, p.52; UAW Brief in regard to the ERA, n.d. (1945– 6), p.12, UAW Research Department Collection, Box 11, Folder 14, ALUA; National Manpower Council, *Womanpower*, New York, Columbia University Press, 1957, p.336; Haener interview, pp.60–4.

27 A comparison of the wage and occupational status of women auto-workers in 1940 and 1963 demonstrates the limited extent to which the sexual division of labor changed in these years. See Harold Hosea and George Votara, *Wage Structure of the Motor-Vehicle Industry*, BLS Bulletin no. 706, Washington, DC, Government Printing Office, 1942, and US Bureau of Labor Statistics, *Motor Vehicle Parts Industry Wage Survey, April 1963*, BLS Bulletin no. 1,393, Washington, DC, Government Printing Office, 1964.

28 *1955 Convention Proceedings*, p.61; 'Report on Conditions Affecting the Equal Status of Women Foundry Workers in the UAW–CIO,' n.d. (April 1947), p.15, Walter P. Reuther Collection, Box 21, Fair Practices Department, 1946–7 Folder, ALUA.

29 Interview with Peterson, 'The Twentieth-century Trade Union Woman,' Oral History Project, p.46.

30 Haener interview, p.34; Peterson interview, p.37.

31 David Brody, 'The Uses of Power I: Industrial Battleground,' in Brody, *Workers in Industrial America*, New York, Oxford University Press, 1980, p.194. For discussions of collective bargaining in the auto industry in the postwar era, see also, Howell John Harris, *The Right to Manage*, Madison, University of Wisconsin Press, 1982; Robert M. MacDonald, *Collective Bargaining in the Automobile Industry*, New Haven, Yale University Press, 1963; and Sumner Slichter *et al.*, *The Impact of Collective Bargaining on Management*, Washington, DC, The Brookings Institution, 1961.

32 Appeal Hearing Report, May 20, 1952, Mazey Collection, Box 40, Local 206-2 Folder.

33 Kessler-Harris, *Out to Work*, p.300.

13

Unionized women in state and local government

Deborah E. Bell

Public-worker unionism has been the most important source of growth in the labor movement in the postwar period, and has brought vast numbers of women into the ranks of unionized workers. In this chapter, Deborah E. Bell explores the historical development of public-worker unionism, and explains the process through which pay equity and other women's issues came to assume special prominence within public-sector unions in the 1970s. Women working in the public sector were not organized into unions 'as women,' Bell argues, but rather, as part of a broader effort to unionize specific occupational groups which happened to be heavily female. An unintended consequence of this was that, as women became a significant part of public-sector unions' membership, they became increasingly active participants as well. In a period of general feminist resurgence, these women succeeded in gaining leadership posts and in putting 'women's issues' on their union agendas, advancing the position of women not only in the public-sector unions, but in the labor movement as a whole.

A new emphasis on women and women's issues has emerged in the American trade union movement in recent years. Unions representing state and local government workers are at the forefront of this trend.[1] They have organized large numbers of women, and, equally important, they have reformulated traditional trade union issues in ways that have particular relevance for women. Most private-sector labor organizations lag far behind. Today, over 40 percent of the 7.7 million women workers in the public sector are represented by a union or association – more than twice the level of organization among women workers in the economy as a whole.[2]

Women work in all areas of government. The majority are in jobs providing educational services, a sizeable minority (about 30 percent) work in health services, and the balance are in social services or public-administration jobs.[3] Because of the public character of certain traditionally female professions – teaching, library and social work – women employed in government are significantly more likely to be working in jobs classified as professional than are women working in the private sector. Twenty percent of women workers in the public sector are classified as professionals, while another 24 percent are paraprofessionals or technical workers. In contrast, in the economy as a whole, only 17 percent of all women workers (public and private) are in the combined 'professional and technical' category. On the other hand, clerical workers are also overrepresented in the public sector, making up 42 percent of its female workforce, as compared to 35 percent in the economy as a whole.[4]

In spite of the high level of unionization and the greater proportion of professionals, the median salary for full-time women workers in government is comparable to the average for all full-time women workers. Non-white women are more often employed in the public sector than in the economy as a whole, making up 24 percent of all women employed in government, as compared to 14 percent of all employed women. One in five public-sector women workers is employed part-time, slightly below the level in the female workforce as a whole.[5] While public-sector employment is in some ways atypical, none of the differences just reviewed account for the extraordinarily high level of unionization, relative to the private sector.

The majority of public-sector labor organizations represent workers in a single occupational category – police officers or nurses, for example – or workers in a cluster of occupations delivering one service – education or health care are instances. Some unions are structured along 'industrial' lines, most notably the American Federation of State, County and Municipal Employees (AFSCME) and the Service Employees' International Union (SEIU), whose members work in a wide range of occupations, performing a variety of services. Some public employees, usually those employed by state governments, have opted not to join international unions but to bargain through independent associations. In 1980, about 320,000 state workers belonged to state employee associations.[6] There are also professional associations which engage in collective bargaining, but are not unions.

The largest all-public unions are AFSCME, with slightly over one million members, 40 percent of whom are women, and the American Federation of Teachers (AFT), with about 550,000 members, two-thirds of whom are women. The National Education Association (NEA) is a professional association with over 1.6 million members, most of whom work in public education. (No sex breakdown is available for NEA members, but the proportions are probably similar to the AFT's.) Among the mixed public/private labor organizations, SEIU probably represents the largest number of public workers. About 250,000 of its members, or one-third of the total, are public workers; of this group, an estimated 45 percent are women. The Communication Workers of America (CWA) represents an estimated 50,000 public workers, about half of whom are women, and the American Nurses' Association represents about 35,000 public-sector nurses, almost all of them women. The Teamsters and the Laborers also represent sizeable numbers of public workers, but most are men.[7]

Women public-sector workers are as likely as their male co-workers to be unionized – more than two in every five – and, for working women, that rate is higher than in any other industry except communications.[8] The high degree of unionization among women in public employment cannot be attributed to organizing efforts directed specifically at women workers. Such efforts were almost non-existent until the 1970s. Rather, their extensive organization is an historical byproduct (indeed, a necessary one) of the general project of organizing public workers, which began in the postwar period. Once organized, however, and particularly in recent years, women assumed expanded leadership roles in public-sector unions, and issues of concern to women workers became more prominent on public-sector union agendas.

The rise of public-worker unionism

The unionization of the public sector is one of the most significant developments in the US labor movement in the postwar era. The overall decline in union membership over the the past thirty years would have been far greater if it were not for the dramatic increases in organization among public workers. By 1978, 6.1 million government workers were represented by labor organizations, compared to 3.9 million in 1968.[9]

Public-sector unionization occurred in three stages. The first, in the years before 1965, was a period of initial efforts to pass collective bargaining laws covering public workers. This period also saw the instigation of organization drives, largely among blue-collar workers and in cities and states where there was a tradition of private-sector trade unionism. The second stage, between 1965 and 1975, saw the rapid expansion of both employment and unionization in the public sector, with service-workers, many of them black, at the center of the organizing. Only in the third stage, from 1975 to the present, a period of reduced growth in unionization and in government budgets, have women workers, especially clericals, emerged as the primary focus of organizing efforts.

Civil service rules constitute the traditional personnel structure in government. Laws establishing civil service systems and regulations, covering primarily white-collar workers, have been passed by states and localities since the late nineteenth century.[10] The designation of collective bargaining rights for public workers also rests with the individual states, for public employees are not covered by the National Labor Relations Act. While some groups of public-sector workers had organized themselves earlier, they rarely gained formal recognition or collective bargaining rights before the 1950s. Important symbolic steps in the development of public-sector unionism were taken with Mayor Robert Wagner's agreement to recognize unions representing New York City workers in 1958, and the executive order issued four years later by President Kennedy, which extended limited bargaining rights to federal employees. Most states passed public-employee collective bargaining laws after 1962, but they vary considerably with respect to categories of employees that can bargain, terms of employment that are bargainable, and dispute-resolution mechanisms.[11] A critical point of difference between the private and public sectors is that most public employees do not have the legal right to strike. Public-sector arbitration procedures are therefore more highly developed.

Before 1965, male blue-collar workers employed in local-government-run parks, sewers and highways were often part-time or seasonal workers and hence not covered by civil service agreements. These workers actively sought unionization in order to achieve full-time status and full-time benefits. They were willing to strike and were loud and forceful in their demands. Their militance often led to the passage of collective bargaining laws, thereby reducing the need for other groups to strike for recognition. Several unions – the Laborers, the Teamsters, SEIU and AFSCME – recognized the implications of this blue-collar militancy. These unions readily signed up workers who came to them, and also initiated their own organizing drives.[12]

Another group which favored unionization, although much less important numerically at the time, was professional white-collar workers in public administration. Covered by state and local civil service systems, many of these workers, particularly at the state level, had historically organized themselves into employees' associations. They tended to be heavily involved in state and local politics, lobbying for improvements in wages and civil service rules and supporting friendly candidates. While employees in some associations steadfastly opposed unionization, others sought collective bargaining over wages and non-politicized grievance mechanisms in order to win greater protection from the vagaries of politics. Unlike the blue-collar workers, they seldom engaged in job actions, but they did use their political leverage to win first informal and later formal bargaining procedures, which ultimately were codified in state law. This general pattern would repeat itself in state after state in the 1960s and 1970s.

During the initial stage of public-sector unionization, politically committed organizers and activists played a critical role. Their politics were usually informed by the experience of CIO organizing drives or left-wing political movements.[13] From the former came a vision of trade unions as a means of gaining institutional legitimacy for the largely immigrant industrial working class, as well as economic gains. From the latter (the Communist Party, the Socialist Party, the 'Wallace for President' campaign), came experience in organizing techniques, a notion of what good government services ought to be and, perhaps most important, political bases of support in several major cities. In New York City, San Francisco, Cincinnati, Philadelphia and elsewhere, the presence of left-wing and progressive political organizations and strong private-sector unions was as important as any other factor in early organizing successes among government workers.[14]

Once the groundwork was laid, public-worker unionization accelerated rapidly. In the period of national economic growth and expanded government budgets under President Johnson in the mid-1960s, the service functions of government, particularly local government, grew enormously. Massive amounts of federal aid were passed down to states and localities to implement the socio-political agenda of the 'Great Society,' a trend which continued until the economic contraction of the mid-1970s. The effort to buy urban peace through more public services and more public jobs also extended to providing improved wages and benefits for organized government workers. The successes of the previous decade – getting laws passed, effective organizing drives, winning more comprehensive contracts – multiplied. Employees' associations began to reconstitute themselves as collective bargaining organizations, or to affiliate with established unions.[15]

Many of the new jobs created in this period were clerical and service jobs in such entities as school districts, hospital corporations and 'Model Cities' programs. There was no legal mandate that such jobs should have civil service protections – job security or pension coverage, for instance. These jobs served a dual purpose: to expand government services and to create openings for the unskilled and the unemployed, frequently women and non-whites. The work was often part-time, for with less than full-time hours and few benefits, more jobs could be created and more people employed. The unions viewed this kind of public-employment policy as a threat, and opposed it, both in the political arena and by organizing the new workers.[16]

Black workers were critical to public-sector organizing in this period. In many cities in the 1960s, blacks were the explicit targets of public-employment programs. Once employed, blacks wanted the rights and protections which they perceived unionization could provide. The multi-occupational unions, most importantly

AFSCME and SEIU, responded by actively organizing service-workers, including large numbers of blacks. Their goal was to achieve full-time rights and privileges and higher salary rates. Organizing black government-workers also led to breakthroughs in traditionally non-unionized areas of the country, most notably the south. Here, black sanitation- and highway-workers receiving low wages and no job security or rights, asked public unions to organize and represent them. 'Dignity' was a common theme in these drives, and links to the civil rights movement were more than rhetorical – civil rights activists were often pro-union activists as well. The civil rights movement defined social enfranchisement as an end; public-sector jobs and public-sector unions became part of the means. It was hardly coincidental that when Martin Luther King, Jr, was killed in 1968, he was visiting Memphis to support striking AFSCME sanitation-workers.

Public-sector job growth and unionization between 1950 and 1975 brought women nearly half the state and local government jobs. Large numbers of women were organized in this period, but very few rose to leadership positions in the burgeoning public-sector unions. During 1965–75, activists were more likely to be male than female – even in organizing drives among professional groups such as teachers and social workers, where female presence was strong. For example, in New York City, the greatest support for the organizing efforts of the United Federation of Teachers (UFT) came from high school teachers, of whom a relatively high proportion were men.

Women clerical workers were organized somewhat selectively prior to 1975. The factors favoring organizing drives seem to have been either large numbers, as in New York City, to make it worth the effort, or small numbers concentrated in one or two locations, such as a hospital, to make it relatively easy. Receptivity to unionization on the workers' part was also a consideration, but when there were large numbers involved or the clericals were the only unorganized group in a jurisdiction, the multi-occupational unions would often try to organize them regardless of their initial receptivity. The strategic reasoning was, first, concern that politicians and administrators might play off unionized and non-unionized workers against one another, and, second, the conviction that a fully unionized public workforce meant power – both at the bargaining table and in the legislature. In localities where clericals were few in number, dispersed locationally, and expressed no interest in being organized, they were more often than not ignored by unions in the pre-1975 period.

But since the mid-1970s, this has begun to change. In May 1977, 34 percent of government clerical workers were represented by a labor organization, compared with 46 percent of government professionals, 44 percent of government blue-collar workers, and 41 percent of government service-workers.[17] Since then, however, the biggest increases in public-sector unionization have been among clerical workers. Between 1977 and 1980, the number of unionized government workers in blue-collar and service occupations increased only about 1.5 percent, while in the white-collar occupations the increase was 20 percent; and among clerical workers in particular, the increase was 22 percent.[18]

What accounts for this upsurge in unionization among clerical workers? First, the simple fact that women have entered the workforce in large numbers in the past few years and plan to remain working suggests an imperative to maximize job security and economic benefits. Also, an ongoing impact of the women's movement has been to legitimate the economic and political activism of women on their own behalf, part of which is a more positive attitude toward unions. The absence of any comparable increase in unionization among private-sector clericals, however, identifies the primary catalyst – the change in the multi-occupational public-sector unions themselves. Part of the change is structural. Over the past twenty years, their occupational distribution has been steadily shifting from predominantly blue-collar to predominantly white-collar. Because there are far more women in white-collar jobs, an increase in the proportion of female members has accompanied the occupational shift and has affected union policy-making in favor of organizing women and women's issues.

Women's issues and women's leadership in public unions

Policy shifts in unions have resulted from increased participation by women members in union activities. Women are becoming more active as shop stewards and running for office. In a survey of its local union officers, AFSCME found that 33 percent of local presidents in 1982 were female, compared to 25 percent several years before, and that women hold 45 percent of all local union offices.[19] In recent years, a woman was elected an international vice-president of SEIU for the first time, and two women were elected to the International Executive Board of AFSCME. Black women have also moved into local leadership positions; this is significant because unions are one of the few places in American institutional life where this is possible in the 1980s. An increased emphasis on skills development among women unionists has helped to increase women's leadership. For example, in the spring of 1981, SEIU held a national conference for 250 women members to discuss women's issues and receive training in organizing, leadership and collective bargaining. At the local level, women's committees often serve the role of stimulating discussion and training among women. There are also more women union staff-workers than ever before. Although they tend to be concentrated in social service, research and editorial staff jobs, women increasingly hold legal, education, safety and health, organizing and collective bargaining positions.[20]

As the number of women members grows and as more women gain concrete organizational, leadership and staff experience, issues of concern to women are more likely to be raised and addressed. Women's issues in the public sector can be categorized in traditional trade union terms – job security, the changing structure of the workplace, and wages and benefits. Because women are concentrated in service and white-collar office jobs, however, the specific issues emphasized are somewhat different.

Changing economic conditions threaten to undermine women's job security in government. Long-term reductions in the rate of growth of government budgets will result in reduced public services and a smaller public-employment base. The push to reduce public services has ideological as well as economic goals: (1) to eliminate institutionalized mechanisms for income redistribution; and (2) to leave service gaps that the private profit-making service sector can fill, in order to stimulate growth in that part of the economy.[21] Under the Reagan administration, there is also an explicit effort to undermine public-sector unionism and gain greater control over the public workforce, as seen in the federal government's conscious destruction of the air traffic controllers' union in 1981.

Public budgetary policy in the 1980s may have a differentially negative effect on women's jobs. This was not the case in previous years. Much of the budget-cutting that occurred at the local level in the late 1970s was due to reduced local revenue growth, and the services suffering the most were those financed primarily from local revenues – police, fire, sanitation, highways and sewers – with male-dominated workforces. Health and welfare services, with a much higher proportion of female workers and a larger share of federal funding, were less hard hit. However, the federal domestic-spending cuts called for since 1980 by the Reagan administration may have a devastating effect on employment for women in the local government growth areas of the past fifteen years – education, health and social services.

A related problem is the increasing support for privatization of the delivery of services traditionally provided by government. Private management companies employing low-paid, non-unionized workers with few benefits are already being hired to run public hospitals and to provide food-preparation and cleaning services for many state and local government agencies. There are even proposals for a nation-wide federal voucher system for primary through high school education, with the vouchers redeemable at public or private schools. Though the rationale for privatization is better-quality services at reduced costs, there is not much concrete evidence that a profit-making company can improve quality *and* reduce costs unless workers are paid the minimum wage with no benefits. Especially vulnerable are entry-level workers, often women, in service jobs where wages and benefits are significantly higher in the public than in the private sector (usually due to unionization), because privatization could lead to immediate savings in labor costs alone.

Even more significant for women are the changes likely to result from automation in office and service jobs. The introduction of technologically advanced equipment – word processing, computerized record-keeping, more automated testing, new types of food-preparation and cleaning equipment – is inevitable, but it has not occurred as frequently or as rapidly in the public sector as in the private, usually because state and local governments cannot afford to buy the equipment as quickly.

The workforce adjustments and changes in the work process that will result from automation are already evident. The popular catch-phrase accompanying these changes is 'increased productivity' – more output per person-hour, which essentially means performing services with fewer workers. New technology is likely to have especially dramatic effects on the structure of the many white-collar and professional functions entailed in maintaining and processing data involved in financial records, welfare cases, medical records and property tax assessments. Computers can process information more cheaply than people, once the information is input, so that many of the tasks associated with record-keeping will be transferred from professional workers to lower-paid data-entry clerical workers and machines. A reduced number of professionals and administrators will then analyze outputs and make decisions. Many of the jobs affected by this 'de-skilling' are female-dominated. This change will also lead to fewer advancement opportunities, because most office jobs will be at the low end of the clerical/administrative career ladder.

Because of 'de-skilling,' automation in the public sector may lead to net gains rather than losses in clerical jobs, but there will be other negative effects, such as the potential for greater control and monitoring of both the content and the pace of clerical jobs. Questions have been raised over possible safety and health hazards associated with the computerized equipment itself (particularly the video display terminals), but perhaps more hazardous are the physical effects – eye strain, back and neck aches, etc. – of the repetitive, monotonous tasks which the equipment imposes on the work process. Further, the pace of work can be monitored, and even pre-set, electronically, making it possible to measure (or to claim to measure) the output and productivity of many public-service functions which were not previously quantifiable. This, in turn, might provide a rationale for productivity-based job cuts without adequate consideration of the effects on the quality of service.

In regard to wage and benefit issues, women's expanded role in public unions has come in an era of sharply reduced budgetary latitude in government and while many private-sector unions are engaged in 'concession bargaining.' Nevertheless, public unions have been moderately successful in raising and addressing some economic issues of concern to women. For example, in addition to negotiating across-the-board wage increases, unions have increasingly exerted pressure for enforcement of affirmative action and equal employment opportunity policies to help women get jobs in non-traditional, often higher-paying, occupations. Public unions are also demanding restructuring of civil service classifications to create career ladders with more promotional opportunities. Demands for training and skills upgrading are also common, and many unions use their own educational resources to provide them.

Dollars alone will not solve the problems facing women who move in and out of the labor force, particularly those with children; alternative work schedules are also needed. Flextime, which permits variation in arrival and departure times as long as the required number of hours per week are worked, often sharply reduces absenteeism among women with children. 'Compressed time' (i.e. three twelve-hour days per week) and job-sharing are other approaches of increasing interest to women.

Child-care is a particularly critical issue for working women. Nevertheless, it is one on which the unions have made little progress. As long as women drop out of the labor force to care for children, they will lose ground over the course of their working life. Studies demonstrate that 'breaks in service' have a seriously depressing effect on wage growth and career advancement for women, particularly in clerical and service jobs, where the effect becomes institutionalized in the 'dead-endedness' of those jobs.[22]

Child-care is costly and usually benefits only a relatively small proportion of a union's members at any one time. Demands for child-care are fairly common, but, in actual negotiations, bargaining committees are rarely willing to give up part of a wage increase to fund such programs, and most public employers are not willing to bear the cost themselves. The national trend since the mid-1970s has been in the direction of individualized solutions to child-care – away from government funds earmarked for child-care centers and toward personal income-tax breaks and financial assistance for low-income families. Full-time enrollment in a child-care center costs upward of $65 per week, more than many working women can afford. Serious attitudinal barriers remain, as well. Women are still viewed as primarily responsible for the care of children by all social institutions, including unions, and there is a deep-rooted ambivalence about making it easier for mothers to work.

The public sector offers unusual opportunities – potentially available physical facilities, concentrations of large numbers of employees and, in some areas, the experience of running day-care programs for the population at large. What is still lacking, however, is a commitment on the part of public-sector unions to experiment with those opportunities, to find ways to provide child-care and to insist on employers' obligation to help provide it. The record to date is not very good. One survey of government employer-sponsored, on-site child-care programs in 1980 found several centers around the country for federal government employees, but only two, in Albany, New York, and Sacramento, California, for state employees. A few centers were also found in public or non-profit institutions, like hospitals and universities, where there are fairly high concentrations of employees in one location.[23]

The most important women's issue to emerge from the public-sector unions has been pay equity. The concept of pay equity, or comparable worth, posits that the principle of 'equal pay for equal work' is inadequate to address the issue of economic discrimination in the workplace because women and men do different jobs in a sex-segregated economy. Rather than arguing for equal pay for all workers performing the same job, pay equity advocates argue for equal pay for work of comparable value. In this view, occupational segregation, combined with wage discrimination, has depressed wage rates for traditionally female-dominated occupations. Moreover, the sex gap in wages is not adequately explained by differences in job requirement (skills, level of responsibility, hazards, and mental and physical effort required) and is therefore discriminatory.

Advances around the pay equity issue have been made in the public sector not only because a lot of working women are concentrated there in female-dominated occupations, but also because wages and job descriptions are public information. Civil service systems offer an easily available basis for job-evaluation studies to demonstrate lack of equity. Generally speaking, this kind of information is not readily accessible in the private sector.[24] Further, public-sector collective bargaining laws and practice and civil service laws and practice contain explicit references to the principle of just and equitable wages. They thus provide a basis for challenging or threatening to challenge existing wage levels and job classifications. Also, politicians are concerned about the voting power of women, and some are receptive to legislative proposals on pay equity for public employees because they provide an opportunity to have a direct effect on the salaries of women in that sector.

A variety of tactics are being employed to achieve pay equity. Legislation and collective bargaining are the primary ones, with litigation and Equal Employment Opportunity Commission complaints as back-up pressure tactics. In many instances, collective bargaining and legislative gains have led to job-evaluation studies which have identified discriminatory wage inequities, but have not yet led to actual wage adjustments. In the context of reduced government growth, implementing pay equity will be costly. AFSCME estimates that winning its pay equity lawsuit on behalf of 10,000 workers against the State of Washington will cost $500 million in back pay and raise the state budget by 2 percent annually for ongoing increases.[25] There are cases, however, where wage adjustments have been made or are scheduled, often because of women unionists, working in coalition with women's organizations and women politicians. For example:

- In March 1982, legislation was passed in Minnesota to determine which state-employee job classes are underpaid relative to others and to make wage adjustments, beginning in July 1983. Funds were approved for that purpose by the state legislature, separate from any general wage increases arising out of collective bargaining. This was the result of a coalition of unions, women's organizations, politicians, and state bureaucrats, working through the Minnesota Council on the Economic Status of Women, a legislative advisory commission.

- Municipal workers in San Jose, California (members of AFSCME), won a commitment to pay equity wage adjustments in addition to general wage increases through a six-day strike in June 1981. (The strike demand was that the money for the wage adjustments not be taken out of the general wage increase.)

- In collective bargaining, the state of Connecticut committed 1 percent of the total state payroll (about $1 million) for pay equity adjustments to state clerical and health care titles. The state legislature has mandated a job-evaluation study, the results of which will be available in June 1984, to determine the distribution of wage adjustments in the context of collective bargaining.

Clerical workers in Santa Clara County, California (members of SEIU), bargained in 1974 for an evaluation of their job classifications. This resulted in wage adjustments such as: extra pay for skills like fast typing and bilingual ability; a new bridge classification between clerical and paraprofessional jobs to provide career opportunities; and establishment of a classification review board to decide on upgradings. After years of bargaining and expedited arbitrations, the clericals received inequity wage adjustments ranging from 1.5 to 15 percent in July 1981, in addition to a general wage increase.

These examples illustrate the importance of generating support for pay equity in the political arena, as well as in collective bargaining, using traditional and non-traditional techniques.[26]

For the public-sector unions that have been active around the pay equity issue, there have been institutional rewards. A strong stand on an issue like pay equity lends credibility to unions as aggressive representatives of women's concerns. This has appeal to potential as well as current members, so that gains on pay equity can be an important part of an organizing strategy. In addition, pay equity represents an innovative wage strategy in public-sector collective bargaining for current members, offering a rationale for shaking loose money for higher wages from a tight-fisted state or local legislature coping with budget-cuts. To paraphrase one public-sector negotiator in New Jersey – we don't care how we get it, through job upgradings or through across-the-board general wage increases, we just want the money.[27] Once established in law or in a contract, the principle of comparable worth as an acceptable imperative for adjusting wage levels – even though it may only be applied to a small number of workers at low initial cost to the employer – provides the basis for a union to negotiate extensions of the principle to greater numbers of workers with each succeeding contract.

In the short run, women in female-dominated professional and managerial occupations in the public sector will benefit disproportionately from pay equity. Their numbers are relatively small, which keeps costs down, and while government professional and managerial salary rates in general are far below comparable private-sector salaries, pay equity is a more palatable excuse for increasing wages than private-sector comparability. In addition, there is a high degree of militance around the pay equity issue among women in these occupations.[28] They are likely to be highly educated, middle-class women with heightened expectations, and to have been affected by the women's movement. In both Washington State and San Jose, where there have been landmark efforts, it was studies of *management* wage rates by sex, leading to wage increases for some management women, that set off the original demands for studies of the rest of the workforce.[29]

The mass of women, in clerical and service jobs, probably will not benefit right away from pay equity; the cost of closing the male/female wage gap is just too great. An indirect approach to pay equity, job reclassification, may offer more immediate relief. The cost of raising wages through reclassification can be rationalized by expanding the range of duties of a particular job, theoretically increasing the productivity associated with that job as well as management's flexibility in assignments. Reclassification can also lead to creating more advancement opportunities at increased wages.

Although some unions have emphasized reclassification as a pay equity strategy, it has some serious pitfalls. For one thing, workers may not want more responsibility, only more equitable wages for the work they are currently doing. The widespread discussion of career ladders may divert attention from the needs at the bottom rungs. The reality is that there will always be many fewer jobs at the top than at the bottom of these ladders. Further, public management has been known to have quite different motives in acceding to reclassification demands. For instance, reclassification may be used to reduce the number of supervisory jobs permitted union recognition rights, or less specific job descriptions may be enlisted by management to give greater flexibility in task assignment. Therefore, unions should be careful to consider all potential costs and benefits. Ideally, the issue should be handled in the context of collective bargaining so that management will be obliged to negotiate explicitly over proposed changes.

Conclusion

Pay equity is likely to play an important role in public-sector collective bargaining strategy over the next few years. As government negotiators become more aggressive in trying to hold down increases in wage costs and become more willing to tolerate strikes, public-sector unions will have to develop greater creativity in their bargaining demands, including pressing for some that will only be applied to select groups of workers. The complexity of the pay equity issue provides a range of strategic options for unions to pursue, depending on specific circumstances.

Success in winning wage adjustments for public-sector, female-dominated job categories, based on the pay equity concept, may have a spillover effect into the private sector. For organizing women workers, however, particularly clerical workers, the public-sector experience is less applicable as a model. The differences are just too great. Pre-existing employees' associations throughout much of the public sector have made it much easier to unionize women public workers than those in comparable private-sector jobs. Furthermore, there is generally less resistance by most public officials to unionization than there is in a private company. In addition, in government, some part of the workforce is usually unionized already, which both lowers management resistance and increases worker receptivity, even when most of the unionized workers are in male-dominated blue-collar or uniformed jobs.

Successful organizing of women workers in government will carry on, and significant union resources will be expended to win these new members. The competition among the multi-occupational unions to win recognition rights has been fierce, and will continue to be. In recent years, for example, clerical workers at state universities and colleges have frequently been the targets of organizing drives by competing unions. In Chicago, where newly elected Mayor Washington agreed to permit white-collar municipal workers to be represented for bargaining purposes by unions, massive organizing campaigns are being mounted by AFSCME, SEIU and CWA, among others.

Today, unionized public-sector women are at the forefront of the fight for improved employment conditions for women. This did not result from a long-range strategy on the part of public-sector unions. Rather, it is the unexpected consequence of the vast influx of women into the growing number of government jobs, and the effects of the complex relationship between the trade union, civil rights and women's movements. An enormous momentum has been generated, and in spite of budget-cuts, the public sector has become a central arena for addressing women's issues. Exciting advances are being made which will affect all working women, directly or indirectly, in the years to come.

Notes

1 This chapter focuses on women working in state and local government. Women working for the federal government are also highly organized, but they comprise less than 10 percent of all women working in the public sector, are represented by different unions, and face different political and economic constraints than state and local government workers. Throughout the chapter, my use of the term 'unions' includes both labor unions and employees' associations which engage in collective bargaining.

2 US Department of Labor, Bureau of Labor Statistics (hereafter: BLS), *Earnings and Other Characteristics of Organized Workers, May 1980,* Washington, DC, Government Printing Office, 1981, p.29.

3 US Department of Labor, BLS, 'Employment and Earnings, March 1982,' vol. 29, no. 3, p.143; BLS, *Earnings, May 1980,* p.28.

4 US Equal Employment Opportunity Commission, *Job Patterns for Minorities and Women in State and Local Government, 1980,* Washington, DC, Government Printing Office, 1982; US Department of Labor, BLS, Special Labor Force Report No. 244, *Employment and Unemployment: A Report on 1980,* Washington, DC, Government Printing Office, April 1981, p.A-20.

5 US Equal Employment Opportunity Commission, *Minorities and Women in State and Local Government, 1978,* Washington, DC, Government Printing Office, 1980, pp.3–266. The spread from the lowest- to the highest-paid women worker is far narrower in the public sector than in the private. In general, government pay for low-skilled jobs is above private-sector pay, while for administrative and professional jobs the government pays less (David Lewin, 'Aspects of Wage Determination in Local Government Employment,' *Public Administration Review,* vol. 34, no. 2, March/April 1974, pp.149–55). Data on all women workers are derived from BLS, *Employment and Unemployment,* and from US Department of Labor, Women's Bureau, *20 Facts on Women Workers,* Washington, DC, Government Printing Office, 1980.

6 Bureau of National Affairs, *Directory of US Labor Organizations, 1982–83 Edition,* Washington, DC, BNA, 1982, pp.14–43.

7 These are my estimates, extrapolated from data presented in the BLS, *Directory of National Unions and Employee Associations, 1979,* Washington, DC, Government Printing Office, 1980, and adjusted to take account of personal communications with union representatives.

298   *Deborah E. Bell*

Most unions representing workers in both the public and private sectors do not maintain separate records based on that distinction.

8 BLS, *Earnings, May 1980*, pp.14–17.
9 US Department of Labor, BLS, *Directory* cited above, note 7, p.66.
10 Robert D. Lee, Jr, *Public Personnel Systems*, Baltimore, University Park Press, 1979, p.22.
11 By the late 1970s, only five states prohibited recognition and/or bargaining rights for state employees, and another nine states had no provisions. Ten states had prohibitions or no provisions covering local government employees, John A. Folsum, *Labor Relations*, Dallas, Texas, Business Publications, 1979, pp.386–9.
12 Jack Stieber, *Public Employee Unionism: Structure, Growth, Policy*, Washington, DC, The Brookings Institution, 1973, chapter 6.
13 Many of the early activists, organizers and leaders of public-sector unions came from these backgrounds. Among those who went on to leadership positions were Albert Shanker, president of the AFT, and Jerry Wurf, former president of AFSCME, both of whom were Socialist Party activists in their youth. Jack Bigel, who emerged in 1975 as a union consultant and one of the architects of the resolution of New York City's fiscal crisis, had been a leader of the United Public Workers (CIO), a union alleged to have links with the Communist Party and destroyed during the McCarthy period. Remnants of that same union in California joined the SEIU and provided the basis for its increased involvement in public-employee organizing.
14 Richard N. Billings and John Greenya, *Power to the Public Worker*, Washington, DC, Robert B. Luce, 1974.
15 Some indication of the rate of growth can be seen in membership data for the three largest all-public labor organizations (Bureau of National Affairs, *Directory, 1982–83 Edition*, pp.70–1).

	1962	1968	1974	1980
		(thousands)		
AFSCME	220	364	648	1,098
NEA	—	1,062	1,470	1,684
AFT	71	165	444	551

16 For another view of these issues, see Frances Fox Piven, 'The Urban Crisis: Who Got What and Why,' in Roger E. Alcaly and David Mermelstein, eds, *The Fiscal Crisis of American Cities*, New York, Vintage Books, 1977.
17 US Department of Labor, BLS, *Earnings and Other Characteristics of Organized Workers, May 1977*, Washington, DC, Government Printing Office, 1979, p.27 (data are not sex-differentiated).
18 *Ibid.*, and BLS, *Earnings, May 1980*, p.29.
19 Personal communication with Marilyn DePoy, Assistant Coordinator of Women's Activities, AFSCME, August 1982.
20 Coalition of Labor Union Women, *Absent from the Agenda*,

Washington, DC, CLUW, 1980, pp.12–13; Ronnie Steinberg and Alice Cook, *Women, Unions and Equal Employment Opportunity*, Albany, New York, Center for Women in Government, 1981, pp.65–7. 1981, pp.65–7.

21 For a more in-depth discussion see James O'Connor, *The Fiscal Crisis of the State*, New York, St Martin's Press, 1973; Union for Radical Political Economics, *Crisis in the Public Sector*, New York, Monthly Review Press, 1982.

22 Nancy F. Rytina, 'Tenure as a Factor in the Male–Female Earnings Gap,' *Monthly Labor Review*, April 1982, pp.32–4.

23 New York State Committee on the Work Environment and Productivity, *On-Site Day Care, the State of the Art and Models Development*, Albany, New York, 1980.

24 The one major private-sector pay equity legal case, which had limited success, involved Westinghouse and the International Union of Electrical Workers (IUE) and was undertaken on the basis of historical records of wage rates and job descriptions going back to World War II, which were in the public domain. See Bureau of National Affairs, *The Comparable Worth Issue*, Washington, DC, BNA, 1981, p.7.

25 'Beyond "Equal Pay for Equal Work," ' *Business Week*, June 18, 1983, pp.169–70.

26 Examples are drawn from the following reports: Minnesota Council on the Economic Status of Women, *Pay Equity and Public Employment*, St Paul, Minnesota, 1982; American Federation of State, County and Municipal Employees, *Pay Equity, A Union Issue for the 1980s*, Washington, DC, 1980, and *Breaking the Pattern of Injustice, AFSCME's Blueprint for Pay Equity*, Washington, DC, 1983; Clerical Council, Connecticut State Employees' Association, *Raising Wages for 'Women's' Work*, Hartford, Conn., 1980; Service Employees International Union, *Pay Equity Issues*, Washington, DC, 1982.

27 Personal communication with Mark Niemeiser, Associate Director for Health Workers, Council 1, AFSCME, in New Jersey, January 1983.

28 Librarians (usually represented by occupationally mixed unions) and nurses (represented by both mixed unions and state nurses' associations) are professional groups noted for their activism around pay equity; teachers are noteworthy for their lack of activism around the issue, perhaps because of their generally superior pay structures.

29 Mike McGuire, 'A New Way to Equal Pay,' *Dollars and Sense*, April 1982, pp.12–14; and Helen Remick, 'Beyond Equal Pay for Equal Work: Comparable Worth in the State of Washington,' in Ronnie Steinberg Ratner, ed., *Equal Employment Policy for Women*, Philadelphia, Temple University Press, 1980, pp.405–19.

14

Women workers, feminism and the labor movement since the 1960s[1]

Ruth Milkman

A resurgence of feminism and a rapid expansion of female labor force participation have dramatically altered the situation of women workers in the US in recent years. In this chapter, Ruth Milkman explores the overall impact of these developments on women's relationship to organized labor, as well as the rise of two important feminist organizational efforts within the labor movement, the Coalition of Labor Union Women and the working women's group '9 to 5.' Milkman is especially interested in explaining why the extent of change in the labor movement has been so limited. For while women are far more fully represented in union membership than ever before, they remain seriously underrepresented at the level of union leadership, and unions' attention to women workers' particular concerns has also been relatively limited. Nevertheless, important groundwork was laid in the 1970s, which might provide the basis for a more extensive feminist mobilization within the unions in the future.

The postwar decades, and especially the 1960s and 1970s, have seen dramatic changes in women's relationship to work. The vast increases in female labor-force participation which occurred in this period produced equally vast social and cultural shifts, transforming family relations as well as women's sense of 'place' in the larger society. And the growth of a mass feminist movement led to enormous changes in consciousness about gender – not only among movement participants, but in the population as a whole. While inequality between women and men has by no means been eliminated, the goal of equality has won popular legitimacy – above all, in the context of the labor market – and women's expectations of work have been heightened accordingly.

Within the labor movement, too, there have been important changes. In 1973, the AFL–CIO endorsed the Equal Rights Amendment. The following year, the Coalition of Labor Union Women (CLUW) held its founding conference, establishing an institutional base for women in the labor movement which the major unions gradually came to accept. Such 'women's issues' as affirmative action, child-care, and equal pay for work of comparable worth were taken up by many unions in the years that followed. Female representation in labor leadership also grew significantly during the 1970s, especially at the local level. And, in 1980, CLUW president Joyce Miller became the first woman member of the AFL–CIO's Executive Council.[2]

Clearly, the rebirth of feminism did not leave organized labor unaffected. And yet, the impact of the contemporary women's movement on the labor movement has been surprisingly limited in a number of crucial respects. The recent gains in women's representation in union leadership, for example, are quite modest in relation to the substantial increases in female union membership which have occurred in recent years. As a 1980 CLUW study concluded, 'With regard to some of the traditional measures of progress and equality – in particular, adequate representation at the power centers of institutions – women are absent from the agenda' of the labor movement.[3] This study also found that those unions which did seriously address 'women's issues' tended to do so at the national level, and were often ineffective in reaching rank-and-file women in their local unions.[4]

The continuing underrepresentation of women among unionized workers is another critical problem. In 1980, only 15.9 percent of the nation's employed women were labor organization members, compared to 28.4 percent of men.[5] To be sure, the gap has been far wider in past years. Because of the recent decline of union strength in some male-employing industries, and increases in labor's recruitment of members in the more heavily female service sector, women today make up a greater proportion of labor organization membership than ever before (30 percent in 1980). Yet a much larger proportion of the total labor force is female (42 percent in 1980).[6]

Women's relationship to the labor movement has never been an easy one, and it would be unreasonable to expect all of the old difficulties suddenly to disappear in the wake of women's increased labor-force participation or the feminist resurgence. Indeed, the period in which these developments occurred has been a particularly troubled one for organized labor. Unions have suffered severe membership losses and have become increasingly isolated from the larger society during these years. But if the dilemma of the unions' relationship to women is not entirely new or surprising, resolving it has never been more critical for the future of the labor movement than it is today. For the dramatic growth in female employment over the 1960s and 1970s directly correlates with the decline in union membership in that period. If the labor movement is to recover from those extensive losses, it must both organize among the vast numbers of unorganized women workers and improve its relations with those women who are already unionized.

This chapter explores the ways in which the dramatic transformation in women's economic and social position has affected organized labor, and suggests some of the reasons why change in women's relationship to the labor movement has been so limited. I begin with a discussion of the recruitment of women into union ranks over the postwar decades. I argue that women were organized without any particular attention to the fact of their gender, but rather as members of occupational groups which happened to be largely female in composition. Because they were organized on these terms, the result of their extensive recruitment over the postwar period is that women are now squarely *in*, but generally still not *of* the labor movement.

Next, I turn to a consideration of the impact of contemporary feminism on women workers in the unions. I suggest here that although women were not brought into the labor movement 'as women,' once they had become a large segment of its membership, pressures to attend to their specific concerns as women grew, largely because of the changes in consciousness about gender which were taking place in the larger society. However, the impact of those broader social changes on the labor movement was limited, both because of the class composition and individualistic orientation of the women's movement, and because of the conservative stance of organized labor toward the new feminism.

Against this background, I then turn to a comparative examination of the two most successful organizational efforts to link feminism and unionism to emerge in the 1970s, namely CLUW and the working women's organization '9 to 5' (9 to 5 is not itself a union, but in 1981 joined forces with the Service Employees' International Union in launching a new, woman-led union for office workers, SEIU District 925). CLUW and 9 to 5 illustrate two different approaches to the project of developing a larger role for women in the labor movement. CLUW has concentrated on gaining more power for women in the unions, particularly in the form of leadership positions, and has pursued this goal without challenging the basic structure or character of the labor movement. In contrast, 9 to 5 has drawn on the tactics of the women's movement in an effort to transform both the image and content of unionism so as to enhance its ability to serve the special needs of women workers. After comparing these two approaches, I conclude with a brief assessment of the future prospects facing women workers in relation to organized labor.

Women workers and unionization: Recent trends

The expansion of the female labor force in the postwar decades was part of a larger transformation in the occupational structure as a whole. As economic growth shifted away from manufacturing and toward service and clerical employment, the historical concentration of organized labor in basic industry grew increasingly problematic. As early as the mid-1950s, the percentage of the workforce represented by unions began to decline.[7] There was some new organizing during the postwar decades, but it failed to keep pace with the growth of the workforce. In 1980, the latest year for which figures are available, union membership hit a postwar low of 20.9 percent of the labor force.[8]

Large numbers of women were recruited into the ranks of organized labor over the postwar decades, and even with the vast expansion of the female labor force, the percentage of women workers who are unionized has been maintained to a far greater extent than among men. The postwar decades were a period of feminization for the labor movement, even as organized labor as a whole has declined in strength. In 1956, women were 18.6 percent of all union members; by 1978, they comprised 24.2 percent of the total. When employee associations are also included in the figure, the proportion of women is even higher, rising from 23 percent in 1973 to 30 percent in 1980. Indeed, in the 1970s, almost all of the growth in labor organization membership was comprised of women workers.[9]

This feminization of the labor movement was not the result of any special commitment to organizing women workers *as women*. Rather, it was the unintended consequence of a series of efforts to offset the general decline in membership by organizing particular occupational groups – at one stage, teachers; later, hospital workers; and most recently, public-sector clerical and service workers. As a result, the composition of the organized female workforce today is very different from the traditional base of the organized labor movement. By 1980, nearly half of the nation's six million organized women workers were in three major employment categories: educational services, medical services and public administration. Only a quarter were in manufacturing, labor's traditional stronghold (see Table 1).

Table 1 Women members of labor organizations, selected industry groups, 1980

Industry group	Number of women members (thousands)	Women members as a percent of		
		Organized women in all industries	All women employed in this industry	Percent of all women workers (organized and unorganized) employed in this industry
All industries	6,056[a]	100.0[a]	15.9	100.0[a]
Educational services	1,737	28.7	33.0	13.2
Manufacturing	1,478	24.4	22.2	17.5
Medical services	689	11.4	13.1	14.1
Retail trade	560	9.2	7.7	19.3
Public administration	452	7.5	23.4	4.9
Services, other than educational and medical	408	6.7	7.7	14.5
Communications	341	5.6	52.6	1.7
Finance, insurance and real estate	71	1.2	2.3	8.5

Sources: US Bureau of Labor Statistics, Bulletin 2105, *Earnings and Other Characteristics of Organized Workers, May 1980* (1981), pp.18–21; US Bureau of Labor Statistics, Special Labor Force Report 244, *Employment and Unemployment: A Report on 1980* (1981), pp.A25, A29.
[a] Totals do not add to 100.0 percent because not all industry groups are included here.

The expansion of unionism among women workers has been quite selective, so that while some occupational categories are now highly organized, others – most importantly, private-sector clerical, service and sales occupations, remain largely outside the labor movement. In the public sector, management opposition to unionization is generally less formidable than in comparable private-sector workplaces, and frequently public employees are already organized in associations (without collective bargaining rights), so that unionization victories are often considerably easier to achieve than in private industry.[10] Consequently, many unions have rushed to organize public workers in order to boost membership levels – and dues – at a time when both are sorely needed. But there have been very few efforts to extend unionism to the millions of 'pink collar' workers in such private industries as banking or insurance. Unionism among private-sector clericals remains very limited, and most of it involves clericals employed by manufacturing firms with organized blue-collar workforces.[11]

The uneven pattern of female representation in the labor movement today validates the feminist perspective on 'organizability' which suggests that women workers are no more difficult to recruit into unions than their male counterparts, once a serious effort to organize them is undertaken. In this view, while some industries and occupations may be particularly difficult to unionize, this is not due to the gender of the workers involved, but rather to other aspects of the situation. Perhaps the most convincing bit of evidence on this point is the fact that the labor organization with one of the largest female memberships today is the Teamsters' union (second only to the National Educational Association). Despite its poor public image, the Teamsters' union has been unusually aggressive in the organizing field, and has nearly half a million female members. Other unions with large numbers of women members are listed in Table 2. The recruitment of women workers into unions is surely a necessary condition for effective representation of their special concerns within the labor movement, but it is not a sufficient condition. The large influx of female members into many important labor organizations in recent years has had remarkably little direct impact on the overall character of these unions or their institutional functioning. Women's representation in top leadership positions, as Table 2 shows, is disproportionately small in relation to their mem-

Table 2 Female membership and leadership in labor organizations with
250,000 or more women members, 1978

Organization	Women members	Percent female	Women officers and board members	Percent female
National Education Association	1,239,500	75	5	55
International Brotherhood of Teamsters	480,974	25	0	0
United Food and Commercial Workers	480,105	39	2	3
American Federation of State, County and Municipal Employees	408,000	40	1	3
Amalgamated Clothing and Textile Workers' Union	330,660	66	6	15
Service Employees International Union	312,500	50	7	15
International Brotherhood of Electrical Workers	303,518	30	0	0
American Federation of Teachers	300,000	60	8	25
International Ladies' Garment Workers Union	278,704	80	2	7
Communication Workers of America	259,112	51	0	0

Source: Coalition of Labor Union Women, Center for Education and Research, *Absent from the Agenda: A Report on the Role of Women in American Unions* (New York, mimeo, 1980), Tables 3 and 5.

bership in all the unions with large numbers of women, and in most
cases the disparity is vast. The general problem of distance between
the concerns of rank-and-file workers and union leaders is especially
severe in the case of women workers. Not only do male officials tend
to resist female encroachment on their leadership, but women themselves often have difficulty in viewing themselves as full participants
in the male culture of the union's internal life. Unaccustomed to
wielding power in the rest of their lives, and intimidated from the
outset by the prospect of self-consciously maneuvering for power
within an organization, women members often decline to enter the
competition at all.[12]

More generally, the dominant cultural imagery of labor organization and of union power remains male and blue-collar. Union
leadership, and to some extent even union membership, has a long
history as a male prerogative. During the major waves of unionization prior to the postwar era, women workers were a small

minority of the workforce in the crafts and industries that formed the cornerstone of the key organizing drives. Women were then seen (not entirely without reason) as temporary workers, marginal to the economy; and unions developed as essentially male institutions. Even in industries with large female workforces, like the textile and garment trades, or in periods when women had a relatively large presence within organized labor, like the World War II years, they never advanced to positions of real power in the unions.

In the 1950s and early 1960s, before the implications of the rise in female labor-force participation had become manifest, and before the resurgence of feminism, the labor movement maintained its traditional posture toward women workers. They were still seen as a special group, in need of special forms of protection, and not as full participants in union activity. Even as the two-worker family began to emerge as the norm in the inflationary era which began in the 1960s, many unionists clung to the old ideal of securing a 'family wage' for their (male) members. As late as the 1970s, male trade union leaders continued to view women workers along traditional lines. But ultimately, the changes which were transforming women's roles and consciousness in the larger society also led to changes inside the labor movement.

Feminism and unionism in the 1970s

By the 1970s, when the process of recruitment described above had greatly enlarged the numbers of women in the nation's labor organizations, pressures began to build for change in the unions' traditional outlook toward women. Women's caucuses and women's committees began to emerge in a variety of unions, and more generally, there was an upsurge in female union activism, beginning in the early 1970s.[13] In addition, some new forms of organizing among women workers began to develop through initiatives originating outside the established unions, drawing on the consciousness-raising techniques and other innovations of the broader women's movement.[14]

This new activity was very much influenced by the rebirth of feminism in the 1960s and 1970s, but the linkage was indirect. The women union activists whose numbers grew in this period typically rejected any direct identification with the women's movement. For

example, Cathy Tuley, an activist in an SEIU women's caucus, told
an interviewer:

> What I knew about the [women's] movement was really limited
> to just what I saw – people in demonstrations and the type of
> women who were professionals and their side of things. That's
> what I think was published more than anything else, so that's all
> I really picked up on . . . Like the woman that started that
> magazine, Gloria Steinem?
>   I think the way she looks is hard to relate to. And also, I think
> her education put a barrier between her and people like myself
> . . . Maybe I have my own stereotype of her, but I think maybe
> she looks above us. I feel she's fighting for women like herself,
> professional women, and that she's not thinking of women in
> the whole sense, just part of them. So I don't consider myself
> part of her movement.[15]

Tuley's view of the women's movement is representative not only of
female unionists, but also of working-class women more generally.
And indeed, the majority of feminist activists are college-educated
women from middle-class families, even if the actual composition of
the movement is more diverse than the media stereotypes would
indicate.[16]

Moreover, while in principle feminism offers collective solutions
to gender inequality, in practice, there is a highly individualistic
thrust to the women's movement. The slogan 'sisterhood is
powerful' notwithstanding, its primary emphasis seems to be on
gaining more power for individual women within American society
– and in the labor market – as it stands. This 'corporate feminist'
orientation has become increasingly dominant within the women's
movement over time, although there are certainly currents within
feminism which depart from it. From a trade union or working-class
women's perspective, the individualistic thrust associated with
feminism serves to reinforce the sense of distance engendered by the
class composition of the movement. And, of course, its individualism
is in large part a product of the fact that so many feminist activists
can reasonably aspire – once sex discrimination is no longer a barrier
– to professional occupations comparable to those held by men of
their class.[17]

Having said this, however, it would be extremely misleading to presume that working-class women have not been influenced by the feminist resurgence. On the contrary, growing numbers of them readily endorse the movement's basic goals, a phenomenon perhaps best captured in the familiar 'I'm not a women's libber, *but . . .*' In particular, and more than any other feminist principle, the ideal of gender equality in the labor market has won enormous popular support.[18] To be sure, structural change in the labor market has lagged far behind the attitudinal shifts. In general (and the only real exceptions here are the elite professions), despite the passage of anti-discrimination legislation, the vast majority of women workers remain in poorly paid, low-status jobs.[19]

Perhaps the most important effect of the resurgence of feminism on women workers has been to raise their expectations. As women with newly heightened expectations of work are faced with unchanged, or even deteriorating job prospects (for example, with office automation), a distinctive new consciousness has begun to develop, particularly among younger women. And under certain conditions, this new consciousness expresses itself in what, for want of a better term, I will call trade union feminism.[20] The identification of 'feminism' with middle-class professional women and with a politics of individualism has set limits on the growth of this kind of activity, but has by no means prevented its development.

Efforts to organize around women's issues within the unions, and the new campaigns to unionize unorganized women workers through special appeals to them 'as women' have generally been initiated by women themselves, rather than by union leaders. Although organized labor has become an important ally of the women's movement in many legislative and other public campaigns over the past decade, where its internal affairs are concerned, progress has been much slower. This is not only because of the historical character of trade unions as institutions of male culture, although that is one factor. In addition, the labor movement is dominated by a siege mentality, and has a deeply rooted mistrust of any efforts to assert the special interests of a group within the membership, particularly if those efforts appear to be associated with a specific ideology (such as feminism).

The defensive stance of the unions toward feminism has historical roots in the immediate postwar period. The attacks on labor during those years, combined with the effects of McCarthyism, led to a retreat from the agenda of 'social unionism' that had been pursued in the 1930s and 1940s, while economic prosperity facilitated a greater emphasis on wage and benefit gains over political challenges to the status quo. By the 1960s, organized labor was no longer at the dynamic center of oppositional politics in the United States, and defined its interests rather narrowly. Indeed, its posture toward the new social movements of the day – the anti-war and student movements, the environmental movement, as well as feminism – tended to be conservative or even hostile. And, in spite of the fact that organized labor stands to gain from developing special appeals to women workers, efforts along these lines were quite slow to emerge, and were generally met with defensiveness rather than ready support from union leaders.

In the 1970s, in spite of all the obstacles, the growing numbers of women both within the labor movement and among the unorganized workforce produced growing pressure for change in the situation of women in the labor movement. It was no longer possible to ignore efforts to assert the special interests of women as a group within the unions, as what was historically a marginal problem for the labor movement now became a central dilemma. Gradually, the pressures began to yield results, amid growing indications that the newly heightened expectations of women workers had created some important new opportunities for organized labor. One survey found that unorganized women workers have a significantly greater interest in joining unions than unorganized men, for example. And, perhaps more significantly, unions are currently winning representation elections in which women's issues are emphasized far more often than other elections.[21]

Among the various feminist organizational initiatives in the labor movement, the two which stand out as most successful are CLUW and 9 to 5. Although both are designed to improve the situation of women workers in relation to the labor movement, their approaches contrast sharply. While CLUW takes the existing structure of the labor movement as given, and directs itself toward increasing the status and power of women within that structure on its own terms, 9 to 5 has opted instead to develop new organizational forms for women workers, which implicitly challenge the established traditions of the labor movement while also working to expand the space of women within it. Each approach has advantages and disadvantages; together they illustrate the range of problems and possibilities facing feminists engaged in union activity.

CLUW and women unionists

Over 3,000 women from fifty-eight different unions attended the founding convention of the Coalition of Labor Union Women in Chicago in March of 1974. From the outset, the new organization committed itself to working within the established framework of the labor movement with the goal of advancing the position of women, both as workers and as unionists. The Statement of Purpose adopted at this first convention outlined four basic goals for the organization: organizing unorganized women into unions; working within unions in support of affirmative action; involving more union women in political action and in legislative campaigns to improve the condition of women workers (including the campaign for ERA ratification); and encouraging participation of women within their unions.[22]

Membership in CLUW was limited to those who were already union members – a policy decision which was made in the planning meetings held prior to the founding convention. This membership policy reflected the new organization's origins: it was established by a group of women with extensive experience in the labor movement, who believed that in order for CLUW effectively to influence the unions, membership had to be limited in this way. Not only in its membership rules, but also in its internal organizational structure, CLUW placed itself squarely in the trade union tradition from the outset, with a full complement of elected officers and a standard committee structure.[23]

The influence of the women's movement was also very much in evidence at CLUW's founding convention. 'One result of this meeting,' president-elect Olga Madar of the United Automobile Workers told the *New York Times*, 'is that fewer and fewer union women will be saying "we are not women's libbers." By coming here, they have proved that they are.'[24] And while criticism of union leadership was restrained, there was a visible determination to impress upon union men the seriousness of the project. As Myra Wolfgang of the Hotel and Restaurant Workers put it in a much-quoted exclamation, 'We have a message for George Meany. We

have a message for Leonard Woodcock. We have a message for
Frank Fitzsimmons. You can tell them we didn't come to Chicago to
swap recipes!'[25]

In the decade since its founding, CLUW has grown into a 15,000-
member organization with sixty local chapters. Its current president,
Joyce Miller, now sits on the AFL–CIO's Executive Council. CLUW
is highly visible within the labor movement and has been effective in
exerting pressure on the AFL–CIO regarding women's concerns. It
also functions as a network of women union officials, who comprise
its most active constituency. Under the aegis of its foundation-
funded 'Empowerment Project,' the organization has developed programs to enhance the leadership skills of women activists. And
locally, CLUW chapters have undertaken a wide range of issue-
oriented activities, often in coalition with other labor or women's
groups.[26]

Although formally the organization remains committed to its
original goal of organizing the unorganized, its sparse resources have
set severe limits on CLUW's abilities to work effectively toward this
goal. In 1982, together with the AFL—CIO's Industrial Union Department, it did launch a 'Women's Organizing Campaign' in the
Washington/Baltimore area, but this effort yielded little in the way
of concrete results and was abandoned entirely after only two
years.[27] CLUW has been far more successful as a vehicle for
promoting women's leadership among those who are already active in
their unions, and this is, in practice, the main function of the
organization. While rank-and-file women are frequently not even
aware of CLUW's existence, women who have already become
union activists see it as very beneficial.[28]

Not only does CLUW's internal structure mirror that of a typical
union, but virtually all of its top officers are full-time union officials,
so that it enjoys limited autonomy from the established union
leadership. While this does secure the organization considerable
respect within the labor movement, there is also a price to be paid. As
one sympathetic critic observed, 'Its [CLUW's] leadership is well-
respected, and it has a good track record with labor, but in my
opinion about half the CLUW board should be rank and file. Maybe
women from the ranks wouldn't worry about their jobs being
jeopardized if they spoke out.'[29]

CLUW has definitely found a niche for itself within the labor movement. But, even by its own standards, it has been less than fully successful in the first decade of its existence. Its membership includes less than 1 percent of the nation's unionized women workers, themselves a minority within the female labor force. And while CLUW has provided support for the few women who are union officials and leaders, and has probably increased their numbers to some extent, the organization has been far less effective in meeting the needs of rank-and-file women unionists.

CLUW's dilemma parallels that of the mainstream women's movement, concentrating as it does on upward mobility for individual women within the labor movement's internal hierarchy, rather than on the collective concerns of women union members. Of course, just as mainstream feminists are in principle concerned with the lot of all women, so CLUW, too, professes a broader concern. But in both cases the actual practice is far more individualistic, and in both, the practice reflects a particular set of presumptions about the most effective way to change institutions. Ironically, CLUW activists (and women union leaders generally), unlike rank-and-file women unionists, are often not so wary of being directly identified with the feminist movement.

CLUW's approach presumes that the key difference between women and men is that women lack leadership skills, self-confidence, and therefore power. While taking account of the fact that women have 'family responsibilities' that obstruct their union activity, CLUW does not view this as the basis for a critique of established organizational forms within the labor movement, but rather as an additional handicap which women must somehow overcome. As the CLUW slogan 'A Woman's Place Is in her Union' implies, all the needs of women can be taken care of within the existing framework of trade unionism. The problem with unions is only that women do not have a large enough role in them; the solution is for women to equip themselves to compete more effectively, on the established terms, for leadership.[30]

Certainly for those women pursuing full-time careers in the unions, CLUW's outlook and strategy have much to recommend them, and it is no accident that female union officials have become the organization's main constituency. Having more women in positions of leadership in the labor movement is important, and additionally CLUW's 'watchdog' role *vis-à-vis* the AFL—CIO on women's issues makes an important contribution. But it is difficult to see how CLUW can effectively expand and overcome its isolation from the nation's women workers so long as its primary energies are consumed in the internal politics of the labor movement. The price of CLUW's success in winning 'insider' status — and still quite a marginal 'insider' status at that — has been very high indeed. And if the organization should ever step too far beyond the boundaries of what is acceptable to the labor movement's leadership, it will risk the loss of its hard-won legitimacy.

CLUW's limitations are to a large extent self-imposed. It was founded by women trade union officials, and has remained faithful to their original vision of CLUW as an insiders' organization. And if pressure from its constituency has pushed CLUW a bit more than its founders intended toward organizing the unorganized and rank-and-file educational work, it is perhaps not so surprising that these have remained nominal goals rather than becoming the practical focus for the organization's energies. If the larger labor movement were revitalized, and rank-and-file activism there grew, CLUW too might develop into something more than a loyal opposition of women officials within organized labor. But any such initiative will have to come from outside of CLUW as it is presently structured.

The 'working women's movement' and SEIU District 925

Another major feminist effort to influence the organized labor movement originated outside of the established unions, as a project of a younger group of activists who were more critical of the labor movement's tradition than were CLUW's founders. In the early 1970s, young feminists with roots in the New Left formed several independent working women's organizations, primarily among previously unorganized office-workers. The best-known and most successful group, 9 to 5, began in Boston in 1973 and is now a national organization with chapters in many localities. Similar groups sprang up in other major cities around the country in the same period.[31]

Initially, the new groups avoided any formal ties to the established unions. The organizers felt that their constituency, women office-workers, could not be expected to identify directly with organized labor. Unions, after all, were popularly perceived as organizations of blue-collar workers, and, culturally, as part of the male world. As Karen Nussbaum, a founder of the original Boston group who would later become 9 to 5's executive director, said in 1976:

> When we started . . . the union people scorned women. They didn't care to take the time with us women, who didn't know anything about unions. I mean, 'union,' 'collective bargaining,' 'contract negotiations' – these words didn't mean anything to us. It wasn't like 'refrigerator' or 'electric light' – things that we had grown up with that were very familiar concepts. These were completely alien.[32]

Initially, rather than taking unionization as an immediate objective, the working women's movement concentrated on consciousness-raising and on public dramatizations of specific issues affecting women office-workers. As some commentators have suggested, the groups essentially functioned as 'pre-union' organizations.[33]

However, 9 to 5 moved closer to the organized labor movement over time. It received a charter from the Service Employees' International Union in 1975, and then began organizing SEIU Local 925 in Boston. Shortly afterward, the SEIU and 9 to 5 entered into a similar arrangement in nearby Providence, Rhode Island.[34] Then, in March 1981, the national office of 'Working Women' (9 to 5's name at that time) and the SEIU announced a much more ambitious joint-undertaking. This was SEIU District 925, charged with unionizing unorganized women clerical workers all over the US. The new district was a division of the SEIU, but drew its staff directly from 9 to 5, and had some autonomy within the union structure. In the words of SEIU president John Sweeney, the district was to be run 'for women and by women who understand their problems.'[35] At the time of writing, after two years of organizing, District 925 represents close to 4,000 workers and is attempting to unionize many more. It maintains interlocking directorates with 9 to 5, which continues its former work outside the boundaries of the union, as a separate entity.[36]

There are a number of contrasts between 9 to 5 and CLUW. The major practical focus of 9 to 5 is on organizing unorganized women workers, and outside of its link to the SEIU, it is not deeply involved in the trade union officialdom. More fundamentally, 9 to 5's strategy reflects an implicit critique of the assumption CLUW relies on – that once women are brought into the trade unions and accorded more power within the existing structure, their needs will be satisfied. Organizational forms traditionally associated with uniomism are seen by 9 to 5 as problematic for women, so it draws on the innovative, relatively unstructured organizational forms developed in the women's movement in its work. Leadership roles are downplayed, for example, in order to encourage participatory democracy within the organization and in order to develop the confidence and skill of as many members as possible.[37]

The focus of 9 to 5 on clerical workers is important in this regard. While CLUW's membership reflects the composition of the labor movement as presently constituted (which is quite different from the makeup of the female labor force), 9 to 5 defines its constituency as clerical workers, by far the largest group of women workers, accounting for over one-third of the female labor force (but a much smaller proportion of organized workers). And rather than limiting itself to unionization, 9 to 5 focuses on issues of special concern to women, such as equal opportunity, age discrimination, and the specific practices of banks and insurance companies toward their women employees. The group's overriding goal is to win 'rights and respect' for office-workers.[38]

The tactics employed by 9 to 5 also depart from those traditionally used in labor organizing. The consciousness-raising process developed by the women's movement is one model here; in addition, the organization has developed several innovative ways of rallying support in highly visible public settings, as well as making very skillful use of the media. Rallies on National Secretaries Day, the introduction of the popular film *9 to 5*, and more recently, a widely publicized campaign focused on the health hazards of video display terminals, are among these efforts.

Unionization is also a goal of the organization, but is conceived of as a long and complex process, with particularly delicate aspects for women. In contrast to CLUW's focus on 'empowerment,' 9 to 5 rejects the traditional 'macho' image of unionism, insisting that women workers, unaccustomed to viewing themselves as powerful, will be successfully unionized only if a different, more woman-oriented culture of unionism is developed. District 925 also strives for more rank-and-file participation and internal democracy than is typical of most unions today. In general, rather than trying to fit women into the existing organizational forms of unionism on an equal basis with men, 9 to 5 focuses on the ways in which women workers and their culture are different from male workers and male culture, and seeks to develop organizational forms both inside and outside the framework of unionism which take those differences seriously and respond directly to the special needs of women workers.[39]

As long as it remained a 'pre-union,' there were limits on 9 to 5's resources and on what it could offer to its constituency of female clericals. The District 925 linkage was intended to expand those resources without losing the conception of women as having special needs. It is an experiment without precedent in the US labor movement: a union led by women, with roots in the women's movement, whose stated goal is to unionize the overwhelmingly female clerical workforce with the backing of one of the largest labor organizations in the country. Yet it *is* very much an experiment, not only for 9 to 5 but also for the SEIU. While careful to negotiate considerable autonomy in their operations, District 925's staff acknowledges that in order to retain (and hopefully expand) the SEIU's support, it needs to garner some quick results in the form of dues-paying members. And that pressure makes the new district's operations quite similar to those of a number of other unions, such as AFSCME and CWA, which are actively engaged – sometimes in direct rivalry with one another, in public-sector clerical organizing. Indeed, with the exception of a recent victory at the Syracuse office of Equitable Life Assurance, all of District 925's organizing successes have been in the public sector. Unlike blue-collar organizing, public-sector unionization has a demonstration effect relevant to unorganized private-sector clericals, as District 925 staffers point out.[40] But the public-sector emphasis is obviously also a product of the constraints imposed by the SEIU, which operates in a fashion more akin to other unions than to 9 to 5's original vision.

The dilemma for 9 to 5, then, is how to preserve its distinctive vision and approach to organizing, now that it is encapsulated in the legal and institutional framework of mainstream trade unionism. Certainly its relationship with the SEIU has put the office-workers' group in a position to go beyond simply consciousness-raising and public relations work, supplying a vehicle through which it can begin to accumulate some real power. Ultimately, the extent to which the SEIU is willing to commit its resources to its new woman-led division, and to allow 9 to 5 to experiment freely with it, will be the major determinant of the future of the venture.

Conclusion

CLUW and 9 to 5 are but the most successful and visible products of the opening toward feminism within the labor movement which developed in the 1970s. There were also a range of smaller efforts within individual unions, many of them locally based, as well as labor-initiated campaigns around issues of particular concern to women workers, such as pay equity. While the impact of feminism on organized labor is historically unprecedented in magnitude, it is nevertheless quite modest relative to the extent of change in the larger society. But the 1970s did lay the groundwork of what could potentially develop into a far more extensive feminist mobilization within the unions.

The wrenching economic downturn of the early 1980s has not done much to encourage further progress. The larger labor movement is in its deepest crisis since the early 1930s, with steep membership losses and extensive 'givebacks' in wages and benefits won in earlier years eroding union power. Although these problems have been concentrated in the manufacturing sector, where women's presence is in any case minimal, the entire labor movement has been thrown on the defensive, and the space which had opened up for women's concerns in the 1970s is in jeopardy. In the longer run, however, the labor movement is likely to be revitalized, and then the feminization of union membership could become the basis of a full-scale alliance between the nation's women workers, with their own distinctive consciousness, and organized labor. In that context, the seeds planted with such difficulty by feminist trade unionists in the 1970s may finally bear fruit.

Notes

1 Special thanks to Deborah Bell, Varda Burstyn, Alice Kessler-Harris and Meredith Tax for helpful comments on an earlier draft of this essay, and to Miriam Frank for research assistance.

2 Very little has been written about these developments. The most thorough single account is Philip Foner's, in his *Women and the American Labor Movement from World War I to the Present*, New York, The Free Press, 1980, pp.478–572.

3 Coalition of Labor Union Women, Center for Education and Research, *Absent from the Agenda: A Report on the Role of Women in American Unions*, New York, 1980, p.5. The representation of women in union leadership is an aspect of women's relationship to the labor movement which has received relatively extensive study. In addition to *Absent from the Agenda*, see Linda H. LeGrande, 'Women in Labor Organizations: Their Ranks are Increasing,' *Monthly Labor Review*, vol. 101, no. 8, 1978, pp.8–14; US Commission on Civil Rights, *Nonreferral Unions and Equal Employment Opportunity*, 1982, pp.10–26; Karen S. Koziara and David A. Pierson, 'The Lack of Female Union Leaders: A Look at Some Reasons,' *Monthly Labor Review*, vol. 104, no. 5, 1981, pp.30–2; and the classic by Barbara M. Wertheimer and Anne H. Nelson, *Trade Union Women: A Study of Their Participation in New York City Locals*, New York, Praeger, 1975.

4 Coalition of Labor Union Women, *Absent from the Agenda*, p.18.

5 US Bureau of Labor Statistics, Bulletin 2105, *Earnings and Other Characteristics of Organized Workers*, May 1980, 1981, p.9. These figures are from a household survey, in which individuals are asked to identify themselves as labor organization members. The US Bureau of Labor Statistics also estimates the extent of organization by surveying unions and associations. The last survey of this type was conducted in 1980, and did not provide a breakdown by sex. However, the overall level of labor organization was somewhat lower than that found in the household survey of the same year (20.9 percent as opposed to 23 percent of the labor force), and it seems likely that the figures for women and men presented in the household survey are also relatively high. See Courtney D. Gifford, ed., *Directory of US Labor Organizations, 1982–83 Edition*, Washington, DC, Bureau of National Affairs, p.1.

6 Gifford, *Directory*, p.3; US Bureau of Labor Statistics, Special Labor Force Report 244, *Employment and Unemployment: A Report on 1980*, 1981, p.A29.

7 US Bureau of Labor Statistics, Bulletin 2079, *Directory of National Unions and Employee Associations, 1979*, 1980, p.60. Here and throughout this chapter, the term 'unions' is used generically, and refers to both unions and 'employee associations.'

8 Gifford, *Directory*, p.1.

9 *Ibid.*, pp.1–3; LeGrande, op. cit., p.9; US Bureau of Labor Statistics, *Directory*, op. cit., p.62.

10 See Deborah E. Bell, 'Unionized Women in State and Local Government,' in this volume.

11 David Wagner, 'Clerical Workers: How "Unorganizable" Are They?' *Labor Center Review* (Amherst, Mass.), vol. 2, no. 1, 1979, pp.20–50.

12 For discussion, see Wertheimer and Nelson, *Trade Union Women*.

13 See Foner, *Women and the American Labor Movement*, pp.478–515; 'Women Workers: Gaining Power, Seeking More,' *US News and World Report*, vol. 73, November 13, 1972, pp.104–7; and 'Working Women Find Movement Has Problems and Potential,' *Labor Notes* (Detroit), no. 7, August 21, 1979, pp.8–9.

14 The best summary account is Nancy Seifer and Barbara Wertheimer, 'New Approaches to Collective Power: Four Working Women's Organizations,' in Bernice Cummings and Victoria Schuck, eds, *Women Organizing: An Anthology*, Metuchen, New Jersey, Scarecrow Press, 1979, pp.152–83.

15 Nancy Seifer, ed., *Nobody Speaks For Me! Self-Portraits of American Working Class Women*, New York, Simon & Schuster, 1976, pp.247–8. Similar examples of this phenomenon are described in various studies of trade union women, for example, Patricia Cayo Sexton, *The New Nightingales: Hospital Workers, Unions, New Women's Issues*, New York, Enquiry Press, 1982, pp. 109–11; and Mary Margaret Fonow, 'Women in Steel: A Case Study of the Participation of Women in a Trade Union,' PhD dissertation, Ohio State University, 1977, pp.155–65.

16 See Maren Lockwood Carden, *The New Feminist Movement*, New York, Russell Sage Foundation, 1974, especially pp.28–30.

17 See Barbara Ehrenreich, 'The Women's Movements: Feminist and Antifeminist,' *Radical America*, vol. 15, nos 1 and 2, 1981, pp.93–101; and Suzanne Gordon, 'The New Corporate Feminism,' *The Nation*, vol. 236, February 5, 1983, pp.129, 143–7.

18 See Lillian B. Rubin, *Worlds of Pain: Life in the Working-Class Family*, New York, Basic Books, 1976, especially pp.130–2; Nancy Seifer, *Absent from the Majority: Working Class Women in America*, New York, National Project on Ethnic America, 1973; Social Research, Inc., *Working-Class Women in a Changing World: A Review of Research Findings*, New York, McFadden-Bartell Corporation, 1973.

19 See US Bureau of Labor Statistics, Report 673, *The Female–Male Earnings Gap: A Review of Employment and Earnings Issues*, Washington, DC, September 1982; and Nancy F. Rytina, 'Earnings of Men and Women: A Look at Specific Occupations,' *Monthly Labor Review*, vol. 105, 1982, pp.25–31.

20 See Myra Marx Ferree, 'Working Class Feminism: A Consideration of the Consequences of Employment, *The Sociological Quarterly*, vol. 21, 1980, pp.173–84; Roberta S. Sigel and John V. Reynolds, 'Generational Differences and the Women's Movement,' *Political Science Quarterly*, vol. 94, 1979–80, pp.635–48. Roberta Goldberg found that most of the women active in the chapter of Working Women that she studied in Baltimore were in their twenties and thirties. See her *Organizing Women*

Office Workers: Dissatisfaction, Consciousness, and Action, New York, Praeger, 1983, p.41. Younger women were also predominant in District 925's organizing at the Syracuse office of the Equitable Life Assurance Society. See David Moberg, 'Clerks Outmaneuver Bosses,' *In These Times,* vol. 7, March 30–April 5, 1983, p.5.

21 The first survey found that while 33 percent of all non-union workers polled would vote to join a union if offered the chance, for women, the figure was 40 percent. See Thomas A. Kochan, 'How American Workers View Labor Unions,' *Monthly Labor Review,* vol. 102, 1979, p.25. A separate report notes that 'labor is winning 59 percent of all representation elections in which women's issues are emphasized, compared to its overall success rate of just 43 percent in 1981.' See Richard Moore and Elizabeth Marsis, 'Will Unions Work for Women?' *The Progressive,* vol. 47, 1983, p.30.

22 '3,000 Delegates at Chicago Meeting Organize a National Coalition of Labor Union Women,' *New York Times,* March 25, 1974; Coalition of Labor Union Women, *Statement of Purpose, Structure and Guidelines* (pamphlet), adopted March 23–4, 1974.

23 See Foner, *Women and the American Labor Movement,* pp.516–20; AnneMarie Troger, 'The Coalition of Labor Union Women: Strategic Hope, Tactical Despair,' *Radical America,* vol. 9, fall 1975, pp. 22–38; and Patricia Cayo Sexton, 'Workers (Female) Arise!' *Dissent,* vol. 21, no. 3, 1974, pp.380–95.

24 '3,000 Delegates.'

25 *John Herling's Labor Letter,* Washington, DC, March 30, 1974, p.1.

26 Elizabeth Weiner, 'Still Sticking to the Union,' *In These Times,* vol. 7, March 30–April 5, 1983, pp.8–9, 15; and *CLUW News,* various issues.

27 Moore and Marsis, 'Will Unions Work for Women?'; 'Labor Letter,' *Wall Street Journal,* August 23, 1983, p.1; 'Labor Letter,' *Wall Street Journal,* March 6, 1984, p.1.

28 Sexton, *New Nightingales,* p.111.

29 *Ibid.,* p.117.

30 For example, see the discussion in 'Union Organizers Exchange Ideas on Recruiting More Women Workers,' *Daily Labor Report* (Washington, DC), January 29, 1981, pp.A6–A8, D1–D4; and Coalition of Labor Union Women, Center for Education and Research, *Empowerment: A Handbook for Union Women,* Washington, DC, 1982.

31 The best general accounts are in Jean Tepperman, *Not Servants, Not Machines: Office Workers Speak Out,* Boston, Beacon Press, 1976; Seifer and Wertheimer, 'New Approaches to Collective Power'; and Roberta Goldberg, *Organizing Women Office Workers,* especially chapter 3.

32 Tepperman, *Not Servants,* p.92.

33 See Karen S. Koziara and Patrice J. Insley, 'Organizations of Working Women Can Pave the Way for Unions,' *Monthly Labor Review,* vol. 105, no. 6, 1982, pp.53–4; Roberta Lynch, 'Women in the Workforce,' *The Progressive,* vol. 43, no. 10, 1979, pp.28–31.

34 See Seifer and Wertheimer, 'New Approaches to Collective Power,' pp.179–80; Karen Nussbaum (interviewed), 'Women Clerical Workers and Trade Unionism,' *Socialist Review*, vol. 10, no. 1, 1980, pp.152.

35 'Women's Group Set to Organize Office Workers,' *New York Times*, March 4, 1981; Anne Hill, 'District 925: A New Union for Office Workers,' *Socialist Review*, vol. 11, no. 5, 1981, pp.142–6.

36 See Moberg, 'Clerks Outmaneuver Bosses.' Figures on 9 to 5's membership are not available. The organization claimed 10,000 members, as reported in 'Women's Group Set to Organize Office Workers,' but this is almost certainly an inflated figure.

37 See Roberta Goldberg, *Organizing Women Office Workers*, pp.45–7.

38 *Ibid.*, pp.33–7.

39 For a discussion of the use of a similar notion of difference among feminist trade unionists in Italy, see Bianca Beccalli, 'Women and Trade Unions in Italy,' in Alice Cook, Val Lorwin and Arlene Kaplan Daniels, eds, *Women and Trade Unions in Eleven Industrialized Countries*, Philadelphia, Temple University Press, 1984.

40 Interview with Jackie Ruff, District 925's executive director, Washington, DC, June 17, 1983; on Equitable, see Moberg, 'Clerks Outmaneuver Bosses' and Ruth Milkman, 'Pink-Collar Unions: Breakthrough at the Equitable,' *The Nation*, vol. 237, December 3, 1983, pp.564–6.

Index

Vogel, Lise, 257
Volunteer Workers' Group, 149
Vorse, Mary Heaton, 232, 256
Votara, George, 278

Wagner Act, 220
Wagner, David, 320
Wagner, Mayor Robert, 283
Walker, Charles Rumford, 201
Walter, Mary, 176
Wandersee, Winifred, 20, 200, 230
Ware, Norman, 18, 19
Washington, Mayor, 296
Webster, Mary Watson, 148
Webster Home, 148
Weiler, N. Sue, 39
Weiner, Elizabeth, 321
Weinzweig, Israel, 128, 137
Weisbord, Vera Buch, 165, 178
Welsenback, Annie, 54
Wertheimer, Barbara Mayer, 57, 87,
  106, 134, 319–22
Western Federation of Miners, 182
Weyl, Walter E., 58
Wheatley Association, 149
White Rose Industrial Association, 142–
  3, 144
White Rose Working Girls' Home, 142–
  3
widows, miners', 67
Willet, Mabel Hurd, 178
Willett, Mabel, 106
Williams, Faith M., 17
Wilson, Bertha, 146
Wilson, Michael, 205
Wilson, President Woodrow, 67
Wolfgang, Myra, 311

Wolfson, Theresa, 39, 116, 122–3, 138,
  134–7
Wolman, Leo, 134, 135
Women, Commission on the Status of,
  271
Women Organizers, Training School for,
  34–5
Women's Bureau, 116, 131–2, 145,
  261–3, 267–9
Women's Christian Temperance Union,
  32
Women's Club Movement, 141
Women's Emergency Brigade, 200
Women's Loyal Union, 142, 149
Women's Trade Union League, see
  WTUL
Women's Voting Association of
  Southern Colorado, 76
Wood, William, 43
Woodcock, Leonard, 268, 312
Wooddell, Jennifer, 176
Woods, Robert, 58
Woodward, C. V., 177
World War II, 14, 146, 224, 261–2
Wurf, Jerry, 298
WTUL (Women's Trade Union League),
  Chapter 2, 122, 131
'Working Women;, 315

Yard, Elizabeth, 204
Yearly, Clifton K., 82
Yeghissian, Patricia, 256
Yoneda, Elaine Black, 203
Yulla, Julia, 52
YWCA, 145, 169, 173
YWCA Industrial Department, 169–70

Zurwell, Louise, 53